Accession
36222041

D0549440

LANGUAGE IN SOCIETY 2

Language and Social Networks

LANGUAGE IN SOCIETY

GENERAL EDITOR:
Peter Trudgill, Professor of Linguistic Science,
University of Reading

ADVISORY EDITORS:
Ralph Fasold, Professor of Linguistics,
Georgetown University

William Labov, Professor of Linguistics,
University of Pennsylvania

Language and Social Networks

SECOND EDITION

Lesley Milroy

LIS LIBRARY

Date	Fund
9/6/16	l-Che

Order No

2739 80x

University of Chester

Basil Blackwell

Copyright © Lesley Milroy 1980 and 1987

First published 1980
Second edition 1987

Basil Blackwell Ltd
108 Cowley Road, Oxford OX4 1JF, UK

Basil Blackwell Inc.
432 Park Avenue South, Suite 1503,
New York, NY 10016, USA

All rights reserved. Except for the quotation of short passages for the purposes of criticism and review, no part of this publication may be reproduced, stored in a retrieval system, or transmitted, in any form or by any means, electronic, mechanical, photocopying, recording or otherwise, without the prior permission of the publisher.

Except in the United States of America, this book is sold subject to the condition that it shall not, by way of trade or otherwise, be lent, re-sold, hired out, or otherwise circulated without the publisher's prior consent in any form of binding or cover other than that in which it is published and without a similar condition including this condition being imposed on the subsequent purchaser.

British Library Cataloguing in Publication Data

Milroy, Lesley
   Language and social networks. — 2nd ed.
   1. Sociolinguistics
   I. Title
   401'.9   P40

   ISBN   0–631–15314–4

Library of Congress Cataloging in Publication Data

Milroy, Lesley.
   Language and social networks

   (Language in society; 2)
   Bibliography: p.
   Includes index.
   1. Sociolinguistics. I. Title. II. Series:
Language in society (Oxford, Oxfordshire) ; 2.
P40.M54 1987   401'.9   87–10370
ISBN 0–631–15314–4 (pbk.)

Printed in Great Britain by Billing & Sons Ltd, Worcester

Contents

Editor's Preface to the Second Edition

The first edition of Lesley Milroy's *Language and Social Networks* arose to a considerable extent out of work performed by the team (led by Lesley Milroy and James Milroy) which carried out the important and exciting sociolinguistic research in Belfast in the 1970s that has been so influential in the sociolinguistics of the 1980s. The book was based partly on the Belfast research itself and partly on work performed by other scholars working in sociolinguistics and anthropological linguistics in many different areas of the world. It represented a novel and exciting synthesis of Labov-type work in social dialectology and Gumperz-type work in the social anthropology of language, as well as work in the social psychology of language.

This synthesis proved to be of such interest that it is no exaggeration to say that it has provided a stimulus for considerable amounts of the best research in the area of language and society which has appeared in subsequent years, especially perhaps in Britain. This second edition has been updated to include discussions of some of the research which the first edition helped to stimulate in this way and which has been carried out by workers in the field in the intervening period; but it also includes new research from Lesley Milroy herself and the Belfast team and, crucially, some new thinking on the topic as well. It also takes account of additional sociological theories, in keeping with the interdisciplinary stance that Lesley Milroy has typically adopted in her work, while always remaining a linguist.

The second edition of the book, as the first, uncovers and

discusses linguistic differences between different areas of Belfast, between different social and cultural groups, and between men and women, as well as differences between the characteristics of particular linguistic variables; furthermore, it explains these in terms of social network structure. It also shows that an ethnographic approach to sociolinguistic fieldwork and a close statistical study of social networks and their linguistic correlates are invaluable for a deeper understanding of linguistic behaviour, language change, linguistic variation, and the maintenance and development of vernacular language varieties. Those familiar with the first edition will recall that the adoption of an ethnographic approach to the Belfast fieldwork was initially dictated by the constraints imposed by the political and social situation in that city in the 1970s. It emerges, however, that— particularly in the hands of the brilliant (and courageous) fieldworker that this author proved herself to be—this methodology produces explanations for the nature of language variation in a complex urban community of a type that could not have been revealed in any other way.

I wrote in the preface to the first edition of this important book that the focus on Belfast would provide a fascinating account of language behaviour in that troubled but important city, while the more general points developed in the work would be of considerable theoretical interest to linguists, social psychologists, anthropologists and sociologists. This remains true of the second edition, but it must be acknowledged that most of the book's considerable impact has been in the field of linguistics itself. Interestingly, this impact has been apparent not only in sociolinguistics, as one would expect, but in historical linguistics also. Perhaps other disciplines will now also take note, but even if they don't there is every reason to believe that the second edition of *Language and Social Networks* will now extend the influence of this pioneering work into the linguistics of the 1990s.

Peter Trudgill

Preface to the Second Edition

The main substantive changes to the first edition of *Language and Social Networks* are to the last section of Chapter 6 and to Chapter 7, which have been updated and extended. I have made very few changes to the earlier part of the text, except to correct errors and inconsistencies. However, the field has advanced considerably since 1980 when the first edition was published; in particular, John Gumperz and Bob Le Page, whose work was quoted extensively there, have now collected and published in more accessible form much of the cited material. Since, however, their views have remained essentially unchanged, I have not attempted to change citations of material published in mimeographed or working paper form at every point in the text. Readers are referred to Gumperz (1982) and Le Page and Tabouret-Keller (1985) for more recent formulations of their ideas.

In Chapter 7 I have discussed only a small proportion of the work carried out since 1980 on language variation and change in Belfast. Many of the publications arising from this later work are cited in the text; but readers are referred particularly to J. Milroy (1981); Harris (1985); Milroy and Milroy (1985b); L. Milroy (1987) and J. Milroy (forthcoming). It is better that this associated material is consulted in conjunction with this extended second edition, than that any attempt be made to summarize it within a single book.

Lesley Milroy

Acknowledgements

The data on which the study of three inner city communities reported in this book is based were collected for a Social Science Research Council project (no. HR3771) carried out between October 1975 and July 1977 as an investigation into the urban vernacular of Belfast. Responsibility for directing that project and working out the ideas presented in this book was shared equally between myself and James Milroy, and it was he who developed the phonological analyses of Belfast vernacular which were an essential prerequisite to any investigation into sociolinguistic structure. Much of the work of transcription and analysis was handled by Rose Maclaren and Domini O'Kane, and I am indebted to the late Sue Margrain for valuable advice and help with the statistical analysis which forms the basis of Chapters 5 and 6.

The second edition of this book makes use in Chapter 7 of some of the data collected during a second Social Science Research Council project in Belfast (no. HR5777), and I am glad to acknowledge here this financial support. James Milroy shared the responsibility of directing this project also, and John Harris helped in the analysis of material discussed in Chapter 7. I am grateful to Susan Gal for introducing me to the work of Mark Granovetter, which provided a useful basis for the extended analysis of the relationship between personal network structure and language variation presented in this second edition.

Several people commented and advised on different parts or earlier drafts of the manuscript, and I gratefully acknowledge the assistance of Fred Boal, John Braidwood, Dick Hudson, John Laver and Mike McTear in this capacity. It will be obvious that this study, like many others, owes much to the example of William Labov. Although it does not always reflect his views, I would like to thank him for helpful comments on a number of preliminary papers in the course of which the ideas embodied here were developed. The ideas of a number of other scholars have also proved relevant and stimulating, and my debt to them will be apparent at a number of points in the text. I would also like to record here my appreciation of the assistance given by Peter Trudgill, the general editor of this series. This assistance took the form both of helpful comments on an earlier draft of the manuscript and (crucially) of much needed encouragement during the long process of writing and rewriting the book. Grateful thanks are also due to Andrina Reid who typed the greater part of the manuscript and to those of her colleagues who completed the remainder.

The warmest thanks however are due to those anonymous informants (for whom pseudonyms are used where convenient) whose language patterns are analysed in this book. Despite the grim conditions in which circumstances obliged them to live, the people of Ballymacarrett, the Hammer and the Clonard areas of Belfast welcomed me warmly and hospitably into their homes and allowed me, over a period of several weeks, to tape record many hours of lively and entertaining conversation to which justice cannot be done in a study of sociolinguistic structure such as this one. I am deeply grateful for the opportunity of meeting these delightful people, whose kindness I will never forget, and for the insights their hospitality enabled me to receive into the complexities of informal social organization in their communities.

Finally, for moral support during the many hours (some of which were inevitably tedious) I spent in writing this book thanks are due to my husband Jim and our three young sons, David, Andrew and Richard. Without this support, the work could not have been completed.

Lesley Milroy

1
Language, Class and Community

This book concerns itself principally with the study of language in the community; that is, the observation and analysis of language in its social context as it is used in everyday situations. It is taken as axiomatic that social significance of various kinds underlies much variability in language use. The perspective we are adopting here is thus distinct from that of the theoretical or descriptive linguist whose analysis is not necessarily based on data collected from live speakers in everyday situations; a great many linguistic observations are made, and conclusions drawn, on the basis of constructed data. The approach in this book is also distinct from the work of those social psychologists whose main object of study also is language behaviour. Characteristically, rather than working in the community, they investigate attitudes to language, or patterns of language use, under controlled experimental conditions. (See the first volume in this series (Giles and St Clair, 1979) for a number of recent studies in the social psychological tradition.)

While the perspective adopted in this book in no way implies any adverse criticism of these traditions of linguistic work (rather they should be viewed as complementing other approaches) I would argue, with Ferguson (1977), that direct and careful observation of the manner in which people use language in its social context is capable of yielding many interesting and surprising results. This is because most systematic linguistic knowledge of the kind which influences social and educational policies is still confined to careful styles or standardized varieties; we still know very little about the *total* linguistic repertoires of individuals or communities. In recent years, such knowledge has begun to shed light on a number of old problems which have concerned investigators in many disciplines. We may quote particularly the connections revealed by Labov's work (1972b) between nonstandard language use (as opposed to some kind of cultural deficit) and general social and educational disadvantage, or by Gumperz's recent work (1977a) which reveals in great detail how misunderstandings of communicative intent, in everyday situations, can fuel hostility between Englishmen and immigrants in London. Recent work in Belfast has suggested that similar communicative breakdowns might arise between subgroups of the same ethnic affiliation more often than is commonly supposed (see Chapter 4 below).

We begin by giving some account of the main methods and findings of those who have studied language 'live' in the sense that they have recorded and analysed real speech events in contemporary communities. It is important, at this point, to consider as fully as possible various methods of obtaining on tape linguistic data which realistically reflect everyday language use; many readers will be aware that the investigator faces a difficult problem here. In fact, fieldwork methods have been the focus of much interest in recent years, and have become considerably refined. It is unwise to underestimate the importance of a careful choice of fieldwork method; for as we shall see, this choice has considerable influence both on the kind of language available for analysis, and on the ultimate analytic procedure.

THE DIALECTOLOGICAL APPROACH

It is convenient to distinguish two somewhat different approaches to the study of language in the community; the *dialectological* and the *sociolinguistic*. However, these two traditions should not necessarily be seen as opposed to each other. On the contrary, most sociolinguistic work has been heavily dependent on linguistic information supplied by the large-scale studies of the dialectologists, and in fact much work carried out on the general principles explained by Labov (1972a) may be seen as an explicit modification of dialectological methods.

Conversely, much recent work in the dialectological tradition has been modified in the direction of modern sociolinguistics.

The main features of the older traditional dialectological approach in its unmodified form are well known and have been discussed critically in recent years by Labov (1972a) and Trudgill (1974). The general aim is a *geographical* account of linguistic differences, and the end product of a dialect survey is a map or series of maps showing the broad areal limits of the linguistic features (usually lexical or phonological) chosen for study. An example of this is the recently published *Linguistic Atlas of England* (Orton, Sanderson and Widdowson, 1978) which is the product of thirty years work and reflects the traditional dialectological approach. Boundaries (known as isoglosses) are plotted on the map which mark out the point where form A gives way to form B. A dialect boundary is said to exist where a number of isoglosses more or less coincide. For example, Wakelin (1972:102) illustrates the boundary between the Northern and the north-Midland dialect areas of England by showing eight isoglosses which mark the southern limit of eight phonological features characteristic of northern English dialect speech. We should note that in order to draw isoglosses in this manner, a pronunciation such as Northern [kuː] *cow*, as opposed to north-Midland [kaʊ] must be said categorically either to exist or not exist in a given area, although in practice, dialectologists know that this is an oversimplification of the linguistic facts. In general, the methods of traditional dialectology are not designed to deal with the fact that the same speaker may use several different pronunciations, or that different speakers in the same area may use a very wide range of different pronunciations. This is not to say that dialectologists are unaware either of intralectal variability, or of the fact that such variability can usually be linked to a number of social factors. In his account of field methods used by the *Survey of English Dialects*, Orton notes:

Great care was taken in choosing the informants. Very rarely were they below the age of sixty. They were mostly

men: in this country men speak the vernacular more frequently, more consistently and more genuinely than
women. Bilingual speakers could not be shunned: as a
result of our educational system the inhabitants of the
English countryside can readily adjust their natural speech
to the social situation in which they may find themselves.
(1962:15)

Although a number of social factors affecting variability are
pinpointed here—age, sex and situational context—the SED
does not set out to analyse systematically their relationship to
language. In general, any reference in the dialectological
literature to the social significance of variability is anecdotal.

The dialectologist is concerned then with the large-scale
linguistic concept of dialect, and with mapping out in a broad
way the areal distribution of linguistic forms. Furthermore, his
interest is specifically in recording *traditional* features of dialect.
Hence Orton's insistence on using as informants men over the
age of sixty. Typically, towns and cities are avoided, and old
members of a population living in an undisturbed rural community are sought out (Wakelin, 1972:1). Frequently this pre-
occupation is seen in terms of the 'pure' dialectal form of the
language as opposed to the form spoken by younger and more
mobile speakers which is 'contaminated' by contact with the
standard and so is not a proper object of study (Widdowson,
1972). Thus, although their research sites are usually 'communities' in the precise sense we shall define later in this chapter,
dialectologists do not claim to be describing the speech of a
community in a comprehensive or socially realistic manner.
Wakelin (whose title *Patterns in the Folk Speech of the British Isles*
reveals this antiquarian interest) notes that the interests of the
original nineteenth-century dialectologists were often historical.
Field methods were seen explicitly as a means of solving historical problems, the main object being to study reflexes of historical
forms in their natural setting relatively free from external
influence. Frequently, this interest in history and origins is
expressed in the literature in terms of geological imagery. For

example, the argument of Mather's (1972) paper is based on a quotation from Schuchhardt who likens the discoveries of linguistic geography to geological stratification. The image is a telling one; for it reveals not only a primarily historical interest, but an underlying view of language as a natural deposit like coal or iron, whose traces can be unearthed without necessary reference to its use by a living community. Reference is seldom made in the literature to the position of the informants in the community, except to emphasize that they are old and locally based. The questionnaire used by the SED typically focuses on eliciting single lexical items; it is extremely lengthy, taking up to four days to record. SED data is therefore, of necessity, based on composite recordings of more than one speaker. As we shall see, all these characteristics of the dialectological approach contrast sharply with the aims and methods of modern sociolinguistics; for this more recent approach attempts to give as far as possible an accurate picture of contemporary language variation and use, taking account of the social identities of individual speakers.

It should be noted that many individual studies in the dialectological tradition modify the characteristically antiquarian approach. For example, recent work in France takes account of variability in an extremely sophisticated manner (Bouvier and Martel, 1973); Kurath's *Linguistic Atlas of New England* records speech from informants with different educational levels; current work in Ireland records the speech of different age groups; Gregg (1972) gives a substantial and clear synchronic account of Ulster dialect phonology, recording a very large number of speakers in a limited area in order to account for some of the facts of variability. However, in general dialectologists do not concern themselves with the interplay between social and linguistic behaviour which is the main interest of the sociolinguist. This difference in emphasis is demonstrated particularly clearly by Wright's (1972) study of the language of coalmining. Although Wright's research sites are two northern English industrial towns—the kind of area of considerable interest to a sociolinguist (see Petyt, 1978)—his concerns are quite different.

They are to document the peculiar and exotic lexicon of English collieries, and the study is seen as important because of the (apparently) imminent closure of the pits and the demise of the coal industry. Thus, the antiquarian interest in preserving a vanishing past is revealed as paramount. In passing, Wright makes a number of observations of considerable interest to any linguist studying a close-knit working-class community, but (and this is the important point) does not follow them up in any systematic way. The strongly vernacular speech of the inhabitants of two northern mining towns is contrasted with what Wright perceives as the more standardized speech characteristic of towns without this traditional and homogeneous form of employment. To illustrate his point, he quotes the *thee* and *thou* usage of grammar school children: [ðaː dɪd ɪt] *thou did it*, [ðiːl kɔp ɪt] *thee'll cop it*, and remarks that they appear to alternate between this extremely nonstandard vernacular and a recognisably standard form of English spoken with a local accent. He further notes that miners characteristically use a more homogeneous vernacular than other occupational groups such as workers in the transport, catering or construction industries. As we shall see, relations between group structure (which may be affected by occupation) and language use are of great interest to us here. Indeed, one focus of interest in this book will be precisely on those points which Wright observed but did not study systematically—the relationship between heavy usage of vernacular speech and the internal structure of the group using that vernacular.

SOCIOLINGUISTICS—SOME GENERAL PRINCIPLES

Much work in this field is dominated by the influence of William Labov whose early research is rooted in the background provided by the dialectologists. In the famous studies both of Martha's Vineyard (carried out in 1961) and New York City (1966) he uses the background of earlier work to locate his own observations in real (or historical) time and to help him discover the directions of linguistic change. This interest in linguistic change is, as we have seen, held in common with dialectologists. But Labov's work is all strongly slanted to the direct observation of linguistic change in the community, to working out its (social) mechanisms and isolating those social groups who are most directly responsible for introducing and spreading linguistic innovations (Labov, Yaeger and Steiner, 1972; Labov, 1972a). Labov makes frequent references to Gauchat's (1905) study of a Swiss village where sound change in progress was inferred from the contrasting speech patterns of both sexes and three generations of speakers.

Unlike the earlier investigator who collected data for the *Linguistic Atlas of New England*, Labov interviewed a large number of speakers drawn from various ethnic groups on the island of Martha's Vineyard (lying off the coast of Massachusetts). He also ensured that he had some representation of both sexes and different ages. He was able to observe linguistic change in progress by focusing on variable realizations of the diphthongs /ay/ and /aw/ (as in *mice* and *mouse*), and noted that a movement seemed to be taking place *away from* the standard New England realizations of the vowels, towards a centralized pronunciation of the second element of the diphthongs associated with conservative and characteristically Vineyard speakers. The heaviest users of the centralized diphthongs were young men who actively sought to identify themselves as Vineyarders, rejected the values of the mainland, and resented the encroachment of wealthy summer visitors on the traditional island way of life.

Thus, a number of assumptions made by earlier dialectologists are shown to be false; the heaviest users of the vernacular are not necessarily old people, nor are conservative dialects necessarily giving way to the spread of standard English. The concept of (almost) unitary dialects marked out by isoglosses is a great oversimplification, and speakers are revealed as exploiting the resources of the dialect as a means of projecting their social identities. This is to some extent independent of their exposure to the educational system, as some college-educated boys in Martha's Vineyard were extremely heavy users of the vernacular diphthongs. As we shall see, this capacity of vernacular features to persist in the face of relentless pressure from standard forms of the language is of very great interest here, for one of the questions we shall try to answer (partly at least) is why people continue to speak low-status vernaculars and even more interestingly, how they manage to maintain vernacular norms, when the social gains in adopting a form of speech closer to the standard are apparently considerable.

Further innovations in Labov's 1961 study should be noted. Instead of eliciting single lexical items from one speaker by means of a formal questionnaire, he based his analysis on the conversational speech of his many informants supplemented by data from reading passages and word lists. As we shall see, his data would probably have given quite a different impression of the language of Martha's Vineyard if he had confined his attention to formally elicited single lexical items. Certainly, without studying a number of speakers, and systematically comparing their language, he could not have noted the regularity and direction of linguistic change, nor could he have drawn conclusions about the social motivations of change. Equally important from the perspective of this book, he would have been unable to interpret his linguistic findings convincingly unless he had first discovered a great deal of background information about the island and islanders. A necessary part of his discussion includes changes in the island economy from one based on fishing to one dependent on tourists from the mainland; the location and ethnic origin of families thought to be most typically Vineyarders; the various ethnic subgroups on the island, their statuses relative to each other, and finally the attitude of the Vineyarders to their own community and to the summer visitors.

Labov's study of the Lower East Side speech community in New York City, completed by 1964, incorporates further methodological refinements and reveals some general facts about sociolinguistic structure in cities which have been generally confirmed in subsequent studies. The reader is referred to

Labov's own book *Sociolinguistic Patterns* (1972a) for a full account of his findings and general principles; the broad outlines of the work are described here only in so far as they are specifically relevant to the concerns of this book.

First, all the informants—340 in number—were selected by means of a random sample, not a judgement sample as in the smaller Martha's Vineyard speech community. This meant that the speech of the sample was truly representative of the speech of *all* Lower East Side New Yorkers.

Second, Labov sampled a range of speech styles, taking formal account of Orton's observation (see p. 4 above) that speakers vary their speech in accordance with the social situation in which they find themselves. He did this by subdividing his recordings of conversation systematically into a careful and a casual style.

The careful style, as we would expect, was the label given to that large part of the interview where an isolated individual was answering questions put by a stranger. Casual style on the other hand referred to the speech produced when the constraints of the interview were over-ridden in a number of fairly clearly defined ways, such as when a stretch of speech was outside the structure of the interview proper, perhaps to a telephone caller or a third person entering the room. Sometimes the speaker became briefly involved in a personal narrative of some intense experience.

Labov additionally collected various types of reading style ordered on a linear scale in accordance with the amount of attention a speaker was paying to his speech. These consisted of a passage of continuous prose, followed by a word list of single lexical items, and finally sets of minimal pairs (such as *god* and *guard* in New York City) which the speaker could differentiate only if he paid close attention to his speech. Thus, five speech styles could be ordered in a single dimension, ranging from least formal (casual style) to most formal (minimal pair style). In his more recent work (1978) Labov notes that he was not here attempting to make a general statement about the possible range of speech styles and that a naturalistic analysis of style would require more than a single dimension. But for the purpose of obtaining a general picture of the norms of the speech community, it is possible to order styles in this relatively simple way.

The key to direct analysis and systematic comparison of this very large amount of data is the concept developed by Labov of the *sociolinguistic variable* as a unit of analysis. A sociolinguistic variable is a linguistic element (phonological usually, in practice) which co-varies not only with other linguistic elements, but also with a number of extra-linguistic independent variables such as social class, age, sex, ethnic group or contextual style. Labov studied the distribution of five sociolinguistic variables in New York City, two consonant and three vowel variables.

The reason why this concept is so important is that it permits *quantification* of language use. In New York City, for example, an important variable is (r). The distribution of the variable may be studied in terms of whether a speaker pronounces or deletes the consonant /r/ in final or post vocalic preconsonantal positions (for example in *car, cart*). Speaker A's use of the variable can be compared with speaker B's, since (r) is a piece of the language which can be counted. The phonetic variants of a given variable are identified in advance and assigned a numerical value which reflects the social values attached to them. In New York City, for example, the characteristic vernacular pronunciation resulting from the application of an /r/ deletion rule was given a score of zero every time it occurred, while for each pronunciation of /r/ a score of one was assigned. Personal scores are assigned to individuals as percentages of total (r) — 1 usage.

(r) is an example of a *discrete variable*, the score being calculated in terms of either its presence or absence. More difficult are continuous variables, usually vowels, which cannot be scored in this way but are given a value in accordance with the position they occupy in phonetic space, to which a social meaning may also be assigned. Thus, variants of the variable (eh), the vowel found in words like *bad, ham*, can range in New York City from [ɪə] (most vernacular) to [æː] (most standard) with two other variants placed at intermediate points on the vowel chart and assigned numerical values. Thus (eh) can be said to vary on the phonetic dimension of vowel height and each occurrence given a value on a 1–4 scale. An index score can be calculated for each individual or group, representing an *average* score.

The reader is referred to Labov (1972a) for a fuller account of this concept. There are many complexities and problems in identifying and analysing variables which are discussed by Knowles (1978), J. Milroy (1980), and Hudson (1980). The main difficulty is often one of ordering continuous variables on a single phonetic or social dimension; for this reason several vowel variables in the Belfast study discussed later in this book were treated as discrete, and scored as percentages. Any linguistic scores referred to in later chapters are calculated using Labov's New York City methods; for whatever the difficulties with the notion of the variable, they are for the moment outweighed by the advantages of a method which allows quantification and comparison of different speakers' language.

The basic methods of presenting information on the speech community's *use* of the linguistic variables were developed by Labov in the same study. Group linguistic scores were calculated for speakers divided according to age, sex and social class; in general Labov considered his informants in groups of this kind and did not present much data on individuals. (We shall return to the question of group versus individual scores later.) The linguistic scores were then considered separately for these independent variables, with the full stylistic range also being taken into account. The broad outlines of Labov's findings are well known and have been confirmed in other surveys of the same type (for example, Shuy, Wolfram and Riley, 1968; Trudgill, 1974). Generally speaking, higher social class groups have relatively high linguistic scores (that is, they approximate closer to standardized varieties); women score higher than men and older speakers often higher than younger, though the pattern may be complex here. Speakers generally score progressively higher as they move along the stylistic continuum. There are many partial exceptions to these regularities; a sociolinguistic variable is not always evaluated in the same way by the whole speech community, and irregularities may provide evidence of linguistic change in progress (this point is discussed in more detail in Chapter 5). But the patterns on the whole *are* remarkably regular and allow generalizations to be made about the social use groups of speakers are likely to make of their language. Labov's basic methods also allow language use to be seen as *probabilistic* rather than *categorical*, any given group being *more* or *less* likely to use a high proportion of a given variable. This insight has been extended, somewhat controversially, in the notion of the *variable rule* as a formal component of a community grammar (see Labov, 1972b: Chapter 3).

A further principle emerging from Labov's early work on which he himself places considerable emphasis is that all speech styles are not of equal interest to the investigator. The most regular structure is to be found in a speaker's least overtly careful style—his *vernacular*. The reason why patterns of variation are clearest there is that conscious correction away from a vernacular tends to be sporadic; yet although the vernacular is the focus of interest to an investigator, it tends to disappear under direct observation. People use their vernacular most of the time (Labov has recently defined this as the form of speech acquired in preadolescent years), and the style used for reading and responding to interviews may be quite different. This is why the findings of traditional dialectology may not always be reliable; for although dialectologists are generally aware of the practical problems created by stylistic shift, they have not developed systematic means of dealing with them. This matter will be discussed in greater detail in the following chapters; but meantime it should be noted that for the purpose of studying the social meanings speakers assign to language, it is important to obtain maximum access to the vernacular.

SPEECH COMMUNITY AND COMMUNITY

As the notions of speech community, and of community in general, are important to the theme of this book, they should be considered briefly here. New York City is defined by Labov (1966:125) as a single speech community because it is 'united by a common evaluation of the same variables which differentiate the speakers'. Thus, all New York speakers from the highest to lowest status are said to constitute a single speech community because, for example, they agree in viewing presence of post vocalic [r] as prestigious. They also agree on the social value of a large number of other linguistic elements. Southern British English speakers cannot be said to belong to the same speech community as New Yorkers, since they do not attach the same social meanings to, for example, (r): on the contrary, the highest prestige accent in Southern England (RP) is non-rhotic. Yet, the Southern British speech community may be said to be united by a common evaluation of the variable (h); h-dropping is stigmatized in Southern England (Trudgill, 1974) but is irrelevant in New York City or, for that matter, in Glasgow or Belfast.

Note then that Labov's speech community is a large-scale concept; speakers from *all social classes* are seen as united by their common evaluation of linguistic norms. Before going on to discuss the quite different notion of *community*, we must look at this concept of social class; for although Labov employs it in his definition of *speech community*, it is not of central relevance to the notion of *community* which is a much smaller-scale and less abstract social unit.

Social class also is a broad, large-scale category. Although it is an apparently simple idea and has undoubtedly enabled linguists to shed considerable light on the social functions of language in cities, it is a very difficult notion to pin down unless consistently used at a high level of abstraction. Basically, the idea is that people can be ordered with respect to the rest of society by quantifiable characteristics like income, education, occupation, residence or life-style (there is lttle agreement amongst sociologists on which characteristics are most satisfactory). All these characteristics can be ordered in accordance with the way they are evaluated by society at large—for example a clergyman would be rated higher than a plumber, a college graduate higher than a non-graduate clerk. If everyone can be given a rating based on numerical values of a combination of these factors, society can be ordered into strata (or classes). The scale can then be segmented into upper, middle and lower class, with as many subdivisions as the analyst wishes to make.

This procedure obviously does reflect social reality to a certain extent and is a sensible way of ordering large amounts of data such as those collected from a large sample of speakers in New York City. But we must not lose sight of the fact that the groups we end up with by segmenting our scale—such as 'lower class', 'working class', 'middle class'—do not necessarily have any kind of objective, or even intersubjective, reality. In using the concept in Norwich, Trudgill (1974:33) points to its abstractness, the general fluidity of status groups, and the difficulty of assigning individuals to specific groups. Membership of a group labelled 'lower-middle class' does not necessarily form an important part of a person's definition of his social identity. Yet smaller-scale categories are available which reflect the fact that there *are* social units to which people feel they belong and which are less abstract than social classes. For this smaller-scale, more concrete, unit we reserve the term *community*, used in a specific, technical sense.

We saw earlier that people living in Martha's Vineyard felt there was clearly a group of people called 'Vineyarders', and that they used the resource of linguistic variability to indicate their affiliation with that group. Although hierarchical orderings do exist on the island, the concept of social class is less useful in explaining patterns of linguistic variation than the less abstract concept of community—Labov does not use this term, but refers to 'categories of local identity' (1972a:299). It must be acknowledged that there is almost as much disagreement on the use of the term *community* as on the use of *social class*, but most writers who use such a unit of analysis agree that they are talking about cohesive groups to which people have a clear consciousness of belonging (Bell and Newby, 1974). Unlike the more abstract social classes, these groups always have a strong territorial basis. While stressing the importance of the notion for some kinds of sociolinguistic investigation, Hymes sums up the problems and restricts the application of the term in the same way as we shall in this book.

> I ... acknowledge the difficulty of the notion of community itself. Social scientists are far from agreed as to its use. For our purposes it appears most useful to reserve the notion of community for a local unit, characterised for its members by common locality and primary interaction. (1974:51)

As we move on to discuss the structure of people's social networks, we will look more closely at what might be meant by 'primary interaction'. Meantime, the importance of a common locality should be noted (see also Cohen, 1982).

Martha's Vineyard may be described as a community by this definition, and also the rural areas usually studied by dialectologists—although as we have seen their work gives us little insight into the relationships between language and community. We may describe as communities those working-class areas of large cities which are often called 'urban villages'; this name is given to them partly because of the characteristic structure of social networks in many working-class areas, but also because the residents have a strong feeling of belonging to and owning 'their' area of the city.

This 'localism' is well documented. Fried observes that data from working-class studies in different parts of the world all emphasize 'the vividness of working-class neighbourhood life, the extension of close knit social interaction patterns in the local area, and a conception of the neighbourhood as an extension of the home' (1973:81). The reluctance of people to change residence (even for superior housing) when they perceive themselves as belonging to a community of this kind is also well documented. In general, community dwellers are fearful of moving outside their areas: the Bethnal Green people studied by Young and Wilmott (1962) hardly moved from the East End into the general metroplitan area of London, and Fried's Boston West Enders are reported as experiencing feelings of anxiety and strangeness no matter how often they venture downtown to shops or hospitals (1973:83). In Belfast the same territoriality has been found (Boal, 1978; Wiener, 1976; L. Milroy, 1976), reinforced (but in view of comparable patterns elsewhere, not caused) by the notorious sectarian lines of demarcation.

Fried contrasts members of the Boston community with the urban middle classes who are not normally deterred by travelling, and may drive considerable distances to work or visit friends. They also characteristically change place of residence with relative equanimity. Like Hymes, Fried links this localism with interactional norms: 'as a regular daily basis for social interaction there were no relationships more important than neighbouring and other affiliations based on physical contiguity (1973:108). Frankenberg (1969) analyses a great many different types of community within the British Isles (using the term in a rather looser sense); he looks at social patterns of various kinds in Irish and Welsh rural areas, in small towns, in urban villages, and in various recently established working- and middle-class areas. In general, it seems that socially and geographically mobile individuals lack these local loyalties and characteristically dense patterns of interaction within a limited area. Middle-class housing developments are described where people may never speak to their neighbours, but interact a great deal *outside* the neighbourhood. Frankenberg also documents tensions between old established communities and 'new people' moving in from outside, who do not share local norms and values (a pattern reminiscent of Martha's Vineyard). He also describes the collapse of the characteristic neighbourhood interactional pattern when a traditional working-class community is moved to the suburbs, several miles from the old neighbourhood.

Knowledge of community patterns and conflicts of this kind can be extremely useful to a linguistic investigator; some will argue that such knowledge is essential. In any event, Labov was able to use information on conflicts between Vineyarders and 'summer people' to help him interpret patterns of linguistic variation; in Belfast as we shall see it has been possible to use this kind of knowledge to account for systematic differences in language use between individuals, and between subgroups in the population of communities which, in terms of social status, are relatively homogeneous. What is clear is that a community might be considered as a social unit whose language patterns are amenable to study. Indeed, the concept of social class was less useful in Martha's Vineyard than in New York City, which, by the definition we have adopted, could not in fact be said to be a community.

Quite different from any of Labov's work is Blom and Gumperz's (1972) study of the Norwegian town of Hemnes. This influential paper also takes the 'community' as its unit of study; the authors are attempting to describe the language patterns of pre-existing groups within a defined territorial area. They do not use techniques of quantifying linguistic data, concentrating mainly on careful discursive description. Both in this paper and elsewhere (Gumperz, 1970) they insist on the importance of the linguistic investigator understanding the general norms and values of the community, before he is able to interpret linguistic behaviour.

Blom and Gumperz are interested primarily in the manner in which speakers use the varieties of language available to them—in this case Norwegian dialect at one extreme and a more standardized code at the other—for signalling a wide range of social meanings. As we might expect from the information we already have on working-class communities, the low-status group in Hemnes have strong local loyalties, perceiving 'local team' interests (the authors' term) to be distinct from the pan-Norwegian values of the élite of the town—the professional classes. The analysis is complex, taking into account various social situations in which dialect and standard linguistic elements are used in different proportions, so that stylistic analysis might here be seen as *multidimensional* (cf. p. 9 above).

What is of major interest here however, is the authors' demonstration that heavy use of dialect is understood by the community to symbolize local loyalty. On the other hand, heavy use of the standard is seen by dialect-speakers to symbolize pan-Norwegian values and rejection of 'local team' values. This is exactly what we would expect as a result of Labov's findings in Martha's Vineyard; but we may in addition reinterpret the New York City data in the light of what appears to be a tendency for low-status people in communities to use vernaculars as symbols of local loyalty. Are low-status New Yorkers rejecting prestige varieties and using the vernacular as a symbol of adherence to those local communities so commonly associated with low-status people in cities? That such a use is made of the vernacular is clear from the two quite different community studies already discussed, and also from recent work in Belfast. When we look at Labov's later studies of the most underprivileged adolescents in New York City, it will be clear that adolescent peer groups use the vernacular in an analogous way, and some of Trudgill's work in Norwich (Trudgill, 1972) suggests that this might happen on a wider scale. A great deal of recent work by social psychologists (see especially Ryan, 1979) has confirmed that low-prestige ethnic and status groups everywhere perceive their language or dialect as a powerful symbol of group identity, despite long-term pressures from the standardized code. Examples can be quoted as divergent as Lowland Scots in Southern Scotland, Catalan in Spain, Canadian French in Canada, Black English in the United States, and the whole range of low-status vernaculars in British and European cities. Low-status varieties appear to have the same social function whether or not speakers attribute a positive value to them when questioned directly. They do not necessarily show any signs of succumbing to the pressures of standardization, despite the social benefits which might accrue to speakers were they to adopt the standardized code. On the contrary, Lambert (1979) considers that the tendency of ethnolinguistic groups to cultivate their own linguistic distinctiveness has actually *increased* during the 1970s (and still continues to do so).

It is necessary to emphasize the importance of these observations which, after all, reflect quite accurately the intuitive sociolinguistic knowledge of a great many speakers of low-status varieties everywhere. The implications of this widespread vernacular loyalty are very different from those suggested by an analysis of sociolinguistic structure based on a division of society into social classes which, intuitively, is equally plausible.

Labov's 1966 model (and subsequent urban studies based on it) suggests an overwhelming tendency for people to aspire to the speech characteristic of the socioeconomic class immediately above them. Yet, Labov's later work, and the work which we have already considered, suggests that language does much more than reflect people's positions in an abstract hierarchical society, demarcating general social class, sex and age groups. This is certainly true at a relatively abstract level, but when we look at language use in a more detailed way, we find that people also manipulate the linguistic resources available to them; they are not 'blobs of clay' moulded by a series of social and situational constraints (Giles and Smith, 1979:64). The resources available for manipulation include low-prestige and stigmatized varieties which may be used, if the speaker wishes, to indicate loyalty to a local community and rejection of metropolitan and national prestige values.

Thus, instead of positing a sociolinguistic continuum with a local vernacular at the bottom and a prestige dialect at the top, with linguistic movement of individuals in a generally upward direction, we may view the vernacular as a positive force: it may be in direct conflict with standardized norms, utilized as a symbol by speakers to carry powerful social meanings and so resistant to external pressures. This may happen in cities, towns or villages and it is likely that it can be observed wherever the linguist's unit of study is based on pre-existing groups in the community. A major concern of this book will be to document in some detail the manner in which low-status Belfast speakers from three different communities use Belfast vernacular in an extremely complex way to demonstrate allegiance to those communities. The social, linguistic and educational implications of these facts are considerable, but our knowledge of them is not yet firm enough to be translated into direct social action.

We may conclude this chapter by introducing the notion of

social network. Blom and Gumperz noted that the heaviest (low-status) dialect users generally were members of 'closed' networks. Considered from a linguist's point of view, this is a similar point to Fried's, that since low-status speakers interact mostly within a defined territory, a given person's contacts will nearly all know each other. The élite of Hemnes on the other hand had 'open' personal networks. They moved (like Fried's urban middle classes) outside territorial boundaries, and a given person's contacts each had his own contacts, none of whom necessarily knew each other. We might show these two general network types as in Figures 1.1 and 1.2, with the individual whose network is being studied shown by a star, and other people in the network by dots. Contact between individuals is shown by a line. The two networks are said to be of *high density* and *low density* respectively.

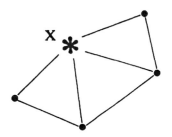

Figure 1.1 *High-density personal network structure: X is the focal point of the network*

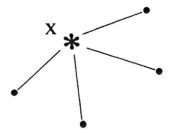

Figure 1.2 *Low-density personal network structure: X is the focal point of the network*

Blom and Gumperz do not analyse systematically the relationship they observed between language and network, nor do they analyse network structure beyond making the binary distinction between open and closed networks. However, it is possible for one network to be described as *more* or *less* dense than another, rather than in absolute terms as *open* or *closed*. Additionally, Blom and Gumperz comment that the *content* of the network ties which bind members of the élite to 'local team' people is 'largely impersonal, focussing around *single tasks*'. In contrast, most local team people 'live, marry and earn their livelihood among others of their own kind' (433). Thus, not only are local team networks dense, but each individual is likely to be linked to others in more than one capacity—as a co-employee, a kinsman and a friend, for example. This kind of network tie may be said to be *multiplex*, or many stranded, and to contrast with the *uniplex* ties of the élite who tend to associate with the local people in a single capacity only.

Although Blom and Gumperz neither analyse network structure in this way, nor posit any kind of relationship between network structure and linguistic choice, we shall see shortly that the notion of social network is amenable to very much further analysis. Ultimately, it can be used to account for variability in *individual* linguistic behaviour in communities, which is something a large-scale analysis like Labov's in New York City does not set out to do.

So far, the general approach adopted in this book to the study of language in its social context has been outlined, and contrasted with a number of other approaches. Two categories which sociolinguistic research frequently makes use of have been discussed in some detail—those of *class* and *community*. Finally, in terms both of methods and findings, large-scale studies, such as the urban surveys, have been contrasted with small-scale community studies. Generally, the latter are able to provide more detailed information on the use which speakers make of language variability—particularly with reference to the less formal parts of the linguistic repertoire. It is already clear that the field methods employed in sociolinguistic work have a very great bearing on the results. The next chapter will therefore examine in a more detailed way the practical problems of studying language in context, the manner in which these problems have been handled, and the kind of data which have become available for analysis.

2

Obtaining Data in the Speech Community: Major Principles

The discussion at the end of Chapter 1 suggested that the vernacular might be an interesting kind of language to study, and that moving beyond 'careful' or 'polite' styles or varieties of language was well worth while. We have already noted that Labov did not consider all the styles he arranged along a linear continuum to be of equal importance; and over the last fifteen years he and his associates have repeatedly shown that the vernacular is in fact the best data base for a sociolinguistic analysis. The reasons for this preference for the vernacular are compelling:

> Its [the vernacular's] highly regular character is an empirical observation. The vernacular includes inherent variation, but the rules governing that variation appear to be more regular than those operating in the more formal 'superposed' styles that are acquired later in life. Each speaker has a vernacular form in at least one language . . . In some cases systematic data can be obtained from more formal styles, but we do not know this until they have been calibrated against the vernacular. (Labov, 1981:3)

There are then good linguistic reasons for making some effort to gain access—which involves obtaining clear tape recordings— to a speaker's vernacular. If information is available only on more careful styles, data may, as a result of sporadic correction, be seriously incomplete so that any description of, for example, the speech of an industrial city, may be quite inadequate. It may be inadequate in the fundamental sense that important phonological and syntactic regularities simply cannot be recovered from the recorded text. This truth is particularly evident if the analyst is working with the working-class speech of a city. Such speech is usually particularly subject to social stigma and little is generally known about its structure. For example, in our own recent study of Belfast working-class speech, we noted a number of features of great importance to an adequate phonological description which did not appear if speakers were interacting in a guarded or careful manner. I refer particularly to the [ʌ] variant (alternating with [ʉ]) in a limited subclass of lexical items. These include *look* and *shook*, but not *cook* or *book*; and there are other limited subclasses of this kind (J. Milroy, 1980). These variables pattern in an extremely significant manner in the community, as we shall see; yet, had informants not been approached in such a manner as to allow vernacular speech to be recorded for at least part of the time, any description of *basic Belfast vernacular* would probably not have been able even to note the existence of these variants. Note that the term vernacular is used here in a manner different from, but related to, its sense in Chapter 1; an *urban* vernacular is defined as the kind of speech the majority of speakers of a city (usually low-status speakers) acquire in their adolescent years. When we speak of Black English Vernacular or Belfast vernacular, we are using the term in this general sense rather than referring to an *individual's* vernacular. Thus, both senses of 'vernacular' (and both are common in the literature) refer to publicly unrecognized language varieties, one on the dimension of personal style, the other on the larger dimension of standardization.

GAINING ACCESS TO THE VERNACULAR

There are two compelling reasons why a speaker's vernacular is hard to obtain in an individual interview of the kind used by Labov in New York City. First, and most obvious, an interview is in our society a clearly defined and quite common speech event to which formal or careful speech is appropriate (this is particularly the case with tape-recorded interviews). This perception of the interview as a speech event subject to clear rules (of a sociolinguistic type) persists, however carefully the interviewer modifies the formality of his approach. It will be shown in the following chapter that interviews are characterized by a discourse structure not found in spontaneous conversations.

Second, informants are usually isolated individuals participating in a series of exchanges with a stranger. They are not normally talking to, or in the presence of, members of their own pre-existing social network. If the family or some friends happen to be present during the interview, this is a matter of good luck, and, unlike the other independent variables discussed (such as the social class or sex of the informant), quite outside the interviewer's control. One consequence of the informant's isolation is that pre-existing norms of behaviour, including linguistic behaviour, do not necessarily apply. The presence of a primary group impels the speaker, to varying degrees (depending partly on its capacity to impose normative consensus), to speak as he normally would in their presence.

The linguistic consequences of this characteristic group behaviour have recently been documented in a study of a Northern Irish village community (Douglas-Cowie, 1978). Speakers from the investigator's own community were recorded on two occasions, first talking alone to an (English) outsider and then amongst themselves. Data adequate for an analysis of the local Ulster–Scots dialect are recorded in sufficient quantity only when the speaker is chatting to the group. Otherwise, extensive code-switching is liable to occur (the speakers are effectively bidialectal in the sense discussed by Trudgill (1983)). Douglas-Cowie makes the point in her conclusion that dialectologists following their traditional methods, especially if they use a nonlocal interviewer, are most probably recording the more standard part of the speaker's linguistic repertoire.

Within the framework of a linguistic interview, Labov tackled these problems in a systematic way by specifying as casual style—i.e. the style nearest to the vernacular—those parts of the interview in which the special constraints of that speech event were temporarily over-ridden. Trudgill (1974) was able to distinguish a more and less formal style by subdividing his data according to topic (see also Blom and Gumperz, 1972; Douglas-Cowie, 1978, for evidence that topic can constrain speech style). We should however note that some sociolinguistic studies employing interview techniques have not been able to show stylistic differentiation. For example, Macaulay (1977) was unable to give a clear account of Glasgow vernacular, or of the direction in which speakers shift in conversational styles, although he considered this to be an important area of enquiry. Like Shuy, Wolfram and Riley (1968), he distinguished only one fairly formal conversational style.

We may conclude then that direct interviewing, however informal the approach of the field worker, is an uncertain means of gaining access to the vernacular. Labov and Trudgill obtained approximations to it under unpromising circumstances by manipulating some of the extra-linguistic features constraining speech style, such as topic, or the speaker's perception of the nature of the speech event in which he was participating. The totality of such situational factors constraining linguistic performance is not known (but see Hymes (1972) for a discussion of the possibilities). What is clear, however, is that the interaction between language and situation is too complex and too little understood for an interviewer to be able to manipulate it reliably. This is probably why Macaulay found Labov's procedure not explicit enough to assist him in overcoming the constraints of the interview situation.

RECORDING GROUP INTERACTION

Labov and his colleagues subsequently tackled the problem of access to the vernacular in a completely different manner (Labov, Cohen, Robins and Lewis, 1968). Their basic objective was to obtain reliable information on the structure and use of Black English Vernacular (BEV), a relatively uniform form of language widely used by black speakers in the United States. BEV is often heavily stigmatized, and at the same time overtly viewed by the black community as a symbol of ethnic identity. With the object of obtaining access to this vernacular, Labov and his colleagues adopted three important procedures. These are as follows:

1. They focused on the speech of adolescents. The closest approximation to the vernacular is apparently found most consistently in adolescents up to the age of about sixteen (Labov 1972b). This is, in part at least, probably for complex reasons relating to peer group network structure which we shall consider in detail in the course of this book. Generally speaking, adolescents have not fully developed the characteristic adult range of superposed styles which may obscure the vernacular.

2. Several field workers were used. Both Robins and Lewis were black, and although nonlinguists, were participants in the vernacular culture and cognisant of its values. Labov and Cohen were white professional linguists. In acknowledging the importance of the ethnic and local identity of the field worker, Labov broadened the range of styles to which he had access by using both 'insiders' and 'outsiders'.

3. More than one method of data collection was employed. Most importantly, several informally constituted peer groups (notably those known as the Jets, Cobras and Thunderbirds) were located. The boys were recorded both individually and in each others' company. During the group sessions, the speech of each member was recorded on a lavalière microphone (round the speaker's neck) on a separate track. The atmosphere of these sessions was party like, with eating, drinking, card-playing, singing and sounding (the exchange of ritual insults) taking place. Although of course the effect of observation and recording was present (the groups had been convened specifically for that purpose), the resulting constraints were not as strong

in their capacity to inhibit the emergence of the vernacular as those generated by the presence of the group were to encourage it. This seems to be the experience generally of those who obtain linguistic data by means of group sessions of any kind (Blom and Gumperz, 1972; Milroy and Milroy, 1978; Reid, 1978; Cheshire, 1982). Labov notes in fact that the control exercised by peer groups over the vernacular is so strict, and supervision so close that a speaker making a single departure from group norms may be taunted for years afterwards. Physical force may even be employed in the exercise of this control. For example, one Belfast boy, slightly older than the Harlem peer group members, has described being beaten up by a shipyard colleague ostensibly because of a single failure to use a vernacular speech variant. (Maclaran, 1976)

Labov and his colleagues took every opportunity to record large amounts of vernacular speech in settings as unlike those of an interview as possible; for example, one very successful recording was made on a coach trip. These recordings have been extensively transcribed (Labov, 1972b) and clearly represent a reliable sample of basic BEV. Just as important, the researchers were able to obtain evidence of a large and varied stylistic repertoire in the BEV community. (A stylistic repertoire is defined as the total range of speech styles available to a community.) Since this speech was recorded during relatively uninhibited group sessions, observed variability went well beyond the unidimensional shifts analysed previously in New York City. It became possible to specify the rules governing ritual insults, vernacular narrative technique, jokes, recitations of 'toasts' (traditional BEV oral poems), and a number of other quite clearly definable speech events. Communicative competence, demonstrated by a full knowledge of these rules and many others, implies an ability to know how to speak on a given occasion. This is as much part of a speaker's knowledge of his language as the syntactic and phonological rules underlying speech production. These rules vary from one community to another (Hymes, 1972) but they are always complex. It is important to be able to demonstrate their existence in a vernacular community, for as Labov has pointed out in his famous polemic 'The logic of nonstandard English' (1972b: Chapter 5), professional educators often make negative judgements about the language capacity of vernacular speakers on the basis of interviews which do not elicit a wide range of styles or even very much speech. It is clear that working-class speakers in the British Isles too have access to an equally wide range of speech styles and verbal arts which remain unacknowledged in the course of the educational process. (See Milroy and Milroy (1977a) for an account of a wide range of vernacular styles.)

The Harlem group data was supplemented by material collected from individual interviews with the same boys, and furthermore by interview data collected from a random sample of adults in two Harlem apartment blocks. By using this combination of methods, Labov was able to obtain a clear view of general community speech norms, as well as focusing as directly as possible on Black English Vernacular. His data were rich enough to allow him to analyse 'internal' grammar; as well as examining general sociolinguistic patterns, he was able to study specifically linguistic constraints on such processes as final stop deletion, copula deletion and double negation.

We should note here in passing Labov's general views both on the social function of this vernacular and the manner in which its norms are maintained in the teeth of strong counter pressures from standard varieties of English: 'it [BEV] defines and is defined by the social organisation of the peer groups in the inner city' (1972b:xiii). Use of the vernacular is then viewed as an important mark of group identity; at the same time (as he argues at several points in *Language in the Inner City*), it is adolescent peer groups who are primarily responsible for using and transmitting the full resources of the vernacular; after adolescence, he contends, speakers progressively move away from intensive use of the vernacular. We shall return later to the questions this argument raises about the social function of the vernacular in the adult community.

Before concluding this discussion of Labov's Harlem work, we must look at his findings on the connection between a speaker's language and his place in the peer group network structure. Copula deletion is a linguistic variable of BEV which Labov studied quantitatively in the manner described in Chapter 1. This means that in a sequence like *He is a bad man* the copula could either appear or be replaced by zero, giving *He a bad man*. The zero form is an important stereotype of BEV. Effectively, Labov was able to relate incidence of copula deletion to the extent to which speakers were integrated into Black English Vernacular culture. To do this, he concentrated particularly on the group known as the Jets.

There were two centres for the Jets based on two apartment blocks where they lived; a core group was associated with each centre. Depending on each member's habitual associates, and on who (reciprocally) regarded whom as a friend, Labov was able to specify four degrees of integration into the vernacular culture, which, in turn, he viewed as dependent on peer group structure. At one extreme are the core groups who are at the centre, then secondary members, peripheral members and finally lames. The lames are isolated individuals effectively outside the street culture who may not even control the full stylistic repertoire. Their use of the zero form of the copula (20 per cent) is very much less than that of the core and secondary members, who use it 46 per cent of the time, and rather less than that of the peripheral members who score 26 per cent. Thus, a speaker's place in a group structure can be seen to be connected with his language at a very much less abstract level than is his place in a social class hierarachy which, as we have seen, is also connected with his language. As we shall soon turn our attention to the related connection between a speaker's social network structure and his language, using rather different methods, the importance of Labov's findings here should be noted. Note also that he does not attempt to extend these methods to study the connection between *adult* language and integration into the vernacular culture.

The major findings of this analysis of group structure and

language use have recently been confirmed in the British Isles in a study of peer groups in Reading. The method has also been extended there by incorporating a study of the behaviour of both boys and girls (Cheshire, 1982).

LANGUAGE IN ITS SITUATIONAL CONTEXT

A completely different approach to the problem of obtaining a reliable sample of vernacular speech is exemplified by Blom and Gumperz (1972) in the paper already briefly considered in Chapter 1. Like Labov, they were interested in observing patterns of language variation in the community. It will be recalled that Hemnes was a bidialectal community: all speakers had access to both the dialect and the standard. In particular, Blom and Gumperz were interested in discovering the specific situational conditions under which speakers shifted from one linguistic code to the other. To accomplish this, they found it necessary to focus their attention on the relationship between use of the two codes and the local social system. This concentration on exact situation of use together with the fullest specification of social context is very different from Labov's methods and is characteristic of much of Gumperz's other work (Gumperz and Hernandez, 1969; Gumperz, 1970; 1976a; 1976b; 1977a; 1977b; see now Gumperz, 1982a).

At this point, an outline of the main findings of the Hemnes study will be helpful. As we have seen, the dialect was strongly associated by Hemnes natives with local team values. Noting this, Blom and Gumperz hypothesized that local team members, when interacting with each other, would not switch at all from the dialect to the standard whatever topic was being discussed. They tested this hypothesis by observing and recording the behaviour of a group of locals at a party given by a friend. The group was self-recruited, so that the researchers did not know in advance exactly who was going to appear at the party. They confined their role to introducing a wide range of topics into the conversation at periodic intervals and then retreating to the edges of the group, so as to allow internal interaction to take over. As they had expected, they found that the locals did not in fact shift from the dialect at all.

The experiment was repeated with a group of Hemnes students at home during the vacation. Although the students considered themselves to be local team members, they also sub-scribed to high-prestige social values with which the standard was associated. The hypothesis was that this group would shift to the standard if a topic relating to these values (such as univer-sity rules and regulations) was introduced. This turned out to be exactly what happened.

A point of major interest was that the students denied using the standard, and were dismayed when they discovered that they had actually done so. It seems, therefore, that these stylistic rules, like linguistic rules generally, operate below the level of consciousness.

The group who did *not* show a shift at the party were restricted in their use of the standard to contexts where it conveyed 'meanings of officiality, expertise and politeness towards stran-gers who are clearly segmented from their personal life' (1972: 434). In complete contrast, the élite of the town viewed the standard as their norm, and used the dialect only for a special effect of some kind such as in telling jokes, or in enquiring about personal affairs in the midst of a business transaction. This kind of switching is appropriately labelled *metaphorical* as distinct from the *situational* switching characteristic of the non-élite group. Amongst this group, use of the standard to another local speaker is seen as an unfriendly act of dissociation.

The findings of the Blom and Gumperz paper clearly call into question the notion of the speech community as formulated by Labov. Their detailed comparative study of small group inter-actions reveals that residents of the same small town are seg-mented into groups—or networks—who do *not* in fact share the same linguistic norms. The social meaning carried by the dialect is different for each group. However the major emphasis of Blom and Gumperz's study is in describing the intimate manner in which choice of code is linked to an integrated system of local values and used to convey social meanings. They argue that linguistic choice takes place as a result of specifiable social and situational constraints and incentives which are quite amenable to analysis. It was already noted that Labov too concludes that language use is closely connected with the local values system; where his approach differs is that he does not examine situational variables as closely nor primarily demonstrate in such detail the manner in which language choice is linked to a local values system. Just as Labov views the vernacular as socially functional in that it is an important marker of group identity, so Blom and Gumperz view the maintenance of *both* dialect *and* standard codes as functional because they express necessary social meanings. They are maintained by a social system which sharply distinguishes between local and nonlocal values. Since the Hemnes élite (like élites elsewhere) usually subscribe to nonlocal values, both sets of values are effectively tied up with the local status system. If maintenance of two distinct codes is supported by a stable social system in this way, we may derive from Blom and Gumperz's work further insight into why conservative and nonstandard dialects (urban or rural) persist. For the 'common-sense' view adopted by traditional dialectologists has, as we have seen, usually been that they will fade out with increasing pressure from the standard language (see also Wyld (1936) who uses this argument to justify his concentration on standard English). If conservative dialects *do* recede, as they often do, their social function is likely to be taken over by another nonstandard variety. This is what in fact appears to be happening in the Ulster–Scots area, studied by Gregg (1972).

It should be clear that rather different field methods from those discussed so far are necessary for the study of 'ethnography of communication' in the manner exemplified by Blom and Gumperz. Most obviously, the researchers needed to know a great deal about local values and the local social system before they could even begin their analysis. They had to understand the strong association of the dialect with localism and the disapproval shown towards locals (such as the students) who used the standard to each other. Before they could form and test their first hypothesis they had to carry out what they describe as 'unstructured ethnographic observations' over a long period. This enabled them to observe in a general way, before forming a testable hypothesis, which people shifted in which direction in which situations.

The ultimate experiments make use of group dynamics in much the same way as Labov's Harlem work. Blom and Gumperz confirm that the operation of stylistic rules is encouraged by the presence of the group, regardless of the fact that strangers and a tape-recorder are also present. This is shown by the fact that recorded conversations usually began with a few polite remarks being addressed in the standard to the researchers themselves, before group norms stimulated a shift to the dialect.

An important point which can be inferred from much of the work discussed in these two chapters—and this point is made specifically by Gumperz (1968)—is that monolingual style-shifting is likely to take place under much the same kind of situational constraints as those specified for dialect or language switching. Different varieties of the same language are likely to have a similar social function to different dialects and even different languages in a bidialectal or bilingual society (Douglas-Cowie, 1978; Trudgill, 1983; Labov, 1972a; 1972b; Milroy and Milroy, 1977a). The point is that the repertoires of some communities can be analysed as consisting only of 'styles' of one language, while others consist of relatively discrete dialects or even different languages. In fact, dialects may not always be as discrete as they appear; according to Blom and Gumperz the main feature of dialect switching which distinguishes it from monolingual style-shifting is the operation of strict lexical, phonological and morphological co-occurence rules. A style shift on the other hand may take place at the phonological level only; but neither kind of shifting is a matter of choice between two discrete entities. Dialect switching, like style-shifting, can be described quantitatively in terms of relative frequencies of key variables (Blom and Gumperz, 1972:415).

The contributions of Blom and Gumperz to the study of language in its social context add to the principles derived from Labov's work in two important ways. First, it is demonstrated that community interactional patterns cannot always be understood without a long period of observation to establish the general norms and values of the community, which may be quite different from more publicly accepted, institutionalized norms and values. This is clear also from Labov's work with participants in the BEV culture, although unlike Blom and Gumperz he is dealing only with young male adolescents. Consequently it is not surprising if patterns of language use in the community are related to a *local, non-institutionalized* social system.

Second, the *situation* in which specific codes are used is particularly important if the impulses behind their use are to be understood. Exact specification of which code is used by whom to whom may be quite as important as quantifying overall usage, as Labov does. Labov himself has shown his awareness of this fact, in a general way, by his observation that social isolates such as the lames may not have communicative competence in the full range of BEV speech events. He is in practice referring to their responses to specific situations of use.

APPLICATIONS OF SOCIOLINGUISTIC RESEARCH

It is worth noting briefly at this point that although the research findings discussed in these chapters have been available for some years, there is as yet little sign that they are being applied in the many contexts of everyday life where they are relevant. We may refer to Bernstein's work in the 1960s as a particularly clear and well-known example of a theory based on very little properly collected and analysed linguistic data; yet, Bernstein's work on linguistic codes was understood to make statements about contrasting patterns of language use between working-class and middle-class speakers and consequently influenced educational training and practice. There is as yet very little indication that educational psychologists and others concerned with the relationship between language and educational attainment are adopting a more accountable attitude to linguistic data. Where real data *are* used, they are usually collected in formal settings, such as the classroom, and certainly as Blom and Gumperz and Labov have shown, cannot give any clear indication of the range of a speaker's linguistic repertoire. Yet, it is the *totality* of this repertoire, rather than merely a small part of it, which provides the linguistic input to the educational process. It has been pointed out recently that this unwillingness to adopt a realistic view of language use has implications far beyond the schoolroom. Taylor (1977) notes that very many standardized language tests are heavily biased against nonstandard speakers. Since standardized tests are used for a very large number of purposes, including the assessment of language disorders, aptitude, achievement, personality, job suitability and employment potential, it is likely that a wide range of human traits is at present being misassessed on a very large scale. However, one person who *has* recently worked on the applications of sociolinguistic research to the resolution of social problems is Gumperz himself (1977a; 1977b). He focuses on the precise factors involved in interethnic conflict in England, usually in work situations, noting that groups typically perceive each other as mutually unfriendly, without understanding that the basis of these perceptions may be misunderstanding of communicative intent resulting from intergroup differences in communicative norms. Once the basis of the misinterpretation is analysed and incorporated into a training programme (1977b), resolution of the conflict becomes a more attainable goal.

In view of Gumperz's findings, it is quite likely that the generalized perceptions of British politicians (and others), that communication problems exist in British industrial life (between workers and management), are quite correct. There is no reason to suppose that different status groups are any more able to interpret mutual communicative intent than different ethnic groups; as we shall see in Chapter 4, research carried out in Belfast suggests quite the contrary. If this is so, there is no reason why the source of the misinterpretation cannot be analysed and incorporated into a training programme; Gumperz's work provides a model for a first approach to the problem.

CHOOSING MODELS FOR LINGUISTIC FIELDWORK

I have concentrated in these opening chapters on a partial account of limited number of studies by Labov on the one hand and Blom and Gumperz on the other for two reasons. First, those areas of their work on which attention has been focused provide the major background to the empirical study of language and social network in Belfast with which this book largely concerns itself. Many of the major principles and findings already discussed will in subsequent chapters be taken for granted. More generally, Labov's three major projects in Martha's Vineyard, the Lower East Side of New York City and Harlem, together with Blom and Gumperz's Hemnes study, are at the moment the most coherent models available to the investigator studying language in the community. And in fact, although subsequent work has not usually replicated their methods exactly, much of it is heavily indebted to these studies. It has already been noted that a number of surveys have been carried out on the model of Labov (1966), and we may refer additionally to a recently published collection of papers by British scholars (Trudgill, 1978). A recent study of a bilingual community in Central Europe (Gal, 1979) is heavily dependent on the categories established by Blom and Gumperz.

In general, very much more detailed information can be obtained from a fieldwork method which takes pre-existing groups as its unit of study; although the observer effect is still present, it is greatly modified. In particular, by making use of the two quite different approaches to group sessions discussed here, investigators have been able to obtain information both on the community linguistic repertoire and the 'internal' grammar of a nonstandard code. Information of this kind is not easily recoverable from texts recorded by means of single person interviews.

Conversely, we should note that although group studies allow a gain in depth, they lack representativeness. No claim can be made that the speech samples collected in this way are representative of the speech of a whole community. Information on some points of interest may be unobtainable—for example it is unlikely that evidence of linguistic change can be adduced unless some kind of sampling from different age groups (and possibly areas or social classes) is carried out. We cannot, therefore, view the survey incorporating individual interviews of large numbers of informants as an obsolete method. Most important of all, it is a necessary means of obtaining a general view of linguistic norms in the wider speech community. The recent work of Labov and his associates in Philadelphia has ambitious goals:

> The project on linguistic change and variation aims to locate decisive solutions to long-standing problems of linguistic structure and language ˙evolution through the quantitative analysis of data drawn from the speech community. (Labov, 1978:1; see also Labov, 1981)

To this end, the project utilizes a very large range of methods, each with its own strengths and weakness. Some, like the neighbourhood study (in which a field worker becomes involved in a single location for a very long period), or the group sessions, obtain a˙ very wide range of the community repertoire but lack breadth and representativeness. To cover this deficit, various types of survey are used. The survey using the individual interview method remains important; the rapid and anonymous survey (see Labov, 1972a), which does not even make use of a tape-recorder, allows a large-scale profile of a sociolinguistic variable to be constructed in a very short time. What is clear is that different methods have different strengths and weaknesses and that any investigator needs to look carefully at his objectives before he chooses one or another.

It will be shown in the next chapter how the fieldwork methods adopted in a community study in Belfast are designed to take account of the principles already outlined here. At the same time, the Belfast project applies insights derived from the concept of *social network* in order to account for the position of the field worker relative to the community which is being observed.

3

Studying Language in the Community: The Fieldworker and the Social Network

The development of satisfactory field methods for the study of language in the community remains a problem, despite pioneering work such as that described in the previous chapters. The nature of this problem, caused fundamentally by the effects of observation on linguistic behaviour, commands a wide area of agreement and is frequently discussed in the literature (Labov, 1972a *et passim*; Gumperz, 1970; Sankoff, 1974; Wolfson, 1976).

It is taken as axiomatic that research of this kind should be grounded in the notion of the speech community (although as we have seen this is not a particularly clear sociolinguistic category) and that a corpus should be collected and analysed which adequately represents linguistic behaviour. It has been shown in Chapter 2 that this involves drastic modification of the old investigative technique of the formal interview, still widely used in many other kinds of social research. Despite the development of special techniques, a linguistic investigator invariably encounters the problem which Labov has aptly named 'the observer's paradox': language in the community can be studied only by collecting large volumes of natural speech on good quality recordings; yet, a stranger who attempts to obtain these dramatically changes the character of the phenomenon he is observing. When a further axiom is accepted, that the data base should be the *wider* community and not a circle of friends or a captive population (such as school children or hospital patients) the investigator must immediately consider the problem of obtaining *representative* data. As we have seen, this problem has been tackled quite properly in the past by the use of sampling techniques; yet, random sampling tends to exacerbate the central problem of the observer's paradox. This is because the population to be studied is usually sampled for isolated individuals, or households, who are then recorded out of context of the social networks within which they customarily interact. Since a single meeting with a stranger is not a particularly auspicious occasion on which to observe a large portion of a speaker's linguistic repertoire, the data obtained are often very sharply limited in their capacity to represent a wide range of speech styles. As Sankoff has pointed out, data collected in this manner may be limited grammatically as well as stylistically; for example, people who are being interviewed seldom use interrogatives (1974:23).

Chapter 1 has described the earliest attempts to overcome this problem, which involved subdividing the data in various ways so as to designate on a linear scale some parts of the interview more 'formal' than others. Because of the obvious limitations of such methods, sophisticated participant observation techniques of studying stylistic variation were designed. Labov and his associates combined studies of self-selected peer groups with a series of individual interviews with members of the groups. For the group studies, two black fieldworkers mediated between the white investigators and the black adolescents who were the focus of the research.

Thus, the significant notion of *both* the insider *and* the outsider as fieldworkers is introduced. Between them, they may have access to a greater stylistic range than either can have, working alone. By making use of group behaviour mechanisms, the Harlem researchers succeeded in demonstrating the existence of a wide stylistic repertoire controlled by speakers of a socially stigmatized vernacular. Note that this study overcame the limitations of a unidimensional concept of conversational style, based on the general notion of greater or lesser formality. *Representative* data was obtained by means of a separate sampling study; no attempt was made to reconcile within a unitary study the aim of obtaining representative data with that of obtaining a wide range of speech styles.

Gumperz's work on code-shifting is also generally characterized by a concentration on specific communicative acts, rather than on obtaining representative data. For example, in one study (Gumperz and Hernandez, 1969) the code-shifting patterns of two fellow workers on Gumperz's own research programme were explored. In Hemnes also, the researchers had little control over the selection of informants; the groups studied were self-recruited in that people brought their own friends to the gathering. Blom and Gumperz also note the methodological importance of self-recruited groups; when previous obligations have been contracted by members of the group to each other and behavioural norms previously acknowledged, participants are likely to fall into an habitual pattern of behaviour. When this in fact happened, the researchers were able to fade into the background allowing group dynamics to carry along the interaction.

It is then fairly clear that sociolinguistic investigators agree substantially on the major problems of fieldwork in the speech community. These may be summarized as follows:

1. It is difficult, if not at present impossible, to reconcile the axiom that data should be *representative* of the speech of a total community with the requirement that a wide stylistic repertoire should be sampled. Labov tackles this problem by carrying out his work in distinct phases. Shuy, Wolfram and Riley's study of Detroit speech (1968)—an excellent example of a rigorous random sampling study—does not attempt to handle more than one fairly formal conversational style. Gumperz, on the other hand, tends to concentrate on the study of code-shifting in conversation, confines himself to small-scale community studies and does not attempt to obtain a representative sample.

2. Where the aim is to study the linguistic repertoire, usually by means of a small-scale community study, some means must be found of accounting for (and reducing) the

effect of an outside observer on the data. Labov in Harlem copes with this problem by using an *insider* as intermediary. Gumperz sometimes uses an insider and at other times combines the use of an insider with inconspicuous observation of a self-recruited group.

APPROACHING FIELDWORK IN BELFAST: A CASE STUDY

The main purpose of this chapter is to show how the second of these two problems might be tackled in a systematic manner. The approach is exemplified by a community study in Belfast which, in accordance with the constraints described in the previous paragraph, sacrificed representativeness in the interest of developing techniques of recording a wide stylistic range.

The fieldwork for a study of Belfast working-class speech was carried out during 1975–6. Three well-defined communities were observed, known respectively as Ballymacarrett, the Hammer and the Clonard. The social characteristics of the three communities will be described in Chapter 4; meantime we address ourselves to the problems of collecting stylistically varied linguistic data, including a large amount of individual speakers' vernacular styles.

Note that although Gumperz and Labov suggested ways of diminishing problems produced by the effect of observation, neither of them set out to account for the influence on linguistic performance of the fieldworker and the recording situation in an explicit manner. Clearly it is important that some attempt should be made to do this, since both the fieldworker as participant, and the fact that tape-recording is taking place, are important components of the total communicative situation. The manner in which this problem was handled in Belfast took account both of Labov's distinction between insiders and outsiders, and Gumperz's technique of retreating to the fringes of the interacting group. The procedure adopted by the fieldworker (myself) is, briefly, as follows. By applying the concept of social network I was able to analyse, and to some extent control, the character of my relationship to the group I was observing. It was possible to equip myself with a status which was neither that of insider, nor that of outsider, but something of both—a friend of a friend, or more technically, a second order network contact (Boissevain, 1974). This status enabled me to carry out prolonged observations and record large volumes of varied interaction over a considerable period. The concept of social network underlying this approach, and its application to sociolinguistic fieldwork, will be discussed shortly. It is best, however, first to take note of a general procedural principle which is likely to be important for any comparable study.

Investigators who work outside their own communities are likely to find that their field methods are constrained by a social barrier of some kind. For example, the design of Labov's Harlem project took into account the black/white conflict in the United States. In Belfast, the barriers constrained fieldwork strategy in a different way. The generally disturbed situation in the city (and the three communities were all in badly affected areas) resulted in three specific constraints. It will be helpful to state these specifically.

1. The fieldworker had to be a woman. Women were much less likely to be attacked than men, and since male strangers were at that time viewed with considerable suspicion in many parts of Belfast, they were likely to be in some danger if they visited one place over a protracted period.

2. The fieldworker had to enter the communities alone (compare the methods of both Labov and Gumperz above). A solitary woman was unlikely to be viewed as a threat and therefore more likely to be able to record large amounts of spontaneous conversation.

3. A fieldworker using recording equipment had to be able to offer some guarantee of good faith of a personal kind: otherwise prolonged observation and recording would not have been possible.

LIBRARY, UNIVERSITY OF CHESTER

While these special constraints on choice of method must be stated, there is no reason to consider social patterns in Belfast to be necessarily different from those in any other city. It seems likely, for example, that the strategy adopted in handling the third problem (see p. 54 below) can go some way to resolving the observer's paradox in working-sclass communities generally.

It is important to remember that although Belfast was dangerous, so also are many inner city areas; some may be more dangerous for a woman than a man, creating analogous constraints on choice of fieldworker. It will be shown in the following chapter that the structure of Belfast working-class communities is, in fact, very similar to those described in Chapter 1. Very probably they too could be successfully entered using similar methods.

SOCIAL NETWORK AS AN ANALYTIC CONCEPT

The notion of social network has already been touched on in several places in this book, but not as a methodological principle underlying fieldwork strategies. Nevertheless, Labov's technique of using an *insider* to collect his primary data, and Gumperz's technique, as an outsider, of *avoiding* interaction with the self-recruited group, both show an *implicit* recognition of the importance of the content of the network ties which link the fieldworker to the group he is studying. The purpose of this section is to show as *explicitly* as possible how the network concept can be used as an analytic tool, rather than as a simple metaphorical device for describing social relations. Blom and Gumperz do in fact use the term in this latter sense in their Hemnes study; both uses are discussed in detail by Mitchell (1969). The network concept is applied in Belfast with reference to the very considerable amount of empirical research carried out, mostly by British and European anthropologists, over the last two decades.

The basic postulate of these recent studies is that people interact meaningfully as individuals, in addition to forming parts of structured, functional institutions such as classes, castes or occupational groups. The other main interest of the approach of these scholars is that it is largely structural. With a view to explaining social behaviour, they concentrate not on the social or personal attributes of the individuals in a social network, but rather on the characteristics of the linkages which bind them to each other (Mitchell, 1969; Boissevain and Mitchell, 1973; Boissevain, 1974). The idea of social network (as an analytic concept) was originally introduced by Barnes (1954) to describe an order of social relationship which he felt was important in understanding the behaviour of the inhabitants of the Norwegian village of Bremnes. He felt that a great deal of social behaviour could not be accounted for by concepts based on status, territorial location or economic activity. A great deal more will be said in later chapters about the capacity of the network concept (it is a set of procedures rather than a fully-fledged theory) to illuminate patterns of specifically *linguistic* behaviour. Meantime, discussion will be restricted to the direct application of network-based procedures to linguistic fieldwork.

NETWORK ZONES (see Figure 3.1 below)

Many recent network studies have succeeded in producing precise and—where possible—mathematical statements of network relationships. Following the principle of *anchorage*, that is, considering a network from the point of view of single individuals, it is possible to begin by making some general statements about the informal social relationships in which everyone is embedded. Each person may be viewed as a focus from which lines radiate to *points* (persons with whom he is in contact). These persons who are linked directly to ego may be characterized as belonging to his *first order* network zone. Each of these people may be in contact with others whom ego does not know, but could come into contact with *via* his first order zone. These more distantly connected persons form ego's *second order zone*. Although a third, fourth and nth order zone could be distinguished, the first and second order zones appear, in practice, to be the most important. Boissevain, for example, has documented in detail the manner in which individuals use second order contacts to attain very varied goals—in one case to seek permission to submit a thesis late to a university department; in another to buy a quantity of scarce foodstuffs. It is the 'friend of a friend' in Belfast (and no doubt elsewhere) who helps to obtain goods at cost price, to mediate in a brush with the authorities, or to secure the services of a handyman. The *content* of the link between ego and the mediating first order contact may be very tenuous, as Boissevain shows; but at the level of informal social relationships, 'friends of friends' in most societies are extremely important people.

EXCHANGES, RIGHTS AND OBLIGATIONS

The general point has often been made (for example by Boissevain, 1974; Kapferer, 1969) that although a network is similar diagrammatically to a communication circuit (see Figure 3.1), its social function is much more complex than is implied by this comparison. A social network acts as a mechanism both for exchanging goods and services, and for imposing obligations and conferring corresponding rights upon its members. Kapferer's study of side-taking in a fight shows that individuals will go to extraordinary lengths to preserve key network relationships. Like social psychology's accommodation theory, which attempts to explain patterns of linguistic code-switching (Giles and Smith, 1979), the network concept has borrowed many insights from *exchange theory* (Homans, 1958). Both Kapferer and Boissevain use exchange theory to explain how individuals act to maintain key social relationships; the principles outlined in this section are also drawn ultimately from exchange theory.

Messages which pass along network links can be seen as transactions, governed by the principle that the value gained by an individual in a transaction is equal to, or greater than, the cost. These transactions may consist of goods and services of many kinds, including greetings, civilities, jokes, information, as well as (for example) sex, child-minding services, or assistance in times of sickness or poverty. When goods and services flow in both directions between links, it is useful to speak of *exchange.* In this sense, most speech events are tokens of exchange. A purely transactional speech event, where messages travel in one direction only, is rare. A *sermon* may be viewed as one example of a transaction, as may the deliberate spreading of a rumour in contrast to the exchange of gossip.

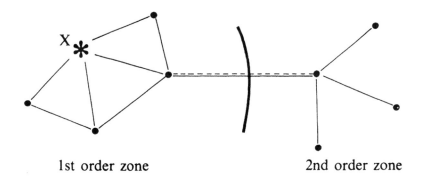

1st order zone   2nd order zone

Figure 3.1   *High-density personal network structure, showing first and second order zones. X is the focal point of the network*

Although he does not express these views explicitly, a skilled sociolinguistic fieldworker such as Labov perceives clearly that if he wishes to engage an informant in prolonged interaction, he must find a way of establishing exchange relationships. Hence Labov's insistence (1972c) that people will generally be willing to talk volubly if the interviewer is sympathetic and genuinely interested. Labov's tokens of exchange are not speech, but sympathy and a boost to the informant's self-esteem. These he is able to offer successfully. The extremely unsuccessful sociolinguistic interview documented by Wolfson (1976:197) may on the other hand be viewed as a transaction rather than an exchange. Here, a young female interviewer is talking to a middle-aged restaurant owner, trying to elicit his view of the city where he works. His replies are curt, and his contempt for the questions obvious. Wolfson analyses the failure as resulting from asymmetrical age–sex relationships between participants. This may be partly true—but the fact is that it is quite possible to record large volumes of speech even where these asymmetrical relationships exist. Using the insights of exchange theory, the failure may also be analysed in terms of the interviewer's inability to provide tokens of exchange, and the absence of any obligation resting on the restaurant owner to provide her with goods and services free of charge (speech in this case). If such an obligation does not exist, it is unlikely that the interviewer will be able to record prolonged interaction unless she can provide tokens of exchange equal in value to those she wishes the informant to give. As we shall see, the goods and services provided by a fieldworker may range from Labov's sympathy and flattering expressions of esteem, to spicy gossip, cigarettes and assistance with transport. The point is, that tokens of exchange of some kind should be available.

The notion of *obligation* is contingent on that of *exchange*. Sometimes more valued goods and services may be provided by one person than another, thus creating an obligation to return them. Again these goods and services may be material, or they may stem from qualities of personality and leadership, an ability to tell jokes or converse wittily. The important point is that, because of this asymmetry, the network becomes a mechanism whereby pressures, resulting from obligations contracted within the network, are applied to influence an individual's behaviour. If the individual wishes to protect social relationships, these constant obligations must be honoured.

STRUCTURAL AND CONTENT CHARACTERISTICS OF NETWORKS

Density

In a useful summary, Boissevain has isolated several *structural* and several *content* characteristics of personal networks which appear to be apposite to any attempt to describe social behaviour adequately. The most important structural characteristic is *density*, a notion already defined briefly in Chapter 1.

A network is said to be relatively dense if a large number of the persons to whom ego is linked are also linked to each other. The density of a network (or portion of a network) may be calculated by a simple formula, which expresses the ratio of the total *possible* links to the total *actual* links in the network under consideration.

This may be set out as follows:

$$D = \frac{100 \ Na \ \%}{N}$$

where Na refers to the total *actual* number of links and N the total number of possible links. Relatively dense networks are generally considered to function effectively as norm enforcement mechanisms, and are characteristic of those sociogeographic units which we defined in Chapter 1 as *communities*. It will be recalled that traditional working-class areas like those in Belfast are usually communities in this specific sense.

Clusters

Clusters are segments or compartments of networks which have relatively high density: relationships within the cluster are denser than those existing externally and may also be considered as being relationships of like *content*. Most people's personal networks consist of series of clusters where ties are, for example, those of kinship, occupation, specific group membership and many others. In practice most network studies, including this one, deal with clusters or groups of clusters. Labov's study of the Jets, Thunderbirds and Cobras is a study of bounded clusters rather than a total unbounded personal network. The adolescents are linked principally in their capacity as gang members (ties of like content), and the density of those clusters is 100 per cent. As Labov has remarked, the capacity of such a cluster to enforce its norms (linguistic and otherwise) on individual members is considerable. Recent network studies (e.g. Cubitt, 1973) have argued that density of key sectors or clusters is in fact a more important norm enforcement mechanism than overall density.

Multiplexity

Interactional or *content* characteristics of networks, though difficult to specify satisfactorily, are of clear importance in considering the influence of a network on behaviour; it is inadequate simply to specify a link without considering the content of that link. For example, the tie of kinship which connects me to my sister has a greater capacity to influence my behaviour than the economic tie which connects me to my newsagent; yet both are first order network contacts.

An important initial observation about content is that a person may be connected to ego in a single capacity only; we may refer to such a relationship as *uniplex*, or having a single content. If however more than one strand or content can be observed in the link, the relationship is, as was indicated briefly in Chapter 1, *multiplex*; the same man may be connected to ego as co-employee, neighbour, kin and in many other capacities. Thus it is possible for ego to relate to relatively few people in many capacities and have relatively *multiplex* network ties, or to relate to a great many people mainly in a single capacity and have relatively *uniplex* network ties. The multiplexity score for an individual, calculated as the ratio of multiplex ties to all relevant ties, can be expressed using the following formula:

$$ M = \frac{Nm \times 100}{N} \% $$

where Nm is the number of multiplex links and N the number of actual links.

The objection to the notion of multiplexity is that the number of strands which can be observed in a relationship may vary from one observer to another, and will also vary with analytic purpose. However, following a number of studies reported in Mitchell (1969), Boissevain and Mitchell (1973) and Boissevain (1974) I have confined my attention in Belfast to the key relationships of kin, neighbourhood, occupation and voluntary association (friendship). It is in fact possible, given this limitation of content, to state whether or not a given link is multiplex, although it is often not possible to tease out the exact number of strands in the link.

The significance of a high multiplexity score is considerable; multiplexity and density are conditions which often co-occur, and both increase the effectiveness of the network as a norm-enforcement mechanism. Relationships in tribal societies, villages and traditional working-class communities are typically multiplex and dense, whereas those in geographically and socially mobile industrial societies tend to uniplexity and spareness.

In the British Isles, multiplexity is linked with social class (Cubitt, 1973; Bott, 1971; Frankenberg, 1969). People in the Belfast working-class communities, like those in comparable communities elsewhere, were normally linked to each other in more than one capacity—simultaneously as kin, neighbours and co-employees for example. It was quite common for relatives to live next door, have frequent voluntary association with each other, and travel together to a common place of work. By way of contrast, a rapid survey of a Belfast housing estate inhabited principally by upper-middle-class professionals (Milroy, 1978: MS) revealed that multiplex relationships there were extremely rare.

We shall examine later the manner in which the concepts of *density*, *multiplexity* and *clustering* can be used to measure an individual's degree of integration into local community networks.

THE FIELDWORKER'S LINKS TO THE LOCAL NETWORKS

Although the analytic principles outlined in these sections have necessarily been somewhat abstract, it is possible to apply them directly to work in the field with the objective of minimizing the effects of observation on linguistic performance. The first and most important application is in defining the fieldworker's relationship to the community under observation.

It has already been noted that, at the level of personal relationships, the second order network contact (friend of a friend) has a definite status *vis à vis* ego's first order zone. If the network is dense, as in all three Belfast communities, the first order zone is in effect a bounded group. Friends of friends perform an important social function by extending the range of goods and services which members of the first order zone are able to provide. Therefore, if a stranger is identified as a friend of a friend, he may easily be drawn into the network's mesh of exchange and obligation relationships. His chances of observing and participating in prolonged interaction will then be considerably increased (cf. the discussion of an unsuccessful sociolinguistic interview on p. 49 above). With this specific purpose, I approached each of the Belfast communities in the specific capacity of 'a friend of a friend'.

This procedure should not be seen as limiting an investigation to communities where a network contact is already available. Indeed, since the purpose of refining sociolinguistic field methods is to broaden rather than narrow the range of language available for study, any acceptable method must be capable of application outside the researcher's own first order network zone. In Belfast, the communities were first selected on the basis of a range of socio-geographic factors (see Chapter 4), and only then were contacts sought who were known in the area, but had no official status of any kind there; approaches to priests, teachers and community leaders were avoided. This last point is very important, as an approach through a semi-official sponsor can result in the fieldworker obtaining access only to relatively standardized speakers (Labov, 1972c). The initial 'link' contact knew the purpose of the research, but did not visit the area with me or introduce me personally; he simply provided lists of acquaintances' names and addresses. I subsequently entered each area alone, always made an initial approach to a specific individual whose name had been passed on and introduced myself as 'a friend of X; he thought you might be able to help me'. Knowledge of X's name acted as a guarantee of good faith, and was received as a claim by X that obligations to him should be fulfilled in the form of help for his 'friend'.

I entered Ballymacarrett, for example, by mentioning the name of a student who had once lived there. The first person to be approached was a middle-aged man (the janitor of a public building) to whom I identified myself as 'a friend of Sam's'. As I became familiar in the area, I was first introduced in this way, and later as 'a friend of Ted's', Ted being the member of the local network who gave most help. Thus—and this is the important point—my social role was definable in relation to the network, the role of researcher being secondary to the extent that it was often not mentioned in introductions.

The important functions of naming a 'friend' in these communities, first to guarantee good faith, but also as a means of becoming rapidly enmeshed in the rights and obligations relationships of the network, can be illustrated by specific examples drawn from linguistic and ethnographic data collected during the fieldwork.

It has already been noted that community network boundaries are often co-extensive with territorial boundaries, and that a very dense network (unlike those of more mobile individuals) can be said to have an existence independent of any individual network member. Because of this, a stranger in a Belfast working-class community, as in others of the same type, is very conspicuous and may be called upon to produce evidence of his good faith. This evidence frequently takes the form of an ability to name residents in the neighbourhood, as the following narrative by Sandy McL, a twenty-eight-year-old Hammer man, clearly shows. He and his wife were returning from a social function outside their immediate neighbourhood late one night, when they were accosted by an armed man who mistook them for strangers on a bombing expedition. Because he was outside his own territory, Sandy was not recognized; he here describes how he established his identity to the gunman's satisfaction:

> ... I just said 'Like, mate, you know there's nothing—I'm just going to try and prove my identity here you know'. So I couldn't find nothing on me at all so I just started to explain—I says 'Do you know anybody that lives round these ways?' He says to me 'Ay'. 'Well my aunts and uncles they've lived here all their days, years and years now', says I; 'do you know Sammy McL, do you know Hester McL?' He says to me 'Ay'. 'Well that's my aunt and uncle'. He just said to me 'That's all right, away ye go'.

This narrative shows that the manner in which I used my status as second order network contact (Sandy's status in relation to the gunman) corresponded closely to neighbourhood norms. Sandy used an identical stratagem to provide evidence of good faith.

The second function of 'naming a friend'—to become enmeshed in exchange and obligation relationships and so observe a range of speech styles over a long period—may be illustrated with reference to my relationship with some young people in Ballymacarrett.

The youths whose network ties formed a cluster within the Ballymacarrett network were all eighteen or nineteen years old. They were core members of a local street gang which had, in the recent past, been violently disbanded by local paramilitary groups. At the time of the research, the boys were resisting pressure to join the paramilitary groups (whose influence in this area was not particularly strong) and had given up street fighting in favour of running a disco group. In fact, in all three communities boys seemed to give up street fighting around the age of eighteen and engage in more peaceful activities. Most of the Ballymacarrett boys were strongly committed to running a good disco group; however, since none could drive a car they made frequent use of a number of first and second order network contacts to transport themselves and their equipment to various destinations. At the time of the observation period, their normal network resources had temporarily collapsed, leaving them in difficulties. I assisted with the use of my van, thus fulfilling a clear role and creating an obligation. The sister of one of the youths quite explicitly expressed this obligation by offering any help that might be required in return for these valued services. In fact, the services were returned in the form of open invitations to visit local homes; it was made clear that I was entitled to call at the houses of the boys' families whenever I wished, with full certainty that I would be viewed as a valued friend. One fortunate, but unpredicted, aspect of this status as a friend to whom obligations were due was that the families asked no questions about the purpose of the recording equipment; it was tolerantly assumed to have some connection with the disco group. Further, my own young children were invited to local parties and other functions, and looked after by local people.

In return I gave miscellaneous help with transport, or with filling in complicated official forms. At no time of course was I identified as a member of the first order network zone; the point is that the relationship established to the network was a recognizable one, neither that of a stranger nor that of a neighbour, but a 'friend of a friend'. It was possible to combine this role with the role of an interviewer working in the area without violating interactional norms, and so gain access to a variety of speech styles in an informal local setting.

At this point, a description of actual fieldwork procedure (taken from notes) will clarify the manner in which free movement between network links, and the direct observation and recording of a number of communicative contexts became possible.

THE CLONARD NETWORK

John R was the man whose name was used to establish a link with the Clonard network. John's extended family lived in the Clonard, and he himself lived in a block of flats nearby. Like many local men, he was unemployed; he had no institutional status of any kind. The first visit was to the house of Martin Convery (48) where I introduced myself as 'a friend of John's', and was immediately invited in and offered tea. Martin agreed to be recorded talking about the way of life in old communities such as the Clonard, which were being swept away by urban redevelopment. Everyone was interested in this topic, and these initial discussions provided information essential for the subsequent analysis of speakers' own network ties. The specific topic of language use in the community was broached with Martin only after a fairly formal interview with a clear two-part question–answer/elicitation–reply structure had been recorded (Coulthard, 1977). At this point, Martin read out word lists and minimal pair lists, and after initial permission to tape-record conversations had been obtained, it was not found necessary to seek this permission again in the Clonard, or explain in detail the objectives of the research. Word quickly spread through the area that I was interested in the way of life in the area (including the dialect) and was tape-recording conversation; Clonard residents themselves usually pointed this out in introductions. The actual recording operation was extremely inconspicuous, as a single hand-held microphone was used. This was quite adequate in the tiny rooms.

Martin invited me to call next day and visit his wife and teenage children. On this occasion Moira (18) was at home and seemed to view me as a friend of her father's, for she began to chat spontaneously as I quite openly switched on the recording equipment. Within a few minutes, four young men had entered the room, and interaction was recorded over a four-hour period, interspersed with cups of tea, sandwiches and cigarettes.

Martin Convery had clearly told the young men (his sons and their friends) that conversations would be tape-recorded; however, although no deceit was used on my part, they appeared to have an extremely unclear perception of how much of the proceedings were in fact being recorded. After forty-five minutes, they saw the tape being changed, read word lists and minimal pairs, and appeared to consider that the 'interview', as a distinct speech event, was over. Nevertheless, they continued to chat amongst themselves, performed lively narratives, and teased each other (a speech event known as *slegging* in Belfast). They raised no objection to the continued and open use of the tape-recorder, most probably because the initial link to the network (through John R) guaranteed good faith and entitled me to claim some of the rights of a network contact. This general pattern of response to my approaches recurred many times.

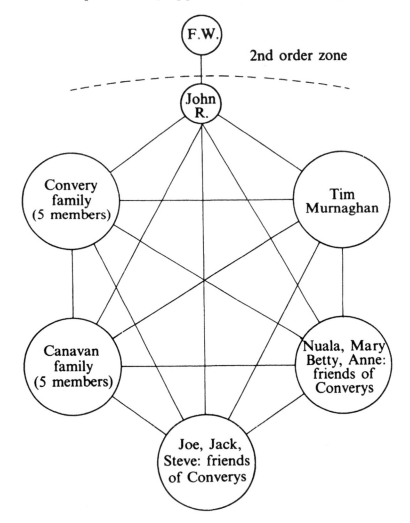

Figure 3.2   *A portion of the Clonard network, showing density of 100 per cent*

Over the next few weeks, I accompanied members of the Convery family to the houses of neighbours, kin and friends, and made many recordings covering a very wide range of different spontaneous styles, as well as some explicit 'interviews'. These styles will be discussed briefly later in this chapter.

The portion of the Clonard network which was studied had a 100 per cent density index: everybody in the network of the original contact (Martin Convery) knew everybody else (see Figure 3.2). Of great importance to this fieldwork was an understanding of the interactional norm of *extended visiting* which enabled me to obtain very long recordings of well-established network interaction. Visiting patterns and other interactional norms will be discussed in Chapter 4.

It is important to note that the speech recorded is not in any sense claimed to be especially 'natural'; the idea of an entirely natural speech style existing independent of situation is not seen here as a realistic concept. The point is, that the initial interview style is the one which informants feel to be appropriate to the situation of answering questions put by a stranger. But additionally, by making use of the rights and obligations mechanisms of the network, I was able to record a number of spontaneous styles which contrasted very sharply with this initial interview style. These were produced in response to a number of complicated situational constraints in which I, as a single participant, probably played a relatively minor part. Much more powerful were the constraints and incentives generated by the rights and obligations mechanism of the network.

DENSITY, MULTIPLEXITY AND LINGUISTIC FIELDWORK

Where networks are relatively dense and multiplex—as in all three Belfast communities—several conditions favourable to the objective of observing and recording a large amount of data close to the vernacular are likely to be present. These are conditions which have often been referred to in sociolinguistic work;

however, an understanding of the network mechanisms discussed in this chapter allows them to be stated more explicitly.

1. The volume of exchanges and therefore of shared knowledge within the network is great. Speakers are therefore likely to use their most casual and intimate speech styles (see Labov, 1972a; Ervin-Tripp, 1972; Levinson, 1978). The validity of this inference was checked informally by observing, where possible, the linguistic behaviour of individuals speaking to outsiders. For example, one Ballymacarrett boy was observed speaking to his future employers. Various proxemic adjustments marked a clear stylistic shift; his voice quality changed and his speech showed a dramatic frequency decrease in the high concentration of vernacular phonological features which appeared on the tape when he was conversing with his friends. It is worth noting that the presence of the tape-recorder in itself, given the fact that it was used carefully in the context of network-linked rights and obligations, seemed less likely to produce a shift away from the vernacular than did conversation with a higher-status participant who was not linked to the territorially based network by informal ties.

2. Persons standing in a multiplex relation to each other are more mutually accessible than if the link is uniplex, and therefore susceptible to the obligation to adopt group norms. These norms include an obligation to use an unmarked style in one another's presence. The strength of this obligation can be illustrated by the following incident.

Early in the recording sessions, one Ballymacarrett youth from a noisy and vociferous group of five suddenly adopted an obviously marked style during a chat about ways of raising money for the disco group. His tempo and loudness range levelled out, some vernacular phonological features became less evident, and he self-consciously fingered his hair and straightened his clothes. One of his friends punched him and shouted 'come on, you're not on television now you know'. The others laughed mockingly. Next time the boy spoke, his style had shifted markedly in the direction of the vernacular. Thus, obligations to the group were stronger than the influence of both the recording equipment and an outside participant, although the remark about television shows that the boys were clearly aware that they were being recorded. The principal effect of this awareness seemed to be the avoidance of dangerous topics. Nevertheless, despite the boys' wariness, at the end of the same long session (four hours) I felt obliged to rub a lengthy account of illegal activities off the tape. Some boys had apparently fallen into their habitual interactional pattern, as a result of the presence of the rest of the group, to the extent of allowing compromising material to appear on tape (see Wolfson (1976) for an account of 'guarded' behaviour during group sessions). When the content of the tape was pointed out, the boys first expressed surprise, then alarm and finally agreed that the tape should be edited. This kind of incident was not uncommon, even in these communities at open war with the authorities and constantly wary of strangers. The simplest explanation of the boys' failure to monitor their speech is that *over a protracted period* they had difficulty in remaining vigilant, because the presence of the rest of the group created a conflicting constraint to talk 'normally'.

3. Extreme density produces a *homogeneity* of norms and values. Since this homogeneity of norms might be expected to extend to interactional and specifically linguistic norms, the density of these networks may partly account for the great consistency with which speakers characteristically show loyalty to vernacular speech norms, despite the social stigma attached to them.

It is important to note that a person's *perception* of density is sufficient to influence his behaviour considerably (Boissevain, 1974). If a potential link is there, whether or not messages actually pass along it, he will be careful to say or do nothing inimical to group values. My own perceptions of density constrained my behaviour considerably; I was keenly aware that anything I said or did to violate group values could become common knowledge to the network extremely quickly. It was the *structure*, not the *content* of the network links which produced this constraint; and the constraint was present whether or not information actually flowed along available channels.

STYLISTIC ANALYSIS

It has been argued here that a fieldwork method which systematically takes account of personal network structures and mechanisms facilitates prolonged observation and recording of spontaneous interaction in communities where networks are characteristically dense and multiplex. The network concept also suggests an initial procedure for analysing the very wide range of speech styles obtained using these methods. This approach to stylistic analysis is based on the recognition that in the communities, the fieldworker was ambiguously 'membershipped' (Schegloff, 1972) both as an insider and an outsider: both as a 'friend of a friend' and as a *bona fide* researcher. This dual role meant that it was possible to record speech either as an outsider by eliciting responses through direct questioning, or as an insider by participating (often peripherally) in group interaction. The initial analysis makes use of this dual membershipping by distinguishing between interview style (IS) on the one hand and a number of spontaneous styles (SS) on the other. Interview style corresponds broadly, though not completely, to Labov's careful style (see Chapter 1). However, the analytic method adopted here employs criteria based on discourse structure for distinguishing IS from SS, rather than defining them by features of the general situational context as was Labov's procedure in New York City. Interview style is defined here primarily by two characteristic features:

1. It displays a clear two-part elicitation/reply structure

(see Coulthard, 1977). Some replies, however, may be very considerably elaborated.

2. One participant (whom we may describe as the interviewer) controls interaction in the sense that he chooses the form of the elicitations and selects the topics. In Sacks's terms (Sacks: MS), this dominant participant exercises a maximum degree of control over the discourse, in that he is able to constrain a selected speaker to produce an appropriate response. Conversely, all spontaneous styles have in common the property that they lack a clear two-part discourse structure; they cannot easily be analysed as replies to an interviewer's elicitations on topics chosen by him. Furthermore, as we would expect, spontaneous styles are characterized by a higher frequency of vernacular speech variants.

The structural differences between interview style on the one hand (A) and two quite distinct spontaneous styles on the other (B), (C), can be demonstrated by considering three short transcriptions. Comparison of (B) and (C) also gives some idea of the wide range of structural features which characterize different *spontaneous* styles.

(A) FW (fieldworker):	/well could you tell me/first of all you say you were born here/could you tell me where you were born/	(1)
I (informant):	. . uh . ./Parker Street in East Belfast/.	(2)
FW:	. ./a wee bit across the road/ and when did you come to live here/	(3)
I:	/here uh/. . just about three years ago/. . .	(4)
FW:	/yeah . and have you ever lived outside East Belfast/	(5)
I:	/uh . for a period/. .	(6)

```
FW:                /when/                              (7)
I:                 . . /a couple of year in
                   Ballybeen/. it's actually
                   Ardcairn/Ballybeen was an
                   extension from that you
                   know/. . . .                        (8)
FW:                /oh yeah/how long for/              (9)
I:                 . ./just a few year/                (10)
```

(B) B: /I got this house 'cos they were
         pulling the bungalows down/   (1)   QUIET
     S: /ah but they didn't move us from
         out of there/so they didn't/   (2)   LOUDER
         we came off our own bat/   (3)
     B: ah we moved ourselves/   (4)   QUIET
     S: squatted/we squatted/   (5)   VERY LOUD
     B: we did not indeed squat/   (6)   EVEN LOUDER
     S: we did/   (7)   LOUD
         we squatted/   (8)
     B: *when you're* a squatter you've no
         rent book/   (9)   LOUD
         I've a rent book to show
         anybody/   (10)
         I've *a rent book*   (11)
     S: /*ah you're* not a squatter now/   (12) LOUD
         but when you first came here
         you were a *squatter*   (13) LOUD
     B: /*I've a rent* book from the very
         first/   (14) LOUD
     S: /*when you* first came here you
         were a squatter/'cos I remember/
         I had to climb over the yard
         wall and all/   (15) BOYS LAUGH
     B: /alright we had to get in that
         way/   (16) QUIET
     S: /squat/   (17) LOUD

B: /we didn't dear/   (18) QUIET
/a squatter is someone that
doesn't pay rent/   (19) BOYS LAUGH
I've my rent book/   (20) QUIET
uh this is about the third or
fourth rent book I've got
issued to me now/   (21)

(C) P: /and we went down to the corner/ (1) LAUGHS
I says here's me. you're not
taking him/   HIGH TESSITURA
and the da gets the soldier by
the neck/   LOUD
and flung him across the wall/   FINAL
                      CONSONANT
                      LENGTHENED
                      IN *flung*

FW: /he's a great big man isn't he/   (2)
P: well he'd this officer by the throat/ (3)
and he's choking him/and he's
shouting.   HIGH TESSITURA
let him go/let him go/
M: /he was going blue in the face/ (4) QUIET
P: /then this other one/y'know   (5)
John McMahon's mother/she
came round she says/I saw him
getting kicked she says but I
didn't think he was your lad/and
the other/the big fat soldier/was
going to kick him in the head
and she says/would you do that
on your own son/. . . and this
other young soldier says/.
MISSUS I had nothing to do   QUIETER
with that/
FW: /Yeah/   (6)

P: /so between one and another we   (7)
       got him out of the saracan and
       we brought him up/the soldiers
       grabbed HER then/
M: /oh ay by the throat/   (8) LOUD

Interview Style

In the interests of clarity, transcription has been kept as simple
as possible. Clear tone group boundaries are marked; pauses are
marked with each dot representing a pause of up to one second
in duration; obvious fluctuations in loudness and tessitura relative to a modal voice quality are noted; overlapping utterances
(interruptions) are marked by italics.

Even such a crude transcription, which ignores many clear
voice features, reveals several distinctive characteristics of interview style. First, the two-part structure of the discourse is
particularly evident, with the fieldworker eliciting and the informant replying. Each move can be coded quite unambiguously
as an elicitation or a reply. Sinclair and Coulthard's description
of *classroom* discourse with the teacher eliciting and the pupil
replying, fits interview style well:

> a more simple type of spoken discourse, one which has
> much more overt structure, where one participant has
> acknowledged responsibility for the direction of the dis-
> course, for deciding who shall speak when and for intro-
> ducing and ending topics. (1975:6)

Comparison with (B) and (C) further reveals that interview
style is characterized by a slow pace with pauses between turns,
no interruptions, and little fluctuation in tessitura and loudness.
The discourse structure of extract (A) is repeated many times
on the Belfast tapes. Interestingly, the same structure was recorded, in my absence, when a young Ballymacarrett man
helping in the research interviewed his sister, eliciting her views
on various local shops and neighbourhoods. The fact that this

sample of IS was structurally identical to the others suggests that discourse patterns are constrained by the speaker's definition of the speech event, as well as by the social relationships of the participants to each other.

A clear two-part structure such as that found in (A) may become modified in the course of the interview, with responses becoming elaborated in various ways as the informant takes partial control of the discourse. However, all interviews have the same structure in their initial stages, and it is from these clear examples of IS that tokens are taken for quantitative analysis and comparison with spontaneous styles.

Spontaneous Styles

Extract (B) is taken from a very long recording of interaction between S (aged nineteen), four of his friends, and his mother, B. The presence of the four friends is important, although their only role in the discourse appears to be to laugh mockingly as S successfully teases B. At this point, I had said little for half an hour, and did not participate in this exchange at all. S is teasing B about the circumstances of a recent change of residence, and for reasons which will become clear shortly this extract may be considered as a distinct speech event. Accordingly, we label it *banter*. There is in this extract no clear two-part discourse structure, and no overt obligation on either participant to control the discourse. Unlike interview style, many conversational moves here, such as for example (2), can be coded simultaneously as reply and elicitation with no clear boundary between these categories. There is much more fluctuation in tempo and loudness than in (A), with many interruptions indicating an overall faster tempo. Finally, the boundaries of the speech event are marked out by quiet speech, relative to the louder voice used in the main part of the banter session. In fact, after (21) the conversation moved into a more extended narrative with B dominating the discourse.

Extract (C) is also marked by absence of domination by the

fieldworker, whose role is confined to giving minimal indications of attention and assent. Again, there is no clear two-part discourse structure. Present in the room are P, a middle-aged Clonard woman who has held the floor at this point for an hour with sequences of narratives, all on the topic of street fights with the soldiers. Her teenage daughter, M, also plays a minimal role in the discourse, corroborating and amplifying her mother's version of events.

This speech event is marked clearly as a narrative in a number of ways. First, there is a dominant participant who has privileges of initiating and ending topics, and who is not liable to be interrupted. A number of clear linguistic features mark her utterances here as performed narrative. First, the so-called historic present alternates with the past tense; the use of the historic present in narratives appears to be commonplace throughout the English-speaking world.

Second, *direct speech* is reported, for dramatic purposes, and introduced by the direct speech markers *here's me* (*him*) and *I* (*she, he*) *says*. These clear genre markings of performed narrative are all present in turn (1). A wide range of what might be described as channel features are manipulated by P for dramatic purposes. In (1) and (3) she uses tessitura, loudness and abnormal consonant length in this function. In (5), she uses dramatic pause and fluctuation in loudness to focus full attention on Mrs McMahon's dialogue with the young soldier.

Clearly, there is very much more to be said about structural characteristics of the various spontaneous styles, which are clearly marked off from each other and produced in response to different sets of situational constraints and incentives; an adequate analysis would need to take account of various components of situation as well as the 'internal' characteristics of the conversation. However, a relatively simple comparison of (A), (B) and (C) is, for the purposes of the argument here, sufficient to indicate the structural simplicity of IS, relative to the complexity of two quite clearly distinguishable spontaneous styles. An initial analysis of a wider range of vernacular styles can be found in Milroy and Milroy (1977a).

CONCLUSION

It is clear then, that the central methodological problem of the observer's paradox is of great importance in that it influences the kinds of data available for analysis, and hence knowledge of the range of a community's repertoire. Although it is important for a variety of practical as well as theoretical reasons to obtain information about vernacular repertoires, most knowledge is still restricted to relatively 'public' styles—effectively variants of interview style. Recent studies by social anthropologists, based on social network analysis, are of direct relevance for two reasons.

First, a network analysis enables the fieldworker to define his relationship to the group systematically. When he has done this he may use the normal, but complex, mechanisms of the network to gain access as a 'friend of a friend' to a wide range of spontaneous speech styles. Since network structures of the kind found in Belfast seem to be common, and possibly universal, in low-status communities the fieldwork methods described here are generalizable elsewhere (see Bortoni-Ricardo, 1985).

The ambiguous status of the fieldworker, both as an 'outsider' and an 'insider', also suggests an initial method of stylistic analysis. The styles which are observed in the fieldworker's role as an insider may be said to represent a reasonable, but not comprehensive, sample of the community's linguistic repertoire. As we have seen in our consideration of *banter* and *narrative*, they may sometimes be clearly marked as distinct speech events; the wider social and situational context of these and other speech events is considered in the following chapter.

4

The Social Context of Speech Events

In acknowledgement of the important principle that the method used to collect linguistic data has the most profound influence on the kind of data which will be available for analysis, Chapter 3 focused on fieldwork strategy. Particular attention was paid to the fieldworker's relationship to the informants. In Chapters 1 and 2 a further principle had already emerged, mainly from Labov's work in Martha's Vineyard and Blom and Gumperz's work in Hemnes. Both of these studies showed the necessity of obtaining relevant background information if small-scale communities are the units of study. This background information may be of several different kinds, but must include some account both of the relationship of the community under observation to a wider society, and of the special norms and values of that community. Since much of the detailed discussion in this book of the links between language use and network structure is derived from data collected in the Belfast communities, this chapter discusses, for the most part, nonlinguistic data particularly relevant to an understanding of the links between a speaker's language use and the structure of his informal social relationships.

The chapter subsections concentrate in turn on the position of Ballymacarrett, the Hammer and the Clonard in the wider urban area; the informal values and everyday social relationships of the inhabitants; and finally interactional norms governing face-to-face communication in the domestic setting.

THE POSITION OF THE COMMUNITIES IN RELATION TO
THE WIDER URBAN AREA

The areas of inner Belfast within which the three communities

are located were initially selected on the basis of general ethnographic factors which seemed likely to give rise to linguistic
differences, even though the variable of social class was held
approximately constant.

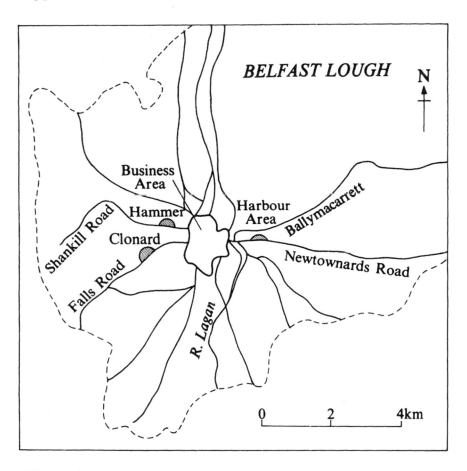

Figure 4.1 *Map of Belfast showing location of the inner city areas studied
(shaded areas)*

Belfast is bisected by the River Lagan (see Figure 4.1) and
Ballymacarrett lies east of the river while the other two communities are on the west. We must note here the existence of
sharp ethnic segregation in Belfast working-class society (to call
this division *religious* is misleading). Ballymacarrett is in the

centre of the largest concentration of Protestants in the city: in fact 42 per cent of all Belfast Protestants live in a continuous line east of the river (Boal and Poole, 1973). Clonard is Catholic and Hammer Protestant. The Falls area, where Clonard is situated, has the largest Catholic working-class concentration in the city, and is divided from the Shankill by a line running due west from the city centre. Boal's (1978) study of territoriality (carried out 1967–8) of two small areas on either side of the divide, suggests almost complete segregation—something in the order of 98 per cent of the Clonard population being Catholic. It is likely that these segregation patterns are replicated in the wider working-class areas and that under the impact of recent events in Belfast the level of segregation is now, one decade later, even higher. The three communities chosen for the linguistic study are therefore distinct both in terms of geographical separation, and of ethnic segregation. The significance of these divisions will be considered shortly.

All three large working-class concentrations are officially described as 'blighted' and have been identified as suffering from a high level of *social malaise*. Social malaise is measured by a wide range of indicators such as unemployment, sickness, juvenile crime, illegitimacy and premature death from disease (Boal *et al.*, 1974; 1978). The highest level and greatest geographical extent of malaise is concentrated in the inner city area west of the river where Hammer and Clonard are located. All the areas are considered locally to be of very low status and contain few skilled workers earning high wages. Their residents probably correspond more or less to the lower-working-class group in Trudgill's Norwich survey.

In Belfast, as in other cities, more highly-skilled working-class families have usually moved out to the suburbs leaving the most vulnerable and exploited members of the community concentrated in increasingly decaying and blighted inner urban areas. We may consider our informants in this study to be victims of the process of 'pauperization' described by Pahl (1975:167). Here, Pahl is referring to structural changes in the working class which result in a tendency for the lower working class to become relatively poorer and lose any chance of upward mobility, as society becomes more skilled. This is because the services of the unskilled and semi-skilled man are less in demand. This split in the working class seems to have had the effect of isolating communities of the kind described here from the mainstream of upwardly mobile urban society, an isolation reflected by the local valence of different, sometimes opposing, sets of values to those publicly acknowledged in the media and educational system. Most important for our analysis here is the very high value placed on social solidarity. In all three communities this was commonly valued above everything else, including improved material conditions; the maintenance of solidary relationships was seen as a necessary buffer in times of sickness or need, or against hostile outsiders, particularly the authorities. These values were often expressed in terms of being 'neighbourly' or 'looking after your own'. Since we would predict from the results of the Hemnes study, and from other work of Gumperz, that the existence of opposing social values of this kind will be relevant to patterns of language use, it is worth looking a little more closely at the relationship of very low status communities to the rest of society.

In fact, poor urban communities have been most extensively and carefully scrutinized not in the United Kingdom, but in Latin American countries. In a careful study of the informal social organization of a shanty town near Mexico City, Lomnitz (1977) presents data which parallels in an interesting way both Pahl's observations on the split in working-class society, and the recurrent observations of scholars such as Fried on the high value placed on the ethic of social solidarity by the poor. It is from this study that we are able to derive information on the informal structure of poor communities which strikingly resembles observations of conditions in Belfast.

In Latin American society, individuals such as the shantytown residents are explicitly recognized by sociologists as occupying a position outside the industrial class structure, and are known as *marginals*. The reason why marginality has been extensively studied is that, contrary to previous assumptions, it has become apparent that this social phenomenon constitutes a problem which does not disappear with time. Marginals characteristically live an economically precarious existence supported by materials rejected by more affluent sections of society. They may be seen as lying outside the industrial class structure in that they have no job security or trade union membership. Their wants and grievances are characteristically not articulated through institutionalized channels (Lloyd, 1979).

Families may remain marginal for generations without showing any signs of upward mobility; typically their sporadic employment (as waiters, tombstone polishers, carpet fitters, domestic servants) is of little direct relevance to industrial production. The ethic of social solidarity is highly developed in marginal communities and is clearly associated with extreme poverty; individuals who become less poor tend to sever network ties with other marginals, reconstructing less dense, less multiplex sets of ties elsewhere.

We touch here on complex problems of social structure which cannot possibly be dealt with adequately in this book. It is particularly important to acknowledge the hazards of attempting to compare the status systems and economic structures of developed and underdeveloped countries, the most striking difference between the two types of societies being that in underdeveloped countries there is characteristically a much bigger gap, in terms of relative wealth, between the poor on the one hand and the professional élite on the other (Lloyd, 1979:13). Nevertheless, it is quite clear that although the poor in this country differ from the marginals of Mexico City in many important respects, the residents of these Belfast communities also *resemble* the marginals quite strikingly in a number of ways. A consideration of these resemblances is relevant to an account of the sociolinguistic structure of vernacular speech.

First, we have already seen that like the marginals, the Belfast communities characteristically valued social solidarity highly. Second, they too characteristically held insecure jobs with little direct relevance to industrial production. Two street sweepers and a street-market fruit vendor were among our male informants; these are fairly typical of the kind of jobs the men held, if they were employed at all.[1] Like the marginals, they showed little sign of ever attaining security or mobility by becoming employed in key jobs protected by powerful unions.

The marginals are of interest to us here in a general way because no study of poor communities, comparable to Lomnitz's, has been carried out in the United Kingdom. More specifically, they are of interest because of the consensus of social theorists that they occupy a position *outside* the industrial proletarian class structure, rather than the lowest position in that structure. That it may be reasonable to consider poor communities in the United Kingdom as occupying a similar position is suggested by Pahl's observation of the split in the working class, which has had the effect of making the poor relatively poorer and more socially isolated, rather than securing a position in a fluid social class hierarchy.

If we consider the implications of these observations, it would seem inappropriate to analyse the social position of the very poor as the lowest point in a class continuum of the kind constructed by the various surveys of urban speech which were described in Chapter 1, this being a slightly misleading model on which to base a sociolinguistic description of urban vernacular speech. The social structure of poor communities may be quite different from structures found in the rest of society, for the reason that the social isolation observed by Pahl debars them, like the marginals, from the upward mobility which is generally assumed to be common in industrialized societies and which is implicit in the continuum model. Certainly this social isolation, together with the presence of opposing sets of social values which might be viewed as contingent on it (Gumperz,

---

[1] Altogether twenty-seven of the men interviewed were eligible for full-time employment (i.e. had completed full-time education but were below retiring age). Of these, ten were unemployed, three were general labourers, three were janitors or porters in public buildings, three were apprentices in the shipyard and three were in semi-skilled occupations. Of the remaining five, one was a milk roundsman, one a barrow boy, one a street sweeper, one a part-time barman (technically unemployed) and one drove a fork-lift loader in a local warehouse.

1972) would lead us to predict very different patterns of language use from those found in the mainstream of upwardly mobile industrial society; we may also need to question Labov's view of an urban population as a single speech community. Much of the remainder of this book will examine, in more detail, the informal social structure specific to these poor communities and the effects of this structure on patterns of language use.

Although all three of the large Belfast working-class areas appear to be similar in their social structure and ethos, there are also some important differences which should be noted here. The area around Ballymacarrett is a very old industrial settlement, antedating the main growth period of Belfast as a modern industrial city (1850–1900). East Belfast is widely felt to have its own separate identity, and many Ballymacarrett people seldom, if ever, cross the river. Heavy industry is located east of the river within easy reach of Ballymacarrett, and the shipyard dominates working-class life there. Although none of the male informants in this area were skilled tradesmen, all were, or had been, connected with the shipyard in one capacity or another. The Northern Ireland Office and all the apparatus of the civil service are located on the Newtownards Road to the country side of Ballymacarrett, and the consequent stimulus to service industries means that unemployment here is less severe than in other parts of Belfast. Even though Ballymacarrett men held very low-status jobs, it was usually possible for them to find work of some kind in the area.

The Catholic enclaves of East Belfast are small, and although the Protestants and Catholics are residentially segregated, both groups share the shopping and work facilities of the Newtownards Road which runs due east from the city centre (as we shall see, the pattern of ethnic segregation is quite different in West Belfast). The population of the Mount, Island and Ballymacarrett Electoral Wards (which roughly cover the East Belfast working-class concentration) is given as 26,173 (Census of Population, 1971).

The area west of the river is characterized by particularly high levels of segregation—although, as Boal and Poole have pointed out, not as high as some levels of ethnic segregation in New York City. In contrast with the East Belfast pattern, religious groups do not share the facilities of a single spinal road, the Catholics confining themselves largely to the Falls Road and the Protestants to the Shankill. Individuals overwhelmingly use public amenities on their own side of the line of cleavage; Boal (1978) has shown in a detailed study that the two groups strongly favour the use of separate bus stops and corner shops even when their choice may commit them to covering an extra distance on foot from their homes. Several old Catholic and Protestant areas lie in close proximity in West Belfast, with the result that this urban sector has been very badly affected by the recent civil disturbances. The whole area also suffers from high levels of unemployment. Official figures are not generally available separately for specific areas of the city, but the level of male unemployment has been calculated at 35 per cent (Boal *et al.*, 1974). More recently, figures of 40 per cent have been mentioned by local politicians and trade unionists, but are difficult to check. Certainly, many informants were unemployed, particularly the younger men; those who were employed often had to travel considerable distances to work. It is relevant to an understanding of personal network structures in the three areas and ultimately an account of patterns of language use, to note that both the Shankill and the Falls contrast with East Belfast in not having a local homogeneous form of employment corresponding to the shipyard. For this employment pattern appears to encourage the formation and maintenance of the dense, multiplex network patterns which are so typical of a traditional working-class community.

West Belfast's high unemployment rate is the consequence of a decline in the linen industry on which the whole area was once dependent. Women do not appear to be affected by unemployment to the same extent as men in the area; most of the older women in Hammer and Clonard had domestic or cleaning jobs of some kind, while the younger ones worked as mill hands or shop assistants in rather poor shops away from the main commercial area of the city. The 1971 population figure for the Falls and Shankill working-class areas are calculated as 30,733 and 30,267 respectively. These figures are derived from those given in the Census for Clonard, Grosvenor, Falls and St James Wards (Falls area) and the North Howard, Court, Shankill and Woodvale Wards (Shankill area).

It is important to note that the inhabitants of the complex of communities which make up these three large working-class concentrations have migrated at different times from different parts of Belfast's rural hinterland. West Belfast is of more recent development than east, and Catholics tend to be more recent migrants than Protestants. These relative 'ages' of subgroups in the urban population are reflected in the personal histories of individuals in the three small communities. Every Clonard (Catholic) informant was conscious of having a rural family background, and middle-aged men usually knew that their parents had migrated to Belfast to find work. One man of fifty-three remembers being brought to Belfast as a very small child; his own teenage children still visit relations in Monaghan. Hammer informants usually had a much vaguer notion that their grandparents were 'from the country' and unless they were very old could seldom provide detailed information. Migration to the Shankill appears to be largely from county Armagh and Antrim; to the Falls largely from Mid-Ulster, West of Armagh. In contrast, no Ballymacarrett informant had any memory of a rural background at all, but the ultimate background of much of the East Belfast population is probably the county Down hinterland (Evans, 1944). These differences are of great linguistic importance, because the Ulster–Scots rural dialect of Down and Antrim is sharply differentiated from the Mid-Ulster dialect (Gregg, 1972). Differences both in rural background and in the relative 'ages' of the communities clearly need to be taken into account in examining linguistic differences between them and in assessing directions of linguistic change (see p. 195 below).

The three small communities (within which some partial personal networks will be examined) are all located at the centre of their respective larger working-class areas. These areas in turn —Falls, Shankill, East Belfast—are made up of a complex of

similar communities. Residents generally have a clear perception of the boundaries of 'their' area which are usually units of
four or five streets. Neighbouring communities are seldom
visited; Hammer people, for example, are not accustomed to
crossing the Shankill Road. This territoriality which, as we have
already seen, appears to be so characteristic of the urban poor
cannot be dismissed entirely as the consequence of Belfast's
religious segregation; all communities on both sides of the
Shankill Road are in fact Protestant. We must relate it more
closely to the structure of the dense multiplex networks which
thrive only within a limited territory and look more closely now
at the structure and function of these networks in each community in turn.

NETWORK PATTERNS IN THE THREE COMMUNITIES

Network patterns in the Hammer and the Clonard have recently
been partially described (Wiener, 1976; Boal, 1978); there is
no independent study of Ballymacarrett. Both Belfast studies
note similarities to traditional working-class communities elsewhere. The typically strong *kin* basis of these networks should
be noted. It is quite common to find several households of
people related to each other within the four or five streets which
constitute the smaller community; in fact Wiener examines in
detail the distribution of members of five extended families in
four streets in the Hammer (1976:72).

A further important consequence of this network structure
emerges from Bott's study, where a high level of marital segregation is linked with a high level of network density. As we would
predict from this link, the sexes tend to polarize in these communities, with a sharp distinction being recognized between
men's and women's activities. This is particularly clear in
Ballymacarrett where personal networks are densest and most
multiplex; indeed in general the literature dealing with working-
class communities suggests that clear definition of sex roles and
network density go together. Conversely, Frankenberg notes

specifically that blurring of sex roles and loose-knit networks go together (1969:253). The most multiplex and dense networks seem to be found where men are employed in such traditional occupations as mining, shipbuilding or steel working. One study of a mining town (Dennis *et al.*, 1957) noted that many of the miners were both kin and neighbours; male solidarity was strong and the level of sex segregation high. Because the miners also took their recreation together in pubs and working mens' clubs, a high proportion of an individual's interactions took place within an almost totally bounded group. Similarly, the Ballymacarrett male informants (all of whom had been connected with the shipyard at some time) often took their recreation in establishments such as the Welder's Club which were associated with the yard. One consequence of the different employment patterns in West Belfast was that male networks were considerably less dense and multiplex; as we shall see, these differences are reflected in language use.

Restriction of movement to those areas within territorial boundaries was particularly evident in Ballymacarrett because of local availability of employment. Although the boys who run their own disco group travelled around the city, they crossed the river only by car; once they were outside their own area they did not venture outside the building where they were performing. In all three areas, the local boys (and sometimes the men) hung around street corners to which they were greatly attached. The street corner was an important setting for male interaction. Each had his own corner, inherited from an older boy; subsequently it would be passed on to a younger brother or friend. If the boys strayed outside territorial boundaries they tended to become involved in fights with other corner groups; sometimes indeed they went beyond their area of three or four streets exactly for that reason.

In general, women were far less subject than men to territorial constraints. This contrast was sharpest in Ballymacarrett, where nearly all the women travelled outside the area to work. Some of the young ones even crossed the city by bus, in particularly sharp contrast to one young unemployed man in Ballymacarrett who refused even to consider seeking work west of the river. It was in fact difficult to find women in the eighteen to twenty-five year age group resident in Ballymacarrett (two age groups were studied in each area); they tended to marry and move elsewhere because of a shortage of local housing. As we shall see, the women's personal networks are in fact measurably and significantly less dense and multilpex than the men's in Ballymacarrett.

Although this characteristic network structure is found in all three areas, it is in general (not only for men) less dense and multiplex in the Hammer and the Clonard. Before examining individual networks in detail in the following chapters, we must note some special features of the local networks peculiar to these two areas.

As a result of an extensive urban redevelopment programme affecting the wider Shankill area many of the little kitchen houses in the Hammer were blocked up or demolished at the time of the fieldwork for the Belfast study.

The population for the most part was dispersed either to housing estates in the outer suburbs, or to a complex of maisonettes and flats close to the city centre. Nevertheless, since everyone I spoke to depended on their old residential area for recreation and for day-to-day social interaction, it is reasonable to identify the Hammer as a *community* in the sense defined by Hymes. Many of the unemployed men came to hang around their old corners rather than staying in the new housing estates; it was common to find young women wheeling prams two or three miles almost daily to visit their mothers, and one young man still expected to walk a mile and a half every day to visit his grandparents. Local conflicts with other communities (the Nick and the Pad) which had also been dispersed still persisted; Nick people and Hammer people who were rehoused side by side did not mix. Men complained about the physical difficulties of corner hanging if they lived in high-rise flats: a visit to the corner had become an occasion, rather than simply a stroll outside the door. Interactional patterns in the Hammer had, therefore, been severely disrupted. The territorially based Hammer network was in fact in the process of breaking up; working-class networks of this kind generally do not survive a change of location (Turner, 1967). Young and Wilmott's study of a similar community of Bethnal Green reports that networks became less dense and multiplex when people were compelled to move from their traditional neighbourhood, and that the destruction of long-standing ties caused considerable distress. Certainly in Belfast, Hammer people who had been relocated outside the area often did not interact with their neighbours, or even know their neighbours' names, and frequently felt cut off from the system of reciprocal support and assistance so characteristic of their old community. Wiener reports considerable distress, particularly amongst the old, at the collapse of network resources. These reactions are reported in the Bethnal Green community also; and Frankenberg further suggests that when networks become less dense and multiplex, people are as a result more anxious to achieve a high social status; 'the less the personal respect received in small group relationships, the greater is the striving for the kind of impersonal respect embodied in a status judgment' (1969:232). Several studies point out a concern with upward mobility and adequate education of children as characteristic of working-class people whose network structures have been disrupted. These are discussed in Bott (1971).

Clearly, there is a link of some kind between network structure and socio-economic status, and since language use is to some extent controlled by both of these factors we may briefly consider here what form this link might take. Frankenberg seems to imply that upward social mobility is sometimes the consequence of *involuntary* destruction of reciprocity networks, rather than the natural result of personal social ambition. However, commenting on the relationship between social status and network structure in Mexico City, Lomnitz adopts a position quite the reverse of Frankenberg's. While the relationship between network structure and socio-economic status is acknowledged, dense multiplex networks along with their characteristic ethic of reciprocity and solidarity are viewed as a basic adaptive strategy for economic survival. Such a network structure, it is argued, would be dysfunctional for a person whose income was greater than the average income of the group; for he would be obliged by the reciprocity ethic to contribute a disproportionate amount to those in need. At the moment, our knowledge of social structure does not allow us to do more than speculate on the relative merits of these views, although important issues involving the competing influence of *status* and *solidarity* factors on human behaviour are implicated. It is worth noting here that the interrelationship of these underlying ideologies is an important variable in analysis of language behaviour in Brown and Gilman's (1960) classic study of the usage of T and V (intimate and polite) pronouns. More recently, concepts of status, solidarity and social distance are considered together in a wider ranging analysis of universal expressions of politeness (Brown and Levinson, 1978). Although further analysis of this kind is quite outside the scope of this book (it is the solidarity factor with which we are principally concerned), some extremely fruitful lines of enquiry for sociolinguistics clearly suggest themselves.

Meantime, we should note that Hammer residents, whose collapsing network structures prompt some consideration of the relationship between status and solidarity ideologies, frequently viewed the demise of the traditional network as the destruction of an important material resource.

Finally, there are some brief observations to be made about the Clonard community. Clonard men, like Hammer men, contrast with their Ballymacarrett counterparts in that they generally moved over a wider territorial area and contracted less multiplex network ties. Since Clonard residents were not, like the Hammer people, in the process of being relocated elsewhere, this pattern was for the most part the natural consequence of lack of local employment. Only two of the eight Clonard men whose personal network ties were studied were in fact employed at all.

The Clonard female informants were on the other hand, with a single exception, all employed, and those in the eighteen to twenty-five age group formed a cluster of the kind usually associated with male networks. Four of them were shop assistants working (or having worked) in the same store; one was a mill hand who interacted frequently with the others. They hung about in a close-knit group during their time away from work in a manner very similar to the young men. In this they contrasted very sharply with the young Ballymacarrett women none of whom were members of any such localized cluster. In fact, their networks are measurably the most dense and multiplex of those studied in West Belfast; this is the reverse of the Ballymacarrett pattern where male networks are significantly denser and more multiplex than female. Evidently network structure is to some extent controlled by economic and housing conditions.

It will be clear in the second half of this book (most of which focuses on specifically linguistic data) that careful quantitative analysis reveals these small local differences in personal network structure to be closely reflected in language use. Knowledge of personal network structures of the kind outlined here permits an understanding of the manner in which the solidarity factor may influence linguistic behaviour of *individuals*, regardless of the social status variable. We have already seen that standard methods which depend on grouping large amounts of data are not designed either to handle or to explain variation at this level of detail.

NORMS GOVERNING FACE-TO-FACE INTERACTION

It appears then that the social networks of many speakers in these three areas are largely co-extensive with territorial boundaries, in that relatively few links cross the river, or the sectarian divide, or even the boundaries of the smaller community. In his detailed observation of the Clonard and a comparable Shankill community, Boal showed that while people sometimes moved outside their areas for *transactional* purposes (to the city, or for shopping), very few *personal* visits of a wholly voluntary kind crossed community boundaries. His study confirms my own observations and agrees well with accounts of working-class interactional patterns found repeatedly in the literature. It is the norms governing these constant interactions—Hymes's 'primary interaction'—within the boundaries of the community which must now be considered.

It has already been noted that a person's knowledge of his language includes more than knowledge of syntactic, semantic and phonological rules. Even if his knowledge of these is complete, he must also acquire communicative competence— knowledge of when to speak or be silent; how to speak on each occasion; how to communicate (and interpret) meanings of respect, seriousness, humour, politeness or intimacy. As we have seen, part of this understanding is associated with the social meanings attached to different linguistic styles or codes. The Hemnes locals were competent to interpret the social meaning of a shift from standard Norwegian to the local dialect; similarly, Harlem adolescents were able to recognize the utterance 'your mother's a duck' as a ritual insult. This interpretation is not accessible to an outsider (Labov, 1972b:304); yet the utterance in context had the effect of causing the addressee to retreat from the argumentative posture he had adopted. Similarly, outsiders may not understand values attaching to specific postures and gestures, or to use of physical space in a community. Yet, since proxemic behaviour is part of the total communicative act, that too must be viewed as a necessary part of a speaker's communicative competence.

Gumperz (1972:16) argues forcefully (cf. Labov, p. 13 above) that a speech community is best defined in terms of knowledge of a large number of shared values of this kind; shared knowledge of purely linguistic norms is not enough. Since shared knowledge of communicative norms and constraints depends on intensity of contact and the structure of communication networks, speech community boundaries may in practice coincide with wider social boundaries such as ethnic, class or national boundaries. Because the dense networks characteristic of the three Belfast communities seldom extend across territorial boundaries, the conditions for shared knowledge of communicative norms such as Gumperz describes are present. Further, because the characteristic network structure entails a large number of interactions and a large amount of shared knowledge, it is not justifiable to assume *a priori* that speakers inside and outside communities of this kind have the same communicative competences. In fact, since all three Belfast communities shared similar norms we must infer that differences in communicative competence, like differences in linguistic usage, are linked to social status in a complex way. The important point is that the patterns of social organization commonly founded in urban working-class communities are able to function as a mechanism of norm maintenance. These norms may not be the same as those which are publicly accepted by the more mobile social groups. Although differences in ethnography of communication (as this area of enquiry is often labelled) are acknowledged to exist cross-culturally and are often studied (see, for example, Bauman and Sherzer, 1974), they are seldom studied with reference to groups defined as mutually heteronymous to the 'same' society. Yet it is clearly possible that such differences exist; we have already seen that the 'local team' in Hemnes effectively constituted a speech community separate from that of the élite who had not contracted dense, locally-based network ties. The two groups attached quite different meanings to shifts between standard and dialectal codes, the élite adopting publicly endorsed values.

Clearly, a comprehensive study of a speech community's total communicative competence would be a massive (or even infinite) task. As it is, much reported work (e.g. Bauman and Sherzer, 1974; Sankoff, 1971; Gumperz and Hymes, 1972) uses part of the framework established by Hymes (1967) and presented in a revised form in 1972. A number of categories are established there which are apposite to any attempt to describe communicative competence.

The basic unit of analysis is the *speech event*, parallel to the *sentence* as a basic syntactic unit, and already discussed briefly in Chapter 3. Speech events are frequently recognized in communities as entities sufficiently clear to merit a label such as, for example, *prayer*, *ritual insult* (and its various synonyms), *interview*, *harangue* or *slegging* (a Belfast label meaning—roughly—*banter*). Speech events characteristically occur subject to specific situational constraints such as those imposed by participant, setting, topic, channel of communication, and many others. At this point it is necessary to take note of a theoretical issue, discussed by Sherzer (1977), namely that there does not at present exist any framework within which cross-cultural/cross-status group comparison and typology of findings from the various studies of communicative norms can be placed. This means that investigators, myself included, tend to study each reference group in terms peculiar to themselves, or to their own society. Hence the following discussion is, of necessity, partial and suffers from the absence of a wider framework within which observations on communicative norms might be interpreted. Nevertheless, a number of important general points emerge, which will be discussed in due course.

Speech and Silence

We begin with some account of the kind of situation in which no speech at all is appropriate: the phenomenon labelled by Hymes as 'the distribution of required and preferred silence'. Anthropologists are well aware of great cultural variability in the regulation of talk (see, for example, Philips, 1976), although most accounts are unsystematic and anecdotal. As Coulthard (1977) has observed, these rules may differ surprisingly even in North-Western Europe. He reports the outrage felt by the Danish in-laws of one anthropologist at the amount of talking an American friend felt was normal; they retreated early to the privacy of their bedroom because constant verbal interaction imposed an intolerable strain on them. Another researcher— this time in Iceland (*sic*—perhaps Greenland is intended?)—is quoted as describing a daily, hour-long visit from neighbouring Eskimos who came to check that all was well; most of the hour was spent in silence with no more than six exchanges taking place. According to Coulthard's account, French children are encouraged to be silent when visitors come to dinner, while Russian children are expected to talk.

Silence may be interpreted very differently according to the situation. In a church it is a mark of respect in our culture, but in a different setting—for example in the period following an introduction of two strangers at a social gathering—silence may carry the meaning of hostility or embarrassment. Basso (1970) reports in some detail the use one Apache tribe makes of silence. In situations such as courtship, an encounter between strangers or a family reunion—in fact any situation where the relationship between participants was ambiguous—the Apaches responded with silence. This seems to be quite the converse of widely accepted British and American norms; it is precisely in situations where social relations need to be established or re-established that silence is avoided and the kind of talk labelled by Malinowski as 'phatic communion' takes place. One purpose of phatic communion is to avoid silence because of the meanings of hostility it conveys in these situations. Another is to assist, preliminary to a more extended interaction, in defining the mutual psychosocial relationship of the participants (Laver, 1974). The linguistic tokens of phatic communion are characteristically highly conventional; for example, remarks about the weather are very common in this function in Britain.

The principal difficulty in describing intergroup variability in the manner in which speakers distribute speech and silence stems from the absence of any systematic study of British or Irish *middle-class* norms and indeed from the absence of a general descriptive framework as noted by Sherzer. Following the implication of Hymes's suggestion (quoted in Hall, 1963), that functionally relevant communicative patterns may be identified by the discomfiture of the subject when norms have been violated, I attempt here to surmount this difficulty by describing localized norms in relation to my own experience. During the early part of the work in the Belfast communities I did not know how to regulate or interpret silence, and I assume that my own norms are those generally accepted in the wider British or Irish social context, since the discomfiture Hymes describes was felt for the first time in prolonged interactions in the early period of the fieldwork.

Certainly the norms appeared to be rather similar to those Coulthard attributed to the Eskimos. A fairly familiar (but not necessarily intimate) visitor entering a working-class house in Belfast may sit in total silence without the host feeling the slightest obligation to say anything to him at all. For his own part, the visitor may settle down in his host's kitchen without uttering a word or giving an explanation for his visit. I adopted a similar behaviour pattern, on one occasion sitting for nearly two hours in complete silence while two brothers completed their football pools in the same room. Two more people (both women well known to me) came in during this period, nodded a greeting and remained silent. Interaction was finally initiated by the brothers arguing over the ownership of a pair of socks.

Similar norms are reported in rural Ulster. Harris (1972) describes how one mountain farmer walked to his friends' house early on an evening, settled down to read a novel, fell asleep and woke to find that the family had retired for the night. He left for home after a visit of several hours without a single word having been exchanged.

A participant in a communicative situation governed by norms different from his own may feel very acute discomfort. Because silence in the situations I have described carried for me meanings of hostility, I found the long periods of silence disconcerting at first. But it seems likely that such differences (which are not generally acknowledged publicly) may sometimes result in serious misunderstandings between social groups; speakers from these communities may, in interaction with middle-class outsiders, be understood to be indicating hostility when this is not their intention at all. Misunderstandings of this kind are in fact reported by Philips (1972) in interactions between white teachers and American Indian children.

Norms of Proximity

A further set of interactional norms governs the physical distance separating participants when communication takes place, and the accepted degree of loudness of their speech. Watson and Graves (1966) report that compared to Americans, Arab students stand closer to each other when conversing, touch each other more, and speak more loudly. If they behave in this way in conversation with Americans, physical contiguity is liable to carry meanings of intimacy (which may be resented) and loudness of speech meanings of hostility. In a detailed study of a conversation between an Asian immigrant and a British teacher, Gumperz (1977a) has reported some misunderstandings arising specifically because each participant assigns different meanings to a given level of loudness at a given proximity.

Some scholars (for example Scheflen (1964), Scheflen and Ashcraft (1976), and Hall (1963)) have shown that it is possible to measure with great precision the normal distance between participants in a conversation in specific situations. As we would expect from the discussion in the previous section, breach of these norms can produce feelings of acute discomfort. Scheflen further notes that if American strangers are compelled to sit closer to one another than their proximity norms permit (on a crowded train, for example) they will erect symbolic barriers. They may cross their legs away from each other, tense their muscles or put their hands up against their faces; they will not lean against each other in a relaxed manner as prolonged direct physical contact of this kind carries meanings of intimacy.

The agreed distances vary from culture to culture, and are contextually determined by factors such as degree of crowding, noise level, age and sex of interactants, and the relationship between them. While recognizing these contextual constraints on proxemic behaviour, Scheflen and Ashcraft are able to quantify the distances acceptable to different cultural groups, relative to each other:

The British, British Americans and Black Americans traditionally occupy relatively large spaces. They stand more than 36 inches apart even in fairly intimate conversations if they have room to do so. . . . Cuban men may stand only

18 inches apart when talking in quiet and uncrowded places. (1976:90–1)

Observations in Belfast suggest that interclass as well as intercultural variation exists; for although the norms described by Scheflen and Ashcraft approximate to those with which I am familiar in middle-class society in a number of British and Irish cities, they differ sharply from norms governing interaction in working-class Belfast. People who are not especially intimate— usually women—commonly converse or sit next to each other with arms linked. I frequently participated in lengthy interactions squeezed close up against people who knew me only slightly; there was very little evidence of barrier behaviour of the kind Scheflen has described. Sometimes a hand was placed on my arm or round my shoulder for lengthy periods and the conversation was interspersed with slaps, squeezes and nudges, usually employed to reinforce linguistic meanings.

It is worth describing in detail one particular posture commonly adopted by men. Characteristically, two speakers stand at right angles within a foot of each other. The roles are prescribed as those of speaker and listener, for the speaker's hand is placed on the listener's shoulder, his mouth only inches from the listener's ear. Eye contact is avoided. Although by middle-class norms such close proximity probably carries meanings of intimacy, it had a different significance in these communities. The whole posture seemed rather to carry meanings of solidarity (an interpretation suggested also by Scheflen and Ashcraft's analysis of body orientation) and to signal that the conversation was private and should not be interrupted. In the Hammer, for example, it was adopted and maintained on one occasion for over an hour by a man of thirty-four in interaction with a male researcher some years older. The two men had not met each other prior to this conversation. The Hammer man was discussing his own illiteracy (which he wanted to keep secret) in a crowded dance hall. Since this posture was adopted spontaneously at a first meeting with an outsider, it is unlikely in these communities to carry the meanings of intimacy which an observer might be tempted to associate with such close proximity. We should also note here that specific *gestures* are assigned quite distinct social meanings. The manner in which different ways of offering cigarettes are linked to the formality of the situation is described in detail elsewhere (Milroy and Milroy 1977a).

Setting as a Component of Situation

The setting of interaction has not often been dealt with in detail in the literature. Usually a given setting (such as church, pub, market-place) is viewed as an important factor in defining the formality or otherwise of a situation (Sankoff, 1971). Blom and Gumperz found that the standardized linguistic code was more likely to be used in public settings associated with business transactions, with a shift to the dialect in those situations signalling more intimate, personal concerns. What I shall concentrate on here, however, is the significance assigned to specific settings in terms of whether they are unmarked (normal) or marked loci of interaction.

It has already been noted that members of working-class communities in both the United States and the British Isles characteristically regard themselves as sharing a common territory; the street is often seen as an extension of the home. The importance of the street corner as a locus of interaction for working-class males has been widely reported in the literature (Whyte, 1955; Fried, 1973; Hannerz, 1974); nor is this norm different in Belfast. In effect, this means that working-class men view the street corner as an unmarked setting for interaction. On the other hand, in middle-class residential areas in Belfast and elsewhere, such a setting is heavily marked; a gathering of adult males on the street corner is likely to signal that some extraordinary event such as a burglary, a death or a road accident has occurred. This interclass difference in the significance of specific settings seems to be related to working-class territorial norms; the street and home are not, as Fried pointed out, seen as contrasting categories of public and private space.

Boissevain (1974:76) discusses in some detail the link between interactional patterns and a community's view of the threshold as a boundary between public and private space. He views differences in perception of the threshold's importance as creating distinctive northern and southern European patterns of interaction; northern Europeans characteristically interact for a prolonged period only with people specially invited into their homes. Although his comments may apply to middle-class northern European society, the corner-hanging groups suggest that working-class norms may sometimes be very different. A further consequence of this 'merging' of the home and the street seems (in Belfast at least) to be that a large number of interactions involving very many participants take place in the domestic setting.

The little terraced houses in the three communities all had an inner and an outer front door. The outer door was usually left open even in the coldest weather, and functioned as a signal that the occupier was available for interaction. Neighbours and friends were then free to walk into the kitchen which, in most houses, was the locus of interaction. Characteristically, large numbers of visitors walked in and out of houses without knocking, frequently giving no overt reason for the visit; often during fieldwork sessions several people arrived unannounced and either joined in the conversation or remained silent. Similar visiting patterns have been noted in Bethnal Green, and in rural Ulster.

These visiting patterns differ from middle-class norms in several respects; first the visit may be prolonged for a very considerable period; second it does not disrupt the domestic routine; and as we have already seen in the section dealing with the distribution of silence, no obligation is imposed either on the host to initiate conversation, or on the visitor to state a reason for his visit. A 'state of open talk' (Goffman, 1976) is maintained during which participants have the right, but not the obligation, to speak.

Knowledge of these interactional norms is of the greatest importance to a fieldworker who is attempting to gain access to a community's vernacular. It was possible in Belfast, using this knowledge, to record large volumes of speech from participants who came into the room, and joined spontaneously in the conversation, often without knowing my identity. The range of vernacular styles recorded during these extended visiting sessions is, as noted in Chapter 3, rather wide. In rural Ulster, extended visiting is known as *ceilidhing*, a habit explicitly associated with the lowest-status mountain farmers and avoided by the local élite. Like Boissevain's paradigmatic north Europeans, members of this élite entertain invited visitors only, in their parlours (not their kitchens). Harris's account of the contrasting social meanings assigned to these visiting patterns bears on Gumperz's insistence that a speech community must be defined in terms not only of shared linguistic norms, but more generally in terms of a wider range of shared norms and values. It is certainly worth noting here that élites appear to stigmatize communicative norms such as visiting habits, in much the same way as they stigmatize the speech sounds characteristic of low-status speakers.

PHATIC BEHAVIOUR AND TERRITORIALITY

So far, factual information has been presented on norms of talk regulation, of bodily proximity, and of the territorial setting of interaction in these urban working-class communities. However, a number of more abstract issues are raised by these observations, which will now be considered.

First, it should be noted that although norms of bodily proximity have been treated here separately from those wider territorial norms which influence the setting of interaction, it is likely that both sets of norms are best considered, following Scheflen and Ashcraft (1976), as related levels constituting part of a unified system of territorial behaviour. An individual's perception of territorial order—of the boundaries between private and public places, of who is a host and who a visitor—requires a multilevel analysis dealing with both boundaries of private space around the body (locations), and boundaries of private space in the neighbourhood (neighbourhood zones). It is not difficult to suggest ways in which interrelationships between these two territorial levels might work together to affect communicative behaviour. Many researchers have noted that speakers in these communities, and others like them, characteristically perceive the neighbourhood as a commonly owned and shared territory. For this reason, neighbourhood boundaries are important thresholds, and as we have seen (p. 54 above) strangers entering them may be challenged. The existence of a clear threshold at the level of the neighbourhood zone, along with the ethos of sharing, may be associated with the relatively unclear distinction between public and private *domestic* space. Neighbourhood residents may cross domestic thresholds more easily than they could if they lived in areas where strangers pass freely into neighbourhood zones. Similarly, where territorial order depends on sharing space within neighbourhood boundaries, it seems likely that insiders are willing to mark out private spaces *round their bodies* less wide in extent than they would be if their perception of territorial order did not include a shared neighbourhood, with clearly defined *outer* boundaries.

Proxemic and territorial norms might then both be seen as different levels of a unified territorial behaviour. Less controversially, it is also clear that norms of proximity are manipulated to carry social messages which define the relationship between the interactants as, for example, one of solidarity or aloofness, of equal or unequal status. Speech itself as well as various features of communicative behaviour such as posture, gesture, body movements and orientations, facial expressions and eye contact fulfil a similar communicative function.

In a careful exploratory analysis of the structure and function of phatic behaviour, Laver (1975) notes that phatic communion characteristically occurs on the margins of interaction, and that it is not in principle different from these various strands of non-linguistic communicative behaviour which usually accompany it. The possibility thus emerges that territorial behaviour *at all levels* is linked in a complicated way not only to nonlinguistic communicative behaviour, but to specifically *phatic* behaviour.

It will be recalled that in these communities phatic communion characteristically did not take place on those occasions predicted by middle-class norms. Laver's basic data are drawn from about 100 student projects and although he is careful to concede that his analysis is only exploratory, his own endorsement of his conclusions (as a participant in British and American culture) suggests that the analysis has some validity for British and American middle-class society. By comparing his data with the Belfast material, it is possible to suggest the nature of the relationship between phatic and territorial behaviour, since Laver does in fact explicitly relate the structure of phatic behaviour specifically to territoriality. The major premisses of his argument are that the linguistic tokens of phatic communion are variable and that the initiating participant varies. One important function of this variability is to indicate the psychosocial orientation of two interactants to each other. A general principle is stated, namely that 'if one participant is static in space . . . there seems to be a sharp tendency both in Britain and America, for the *incomer* to initiate the exchange of phatic communion' (p. 8).

Laver suggests that this initiation act constitutes an acknowledgement that the static participant has a stronger claim on the shared territory than the incomer, and so functions as a token of propitation or submission. The incomer places himself momentarily in the power of the static participant who may rebuff his advances or respond with hostility. Thus, Laver suggests that territorial imperatives lie behind the principle that the incomer speaks first.

One conclusion which immediately springs from this argument is that rules of phatic behaviour may be variable where perceptions of territorial order are variable. This variability may account for two facts; first that the incomer in the Belfast communities was not necessarily constrained to speak first, and second that phatic communion often did not occur at all where it might be expected. Following the implications of Laver's analysis we may draw two more tentative but plausible conclusions.

The general principle that the incomer speaks first to indicate acknowledgement of territorial rights may not apply, for the reason that it is redundant in communities where a territory is perceived as shared. This sense of shared territory is reflected by the location of a threshold at the level of the neighbourhood zone, and in the free movement of residents in and out of each other's houses. The place where an incomer is likely to be challenged and to avoid infringing territorial rights is at the neighbourhood boundary. He may not need to repeat an acknowledgement of his status as incomer every time he interacts within the shared territory. Thus, phatic behaviour may be considered to be governed (partly at least) by territorial imperatives.

Second, if as Laver argues one of the social functions of phatic communion is to define or redefine relationships of status or solidarity between participants, it may be partly redundant in communities where relationships between participants are well-defined and unambiguous. Characteristically, as we have seen, relationships within these communities are assumed to be solidary and are not governed by status differentials. Moreover, the close-knit network structure implicates constant interaction and so constant reaffirmation of these solidary ties. Thus the solidarity ethic and the dense, multiplex network structure, both of which co-occur with perceptions of shared territory, may be seen as encouraging a pattern of phatic behaviour where silence at the margins of interaction is tolerable. The nature of the relationship between the speakers, which could in principle be defined by patterns of phatic behaviour, has already been defined by other means.

Although these remarks are speculative, and are intended to explore possibilities rather than to offer firm conclusions, the available evidence does suggest that territorial imperatives influence patterns of both phatic and non-phatic communicative behaviour in an extremely complex manner. Certainly, the links between territorial and communicative behaviour are quite amenable to further empirical investigation, and offer a very rich and suggestive field for study.

CHANNEL

One important area of description in any account of communicative norms is the choice of *channel* a community makes in a specific situation; by this is meant the choice of for example oral, telegraphic, semaphore or written mediums for the transmission of language. Hymes also notes that some description of the *evaluation* given to each channel may be important (1972:63).

The two channels most commonly used in Europe are of course the oral and the written (a student of African culture may have to take *drummed* messages into account in his description). The relative evaluation given to speech and writing in Britain and America has been indirectly investigated by the urban linguistic surveys such as those of New York City, Detroit and Norwich, all of which compared the kind of language used for reading with the kind of language used for conversation. Information on channel evaluation can be extracted from the results of these surveys, even though they do not set out explicitly to contrast attitudes to speech and attitudes to writing.

Since Western urban culture has for some centuries now placed a very high value on written language (a value stated in its clearest form by eighteenth-century scholars such as Dr Johnson) it is not surprising that this important norm is reflected in those urban sociolinguistic studies which find quite extensive style shifting in the direction of publicly recognized prestige norms when speakers read aloud. It is also possible to see this shift in Macaulay's Glasgow study. Since Macaulay was not able to demonstrate the existence of two *conversational* styles, we must infer that the shift between conversation and reading in his data was considerable.

Our awareness of this communicative norm is constantly reinforced by the value placed on a high level of literacy in the educational and status systems. Europeans and Americans may therefore feel that it is somehow 'natural' that writing should be evaluated more highly than speech, although a little thought

will make it clear that this ordering is by no means universal
Many of the reports in Baumann and Sherzer's volume, for
example, make it clear that anthropologists often deal with communities who value oral linguistic abilities of various kinds very
highly; others have a very highly developed oral literature of
great antiquity (Finnegan, 1970). Instances have also been reported of individuals performing amazing feats of memory in
reciting long oral poems (Goody and Watt, 1963). However, in
industrialized countries purely oral skills of this kind tend to be
the prerogative of peripheral or underprivileged groups such as
the school children studied by the Opies (1959), or the poor
blacks in Harlem studied by Labov.

The Opies have documented a thriving oral lore, some of
which can be traced back several centuries, amongst British
school children. Labov has reported considerable skill in various
verbal arts, all orally transmitted, in the black community.
These arts include not only well-defined speech events such as
ritual insults where a high premium is placed on a quick wit and
ready response, but also recitations of long traditional oral
poems. Labov also reports that some adolescent boys who are
poor readers show a perfect command of the principles of logical
argument *orally*; they cannot however transfer their expository
skills to the written channel. In general, the level of reading
attainment in the black community is very low. This fact, along
with the strongly oral and rich character of BEV verbal culture,
suggests that the BEV community does not evaluate the oral
and written channels in the same way as the wider New York
City community. Of course, the wider community's evaluation
reflects institutionally accepted norms.

We have already seen that like the black community in
Harlem, the three Belfast communities are relatively socially
isolated and cut off from the mainstream of upwardly mobile
society. In view of Labov's findings, it seems at best unwise to
assume that the 'common-sense' relative evaluation of oral and
written channels which is so evident in the results of the urban
surveys will automatically be the same in such communities. An
additional reason for caution is that small-scale community

studies investigate communicative values at a much lower level of abstraction. In fact, in the Belfast communities too, speakers valued various kinds of conversational arts very highly. Many hours were spent simply chatting, and a great many of the recorded conversations are lengthy, lively and witty. A common compliment in working-class Belfast is to describe a speaker as a [kwər gɛɪg] ('queer gag')—a witty conversationalist capable of sustaining interest for a long period and of making people laugh.

As might be expected, many of these speakers were illiterate or semiliterate—this latter group could handle only three-letter words on the word list. Those who *were* able, read the word list at great speed, often showing little sign of carefully monitoring their speech. On the contrary, stereotypical vernacular pronunciations (such as [bɛɪg] for the lexical item *bag*) were often used. In contrast, those same fluent word list readers invariably tackled the task of reading a passage of continuous prose extremely unwillingly in a halting, dysfluent manner. Certainly it was not possible to assume an ordering of styles of the kind usually adopted in urban surveys, with the word list style occupying a position closer to the prestige norm than the reading passage style. In fact, quantitative comparison of word list and reading passage styles was not possible since so few speakers were able or willing to tackle the reading passage at all.

This unwillingness seemed often to result from attitudes to the act of reading aloud, rather than from literacy problems; for on the whole, informants felt embarrassed and self-conscious about reading aloud a passage of continuous prose, even when they tackled the word list with equanimity. Attitudes to reading aloud in these communities are reported more fully elsewhere (Milroy and Milroy, 1977a), but similar attitudes in other cities are not commonly discussed in the sociolinguistic literature. Yet, significantly from our point of view here, they reveal fairly clearly certain aspects of the community's relative evaluations of spoken and written channels of communication. We should note that linguists usually assume an evaluation of the kind reflected in the urban surveys to be inevitable; contrary to what actually happened in these working-class areas it is also often assumed that data can be elicited more easily using a reading passage than by recording conversation (Labov, 1972a:211). Such an assumption ignores the very positive value placed on oral skills in communities such as these, or the black community in Harlem, where *literacy* skills may not be as highly rated as in the wider community. Further investigations of working-class communities may reveal this evaluation to be rather general.

These observations suggest that the stylistic range in the Belfast communities cannot be analysed effectively using Labov's early model of the single linear continuum with 'casual' and 'careful' conversational styles ranged alongside reading passage, word list and minimal pair styles, each of which approximates progressively more closely to a prestige norm. In fact, if we systematically compare speakers' language in word list style, interview style and spontaneous style by counting the frequency of phonological variables, we see that speakers do not necessarily adopt a pronunciation closer to the prestige norm when they read aloud. Table 4.1 gives the scores for the variables (a) and (th) of all those Ballymacarrett speakers who both read word lists and produced a large amount of conversation speech in a range of social contexts. The phonetic properties represented by the linguistic scores are explained in the following chapter; for the moment it is sufficient to note that the higher the score, the closer the approximation to the vernacular.

Three facts are clear immediately from Table 4.1. First, both variables are sensitive to the kind of situational constraints discussed by Gumperz and Labov, in that in an interview situation they show a shift away from the vernacular which is appropriate to spontaneous interaction amongst neighbours, kin and friends. Second, this shift does not continue in the expected direction with (a); rather, word list (a) scores are usually closer to the vernacular than interview style (a) scores. Third, the (th) scores shows a striking uniformity in word list style. They refer in fact to percentage deletion of the fricative [ð] in intervocalic positions (as in *mother, brother*) and reveal that even speakers who delete [ð] a great deal or completely in conversation do not delete at all when they are reading a word list. In this respect, contrary to what we should predict from the linear continuum model, they do not differ from speakers (mostly women) with a *low* deletion rate in conversational speech. Only one speaker deletes [ð] at all in his word list. These apparently different patterns for a consonant and vowel variable require some explanation, as does the failure of (a) to pattern stylistically in the manner we would predict from previous sociolinguistic work.

Table 4.1 *Two linguistic variable scores in three styles for thirteen Ballymacarrett informants*

	(a) (index score)			(th) (% score)		
	SS	IS	WLS	SS	IS	WLS
Donald B	3.00	2.66	3.00	56.25	90.00	0.00
George K	4.15	3.40	4.62	88.89	55.56	0.00
Mary T	2.05	1.40	1.00	50.00	7.14	0.00
Elsie D	2.65	1.60	2.31	25.00	33.33	0.00
Millie B	2.80	1.85	2.69	66.67	53.85	0.00
Brenda M	2.80	2.15	2.69	33.33	33.33	0.00
James H	3.30	2.75	2.92	100.00	100.00	0.00
Terence D	2.90	3.35	3.15	94.74	69.23	0.00
Brian B	3.65	2.65	3.00	93.75	75.00	75.00
Stewart M	4.05	2.80	3.00	75.00	66.67	0.00
Alice W	2.55	2.20	2.69	25.00	22.22	0.00
Lena S	2.40	1.92	2.46	20.00	0.00	0.00
Rose L	1.35	1.55	1.50	0.00	40.00	0.00

SS   = Spontaneous style.
IS   = Interview style.
WLS = Word list style.

The significance of observed variability between styles in the (a) scores was checked by subjecting the data to appropriate statistical tests. Applications of statistical techniques to socio-linguistic data will be discussed more fully in the following chapters; meantime it is sufficient to note that simple checks allow us to be sure that stylistic patterns of the kind we have inferred from the variable data of Table 4.1 do in fact represent significant differences in the data; that is, differences which cannot be attributed simply to chance variability.

There is little point in subjecting the (th) data to tests of significance since the general trends are extremely clear. However, the rather less regular (a) data was analysed with the following results.

First, a test known as Friedman's Two-Way Analysis of Variance revealed that there were significant differences between the three sets of data (SS, IS and WLS) without indicating where those differences were located. A series of Wilcoxon tests, designed for analysing paired sets of data, were then applied to discover the location of the significant differences. The results confirm our initial impressions of the three sets of (a) data in Table 4.1.

First, as we might expect, there is a significant difference ($p < 0.05$) between SS and IS, indicating that the figures for these styles do not represent chance variability. Second, there is *not* a significant difference between SS and WLS; this result reflects an earlier remark that the norms observed in spontaneous styles are usually rather close to those in word list style. Finally, there *is* a significant difference ($p < 0.05$) between IS and WLS, again reflecting the observation that the variability generally suggests a shift away from the vernacular in interview style, rather than a quantitative progression towards a standardized norm, to which the closest approximation is found in reading styles. On the contrary, SS and WLS are *both* significantly different from IS, but not from each other.

The statistical tests of course merely confirm the validity of our impressions; they do not tell us *why* this pattern should occur. We will return shortly to a discussion of this question with regard to the variable (a); first, it is best to look at (th).

The fact that some speakers have a near categorical *deletion* rule in conversation, which never operates when they read aloud, suggests some kind of dual norm which has little to do with paying more attention to speech during reading. It is clear that there is a vernacular rule of deletion which is applied in conversation subject to situational constraints. However, a rule of [ð] *insertion* in reading is nearly always applied. Presumably the single speaker who applies the vernacular rule in word list style is deliberately using it to assert vernacular values in much the same way as the young men in Martha's Vineyard. Although Brian B appears to be unusual in his extension of the vernacular rule to word list style, strategies of this kind are open to all speakers. Some may choose not to use them.

The striking uniformity of the (th) scores in word list style can most plausibly be accounted for by a low-level rule of the English spelling system which consistently uses *th* to correspond to the pronunciation [ð] in intervocalic positions. The influence of spelling pronunciation in restoring deleted consonants in English over several centuries has been extensively documented by Wyld (1936). More recently, the same phenomenon has been noted by Beatriz Lavandera (pers. comm.) as accounting for presence versus absence of Spanish [s] in preconsonantal and word final positions. Thus, the influence of the written form produces here variability which is *qualitative* rather than *quantitative*.

Although spelling pronunciation cannot be invoked to explain large-scale linguistic changes (see Labov, Yaeger and Steiner, 1972 for the problems inherent in such an explanation) it is likely that in reading aloud, an informant may be guided by clearly rule-governed aspects of the spelling system if simple alternation between presence and absence of a consonantal segment is involved. Such an explanation accounts for the (th) data of Table 4.1 better than the one advanced by Labov to account for stylistic variability in New York City—namely that speakers approximate more closely to a prestige norm when they read, because they are monitoring their speech more carefully than in conversational styles. Such an explanation is unsatisfactory here in that it cannot account for the fact that nearly all the Ballymacarrett speakers, regardless of their scores in conversational styles (which vary very considerably), consistently pronounce [ð] when they read.

This argument cannot, however, apply to stylistic variation in *vowel* variables such as (a). Spelling is a poor guide to the prestige pronunciation of syllabic sonorants, which are not subject to variable deletion like the dental fricative in intervocalic positions, or the stop in final positions (Fasold, 1978:88). Speakers can only know the prestige pronunciation of vowels if they have some knowledge of the linguistic norms of the wider speech community. It is in fact this kind of shared knowledge of linguistic norms which, as we have noted, Labov sees as the defining feature of a speech community. The difficulty of defining one, and only one, 'prestige' variety of English in Belfast makes the concept of the speech community difficult to apply in Labov's terms, and provides a partial explanation of the failure of these working-class informants to continue a shift way from the vernacular when they read word lists. Much sociolinguistic work has assumed that prestige forms can be fairly easily identified, as they can in Norwich for example, where Received Pronunciation influences speakers very considerably. However, researchers working in Scotland (Macaulay, 1977; Romaine, 1978a) have mentioned encountering difficulties in using the concept of a prestige norm. Similar problems are encountered in Belfast where a range of educated accents can be heard, some of which sound Scottish, some Hiberno-English, while others are apparently modelled on RP. Educated speakers appear to have a range of linguistic choices open to them quite different from the range open to, for example, educated Londoners. Romaine (1978b) has described the consequences of this situation in Edinburgh. Two upper-middle-class informants, both Edinburgh native speakers, attended the same fee-paying school. Yet one speaks RP and the other the local (rhotic) prestige accent known as 'Morningside'. The same difficulty in Northern Ireland in identifying a single linear progression from most to least vernacular suggests that a vernacular speaker in Belfast may sometimes have difficulty in identifying a 'correct' variant appropriate for his use when he reads words in isolation in an unfamiliar situation. Unless the spelling system can help him, as in the case of (th), he is likely to approximate to the strong linguistic norms with which he is familiar as a refuge from acute linguistic uncertainty. The shift in *interview* style as consistently evident in Table 4.1 may then be seen as an avoidance, or modification, of a vernacular norm under the specific situational constraints to which conversation is subject. The direction of shift—which is constrained by both social and systematic phonological factors—can be more appropriately described as being away from a localized norm than towards any identifiable prestige target.[2]

An important conclusion which may be inferred from this discussion of the relative evaluation of communicative channels, is that speakers appear very consistently to modify their conversational speech away from the vernacular in response to situational constraints. However, when they read aloud they do not necessarily continue to modify their speech in the direction of the prestige norm (the (a) pattern is repeated in the Belfast data for several vowel variables), unless they are able to use the spelling system as a reliable guide. It has been suggested that one reason for this stylistic patterning is the absence of a clear set of prestige norms; but whatever the reason, it cannot be assumed that people always use a specially correct kind of speech for reading. It is therefore reasonable to suggest that the widespread communicative norm which places a higher value

---

[2] The question of the direction in which speakers 'correct' their accents is discussed more broadly in Chapter 7 (see p. 181 ff below). For a discussion of constraints generated specifically by the phonological system see J. Milroy (1981). An excellent illustration of the way in which 'careful' pronunciation may be constrained by *community* norms is provided by the response of Stewart M (18) to a minimal pair list. He merged *chop* and *chap* as [tʃäp], expressed surprise at the merger and attempted to differentiate the pair by raising *chap* to [tʃæp]. The similarity of this pronunciation to RP embarrassed him; he mimicked effeminate gestures and laughed mockingly with his friends. Some of the young men successfully differentiated this pair, when pressed, by *backing* and lengthening the second item to [tʃɑ p]. The point is that the raising strategy was proscribed in Stewart's community, apparently because of the social values attached to the RP pronunciation it produced.

on reading than conversation does not apply in these communities. Moreover, if (as Table 4.1 suggests) reading styles are not subject to the same kind of situational constraints as conversational styles, then the two sets of styles should, in any model of communicative competence, be characterized as different parts of these speakers' repertoires, rather than points on a single linear continuum. However, the linear continuum model may well be valid for speakers with a clear knowledge of the linguistic norms of the wider community, who also place a high value on reading skills than conversational skills. It is probable that most informants located by the use of random sampling techniques are of this kind.

SUMMARY

The picture acquired in this chapter is one of underprivileged and low-status groups living in communities characterized by dense, multiplex network relationships which are contracted within clear territorial boundaries. Most interactions which are not transactional and explicitly goal-oriented take place within the territorial boundaries. Under these circumstances (see Gumperz's comment discussed on p. 85 above), it is not surprising if communicative norms are different *inside* the communities from those widely accepted in upwardly mobile Irish and British society. We find, for example, that rules for the distribution of silence are different from those described as 'normal' (Trudgill, 1983b:13). Norms governing physical proximity and appropriate settings for interaction also appear to be different. Finally relative evaluations of written and spoken channels of communication are different from those we can infer from the large-scale sociolinguistic studies which examine *conversational* and *reading* styles in the speech of a wide range of social groups. It is tempting to agree at this point with Gumperz's insistence that a speech community cannot be defined satisfactorily only in terms of speakers' agreement on the social value of purely linguistic norms like (h) in Norwich, (r) in New York City, or (th) in Belfast. A fully competent member of a speech community also needs to know how, when and where to speak. Knowledge of this wide range of norms, if they are different from publicly accepted norms, depends on a large amount of interaction with a limited number of people in a limited territorial area. This interactional pattern is characteristic of communities where networks are very dense and multiplex. It has already been suggested in Chapter 3 that this kind of network functions generally as a mechanism for maintaining normative consensus. We may now more specifically suggest that it has the power to maintain a set of communicative norms different from those which govern the behaviour of people not linked to a localized community by a large number of ties. The capacity of the dense, multiplex network to maintain nonstandard norms of a specifically *linguistic* kind will be examined in the following chapters.

5

The Quantitative Analysis of Linguistic Data

In recent years, a large number of those quantitative studies described in Chapter 1 have succeeded in showing close links between social patterns and patterns of language use. This has been done by using the technique of correlating average group scores for sociolinguistic variables with a wide range of independent variables. The list of such variables which can be seen to influence a speaker's language is very large, and I do not give a complete list here nor discuss any variable exhaustively. The reader who requires fuller information is referred to a more general sociolinguistics text book such as Labov (1972a); Dittmar (1976); Trudgill (1983); Hudson (1980). The particular social variables we need to discuss briefly in this book are as follows: (1) social class; (2) sex of speaker; (3) age of speaker; (4) regional origin of speaker; and (5) (more complex) group identity of speaker. We may additionally remind ourselves in passing that language reacts in a very sensitive way to the variable of *situational context*; variations in the way speakers use the variables (a) and (th) in Belfast for example can be accounted for partly at least by situational variables. This parameter of variation will not be discussed further here, except in so far as it interacts with other variables, such as sex or social class.

EXTRA-LINGUISTIC VARIABLES

Social Class

All studies undertaken in cities have shown a very clear link between a speaker's language and his position in a social class hierarchy. To illustrate this we may refer again to the scores reported for (r) in New York City by Labov (see pp. 10-11 above). Clearly, the higher the social class of a speaker, the more likely he is to pronounce [r] in postvocalic positions. Similar patterns of linguistic stratification have been reported for a wide range of sociolinguistic variables elsewhere.

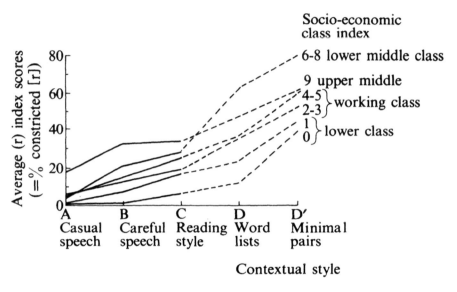

Figure 5.1

For linguists who are particularly interested in the direct observation of linguistic change, the main interest in the link between language and class is frequently the kind of irregularity in the stratification pattern apparent in Figure 5.1. Labov interprets a crossover pattern like this as a sign of linguistic change in progress from above; what is happening, he argues (1972a: 122), is that the *second highest* social group, in their most careful styles, are adopting, and emulating, a pronunciation characteristic of the *highest* prestige group. Similar cross over patterns may occur at the opposite end of the social class continuum with the *second lowest* social group using more of a stigmatized form than the *lowest*, as exemplified by the (a) pattern in

Norwich (see Figure 5.2). This may be interpreted as a change in progress from *below*—that is *not* in the direction of a conscious prestige norm. We shall refer again to this kind of crossover pattern when the notion of *interaction of variables* is discussed later in this chapter. Meantime, note that in order to infer that linguistic change of some kind is taking place, it is necessary to consider more than one extralinguistic variable; in the case of (r), both social class and contextual style. As Trudgill explains in some detail, the (a) pattern in Norwich involves consideration not only of class and style, but also of age structures in the Norwich working-class population (Trudgill, 1974;111).

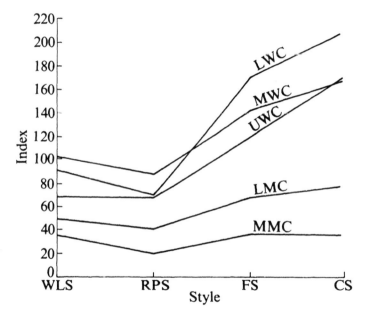

Figure 5.2

Figures 5.1 and 5.2   *The distribution of two linguistic variables according to social class and contextual style. Figure 5.1 refers to (r) in New York City after Labov. Figure 5.2 to (a) in Norwich after Trudgill*

The other point to be noted here is that all the Belfast informants are drawn from the lower end of the social scale. We can therefore infer on the basis of findings such as Labov's and Trudgill's, that the vernacular norms observable in spontaneous styles and subject to correction in interview style, are likely to be avoided by speakers from higher social groups. For it is this observation of the links between stylistic variation and social class stratification which often enables us to identify the salient linguistic norms of a community.

Sex of Speaker

Differences in language according to sex have been observed in many kinds of society and may themselves be of many different kinds. For example, Salisbury (1962) reports that multilingualism is highly valued by the males of a New Guinea complex of tribes who frequently switched between languages, but disvalued by women who spoke only the language of their native tribe. In Western urbanized society one of the most general findings of all the recent studies is that sexual differences in language usually take the form of women approximating closer to the prestige pattern, and style-shifting more extensively, than men. Women are also sometimes thought to initiate linguistic change (Labov, 1972a), although the evidence is confused and conflicting here. Problems in formulating an adequate generalization usually arise as a result of other factors, such as whether the change is in the direction of a prestige norm, or the nature of the motivating source of the change (which may be complex). For example, in Martha's Vineyard, the young men seemed to be responsible for a movement away from the standard norms. Labov explains the motivation for this change as a desire on the part of young men to identify themselves as Vineyarders; if Labov's explanation is correct, sex would be a less important factor in determining leadership of a linguistic change than the social values peculiar to various subgroups in the population. In principle, the young Vineyard women should be capable of leading the change also, if they shared the same social values as the men.

The data from the Belfast communities shows in general the

expected pattern of women conforming less closely to vernacular norms than men. But in the matter of who initiates linguistic change the situation is complex. Men seem to be generally more conservative, in that several very archaic urban vernacular features usually traceable to a specific rural hinterland are consistently observable in male speech only. We may refer to a dental variant of /t/ in words with a following /r/ like *petrol*, *water*, *pottery*. This variant is clearly observable only in the speech of middle-aged men and older men in the Clonard (the area where migration to the city is relatively recent). A similar pattern affects the distribution of a palatal glide introduced after /k/ usually before front vowels in such items as *cap*, *cat*, *car*.

The [kj] pronunciation, like [ʈ], is a rural stereotype and hardly appears in the speech of women, although all the men over forty in the Clonard use it extensively, even when reading word lists (Milroy and Milroy, 1977b). Thus, in this instance, women do seem to lead change in the sense that they abandon conservative linguistic features more readily than men. However, a generalization based on the sex of the speaker rather than, for example, his social values, or the structure of his social network, is unwise. For as we shall see, the Clonard data also provide evidence that women are capable of introducing to their own small communities a linguistic feature associated with *men* in Ballymacarrett which is, moreover, not particularly close to any publicly recognized prestige norm.

Speaker's Region of Origin

It is clear from the foregoing discussion that areal differences play quite a large part in variations observable in Belfast working-class speech, which we will refer to again in due course. Generally speaking, area has *not* in the past been an important variable in quantitative studies, although it has been the focus of interest in the predominantly non-quantitative studies of the rural dialectologists. However, in Norwich area was important in explaining the distribution of the variable (h), since aitch dropping is a vernacular norm in Norwich but not in the sur-rounding countryside. Therefore, speakers born outside Norwich show a different pattern of linguistic behaviour from those native to the city (Trudgill, 1974).

Age of Speaker

This variable has already been touched on in some of the dis-cussions above; indeed, one of the best-known studies of the effect of age on speech is the Martha's Vineyard study. There, younger speakers approximate more closely to an island ver-nacular than middle-aged speakers; and in fact, in very many places younger speakers, especially males, approximate more closely to the vernacular than middle-aged speakers. For example the (a) variable in Norwich (already mentioned in the discussion on social class) has a diphthongized reflex (in items such as *bad, man*) which represents a movement *away* from the RP norm and is particularly associated with people under the age of thirty.

Group Identity of Speaker

In a sense, it is clear that all the independent variables outlined above might be considered as various categories of identity. Thus, a speaker's language may simultaneously mark him as male, young, working-class, and of a particular regional origin. The extent to which he allows his speech to symbolize his social identity in this way may vary according to other factors (social and psychological) which investigators have not been able to examine quantitatively. One or two small-scale studies—such as Labov's account of the gangs in Harlem—show that a speaker's desire to identify with a particular ethnic culture can cut across social class differences. Labov demonstrated that copula dele-tion, a feature associated with blacks, is used variably depending on how far the speaker is integrated into the vernacular culture, and it is in fact a matter of common observation that people use language in this way to express membership of groups of many kinds—for example, regional, ethnic or occupational. However, correlating language scores in a systematic way to the various aspects of a speaker's social identity is complex, and is not often attempted. It is this kind of multiple influence on language which has led Le Page (1975a; 1976) to refer to each utterance a speaker makes as an 'act of identity' and to plot *individual* speakers' language *multidimensionally*, with reference to several sources of influence at once. For example, in an analysis (still in progress) of the speech of school children in the Caribbean island of St Lucia, he identifies four ways of expressing habitual aspects of the verb *live*. Each variant is associated with a different source of influence in this multilingual community: (1) *I live* (educated usage); (2) *I lives* (nonstandard English dialect speech); (3) *I living* (former French patois-speaking communities); (4) *I does live* (the influence of Barbados on Castries, the Capital of St Lucia). As speakers variably use one or another of these choices, Le Page sees them as expressing different aspects of a fluid social identity as they move through a multidimensional sociolinguistic space (cf. Le Page and Tabouret-Keller, 1985).

Such an analysis is clearly much more complex and difficult than those we have outlined in this chapter; yet the fact that, for example, sex, age, social class and a more concrete group identity can interact with each other in a complex way suggests that Le Page's approach captures a sociolinguistic reality.

The analysis in this chapter and in Chapter 6 presupposes a point of view (although not an analytic method) similar to Le Page's—that speakers use the resources of variability in their language to express a great complex of different identities. No method of analysis in the present state of knowledge is likely to capture completely the complexity of the way speakers use variability; but to add in a necessarily limited way the dimension of individual choice to those variables already considered (which may be seen as lying outside the speaker's control) we use here the analytic tool of *social network analysis*. This allows to some extent quantification of the character of an individual's everyday social relationships—the influences to which he is constantly open. We further examine the links between the way in which these network structures on the one hand, and the other 'identity' variables of age, sex and area on the other can influence a speaker's language use.

Before proceeding further with a quantitive analysis, it is necessary to give some account of the *linguistic* variables in Belfast which are the main focus of our study in these chapters.

Irish and Scottish accents of English differ fundamentally from most Anglo-English accents in many ways. Most obviously they are *rhotic*, and also they are different in the manner in which they employ distinctions based on vowel length. Belfast vernacular shows these characteristics and also shows a much greater degree of phonetically conditioned allophonic variation (it is not known how far this may be a property of urban vernaculars in general) than has usually been reported in the literature.

For example, Belfast vernacular does not have a distinction corresponding to the /ɑː/v./æ/ distinction found in RP: *Sam* sæm/ v. *psalm* /sɑːm/. However, the phonetic reflexes of the single /a/ vowel vary from a front variant with a closing glide near the half close position, to a back rounded variant near to cardinal 6 (see Figure 5.3), sometimes with a centring glide. Many speakers show in addition a sharp distinction in *length* between a short variant which occurs most often before voiceless stops, and a long variant which occurs before all other single consonants and most clusters. This phonetically conditioned length distinction is in fact a general feature of the mid and low peripheral vowels of Belfast vernacular, and is discussed in greater detail elsewhere (J. Milroy, 1981 and forthcoming).

The extreme front variation of /a/ is found only before voiced velars—in which we might call the /ag/ class which consists of items such as *bag, lag, rag*; but slightly *less* front-raised variants are found before voiceless velars. Centralized or back-raised variants never occur in environments with a following velar consonant. Variants followed by a non-velar may range between [æ] and [ɔᵊ]. Further complexity is introduced by the clear tendency of a following labial or nasal (*man, grab*) to encourage an extremely back-raised and rounded variant. Knowledge of these complexities of phonetic conditioning is extremely important if a quantitative study is being undertaken, since any scale which measures backing of /a/ must at the very least exclude items where a velar consonant follows the vowel.

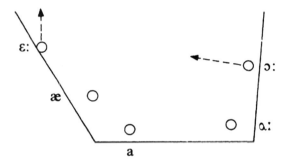

Figure 5.3 *Variation in /a/. Arrows indicate direction of glides*

Similar complexities are encountered in defining the scope of other variables. We find, for example, that the /ɛ/ vowel in Belfast varies between (1) a low slightly centralized variant [æ] in monosyllables which are closed either by a voiceless stop *or* by a liquid or nasal followed by a voiceless obstruent (*bet, peck, rent, else*), and (2) a higher longer vowel with a centring glide [ɛ'ᵊ] which, in monosyllables, is nearly categorical before all other consonants. Thus there is often a dramatic contrast between *bet* [bæt] and *bed* [bɛ'ᵊd] in terms of both the length and the quality of the vowel.

The complicating factor is that in monosyllables with the *bet, rent* type of environment, the [æ] variant is almost categorical for male speakers while women more variably use both [æ] and [ɛᵊ]. If we consider polysyllables, the situation is quite different. In items such as *electric, textile, heavy*, the low vowel is generally favoured. Although there is variability between the two variants, it seems to be influenced largely by the kind of extralinguistic variables we discussed in the last section, rather than by the phonetic environment. Because of the stronger phonetic constraints on variability in the monosyllables, it is practical and convenient to treat the /ɛ/ class as consisting of *two* variables which we will refer to as (ɛ¹) and (ɛ²). In defining the scope of a linguistic variable (see below) the main object is always to exclude as far as possible those phonetic environments which do not permit variability.

Yet another kind of linguistic complexity is presented by the variables (ʌ¹) and (ʌ²). Like the /ɛ/ class, but for a different reason, the word class of /ʌ/ as in *cut, mud*, has to be treated as consisting of two variables. The variable labelled as (ʌ¹) affects all items in the class. Two variants are distinguished, one rounded [ɔ̈] and one unrounded [ʌ]. There is also an |ʉ| word class consisting of items like *good, food, cook, would*. There is no class corresponding to RP |ʊ|, so that in Belfast the two lexical items in the phrase *good food* [gʉd fʉd| are assigned to the same class rather than to different classes as in RP /gʊd fuːd/.

However, there is a small set of lexical items which alternates between the two phonetically divergent classes, /ʌ/ and /ʉ/. The total membership of this set cannot be predicted on phonological grounds, nor do speakers themselves have reliable intuitions. For example, *foot, took, shook, look* have all been attested as alternating between [ʌ] and [ʉ], while *soot, cook, book, hook* seem always to be pronounced with [ʉ]. Altogether, eighteen items have been assigned on the basis of observation to this alternating class; these items are considered to be tokens of (ʌ²). Although there are clear difficulties in defining its membership, this lexical set is very important from a sociolinguistic point of view as the [ʌ] variant (all of the words in which it occurs are very common) is a stereotypical vernacular pronunciation, carrying symbolic value similar to the zero form of the copula in the black communities of the United States (Maclaran, 1976).

Clearly then, establishing the phonetic and phonological scope of the variables is a complex matter, requiring considerable preliminary analysis of the phonology of the vernacular.

When we come to consider the *social values* associated with these variables, it is generally clear which of the variants approximates most closely to the vernacular norm. This is best established by observing the direction of shift in the formal interview situation, and taking the variants most frequently found in spontaneous speech as approximating closest to vernacular norms. It is however important to remember that data collected from working-class communities cannot be used to establish prestige norms, in the same way as Trudgill, for example, is able to do in Norwich where speakers from a range of social classes are studied. For this reason (and also because of the difficulty discussed in Chapter 4 of establishing the identity of prestige norms) it is convenient in this account to consider variants as approximating more or less closely to a *vernacular* norm, rather than more or less closely to a *prestige* norm.

The eight variables and their phonetic variants analysed in these chapters are described below. Where possible, the total number of tokens of each variable for each speaker is between sixty and eighty. These are the numbers on which the individual scores in the appendix are based for all variables, except those with a limited phonological or lexical distribution—(th) and (Λ^2) in this study. The scores for (th) are based on only sixteen to twenty tokens per speaker, those for (Λ^2) slightly more. The total number of tokens scored for (Λ^2) is 1,500, compared with 856 for (th). In all cases, scores are based on two separate styles for each speaker (interview style and spontaneous style) and therefore refer to language samples drawn from two different sections of tape.

   1. (a) *Index* scores are used, measuring degree of retraction and back-raising in items such as *hat, man, grass.* Items with a following velar are excluded. A five-point scale is used ranging from scores of one for tokens with [æ] to five for tokens with [ɔə].
   2. (ai) *Index* scores measure on a three-point scale degree of fronting and raising of the first element of the diphthong in closed-syllable items of the /ai/ class—*pipe, line, life.*

3. (ı) *Index* scores measure on a three-point scale degree of lowering and centralization to [ë ∼ ӓ] in items of the /ı/ class—*hit, kill, tin.* Scores range from one for [ı] to three for [ë ∼ ӓ].

4. (th) *Percentage* scores measure deletion of intervocalic [ð] in a small lexical set, for example *mother, brother.*

5. (ʌ¹) *Percentage* scores measure frequency of lip rounded variant in items of the /ʌ/ class—*hut, mud.*

6. (ʌ²) *Percentage* scores measure frequency of [ʌ] variant in a small lexical set which alternates between [ʌ] and [ʉ]: for example *pull, took, shook, foot.*

7. (ε¹) *Percentage* scores measure frequency of a low vowel (as opposed to a mid vowel) in items such as *bet, peck, rent, else.* The analysis is restricted to monosyllables closed either by a voiceless stop, or by a voiceless obstruent preceded by a liquid or nasal.

8. (ε²) *Percentage* scores measure frequency of the same low vowel in di-and polysyllables.

Neither this brief description of the variables nor the foregoing discussion of four of the most complex of the eight do full justice to the greater complexities of Belfast vernacular phonology, nor to the historical and theoretical questions raised by closer study. The reader is referred to J. Milroy (1980) and J. Milroy (1981) for a fuller account.

SOCIAL DISTRIBUTION OF THE VARIABLES

The general links between patterns of linguistic variation in the Belfast communities, and the independent variables of age, sex and area have been described elsewhere (Milroy and Milroy, 1977b). The scores of forty-six individual speakers representing males and females, divided into two age groups (18–25; 40–55) are to be found in the appendix; all subsequent analysis discussed in this book is based on these scores. To check the *reliability* of the links between linguistic and extralinguistic variables, a statistical technique known as *analysis of variance* (already mentioned in passing in Chapter 4) is used. Although it has not in the past been common in sociolinguistics to find any but the most basic statistical techniques routinely used—such as the calculation of averages—it is wise to subject data where possible to simple statistical checks of *significance*. That is to enable the analyst to be sure that observed variability is not simply the result of chance; one needs to be reasonably certain that if the same speakers were recorded again, or if a comparable group of speakers were recorded, similar patterns of variability would be observed.

Sometimes of course the patterns of variation are so clear, and a number of converging trends so regular (as in the (r) distribution in New York City or the (a) distribution in Norwich discussed earlier in this chapter) that statistical tests of significance seem redundant. However, the sociolinguistic literature contains quite a large number of examples of patterns of variability, including some in Belfast, of which the significance is not at all clear without some kind of statistical check. Wherever quantitative methods are used, there is generally some statistical method available to help the analyst interpret his results. Two techniques are used in these chapters for different analytic purposes —*analysis of variance* and *correlation*. Analysis of variance is applied first.

Analysis of Variance

This is an extremely powerful and versatile technique applicable to many different kinds of quantitative work wherever the basic problem is to compare *means* and the scatter of scores around the means. Since the basic technique of quantitative sociolinguistics is to compare mean linguistic scores of social subgroups of various kinds, this technique is employed here to look at differences in the way the linguistic variables are distributed among the age and sex subgroups in the three areas—Clonard, Hammer and Ballymacarrett. What we are doing is looking for significant differences between mean linguistic scores among subgroups of various kinds into which we divide the forty-six subjects. We can reach conclusions about sex differences in language, for example, by comparing male and female means; area differences by comparing area means; and so on. The next step is the important one, especially when dealing with small groups of speakers as we are when the total number (N = 46) is divided into three or four subgroups. If differences are found between the mean scores of the sexes for a given variable—let us say (th)—we must be sure before concluding that (th) functions as an important sex marker in Belfast vernacular that this variability is not the result of chance. We can do that in the following way.

Analysis of variance employs a fairly complicated formula in comparing means; the formula need not be explained here, although the important principles will be. A statistic known as the F-ratio is produced which is affected not only by the raw scores, but also by the size of the group and the manner in which the scores *within* the group are distributed or vary round the mean—that is, the relative homogeneity of the group. The F-ratio is then tested for significance, using a further statistical technique known as the t-test. If a given level of F proves to be *significant*, we can be confident that even with very small groups any difference we have observed is very unlikely to be the result of chance, and that the figures are reliable.

We must now explain exactly what is meant by the term *significant*, in its technical sense. The application of the t-test to the F-ratio produces a further statistic which indicates the probability (p) of that particular level of F occurring as a result of chance. If the probability is less than one in twenty ($p < 0.05$) it is accepted that the difference between the means—let us say of the male and female (th) scores—is not the result of chance, but that there is a real and reliable relationship between sex of speaker and linguistic score. The figure of one in twenty is in fact arbitrary, but is conventionally accepted as the minimum level of probability (that the difference between means could have occurred by chance) to aim for, and is as such a rather stringent test of significance against the results coming about by chance. A *highly significant* result is an F-ratio which would occur only one time in a hundred by chance ($p < 0.01$). If we emerge with a result which gives this figure, we may conclude with even more confidence that our figures represent a real and reliable difference between, say, male and female language.

If on the other hand the t-test shows that a given level of F could occur *more* than one time in twenty by chance ($p > 0.05$) we may conclude that the differences are not significant. However, if the figure is close to 0.05—say 0.0516—it is reasonable to talk in terms of a *trend* rather than a significant difference.

Table 5.1 summarizes the results of the analysis of variance tests. Significant differences between subgroups divided according to sex, age, and area are presented.

Table 5.1 *Mean differences between male and female groups for five linguistic variables. In all cases, male scores are higher and therefore closer to vernacular norms*

Variable	F-ratio	Probability
(a)	22.6064	$p < 0.01$
(th)	19.3795	$p < 0.01$
(Λ^1)	6.3769	$p < 0.05$
(ε^1)	21.8974	$p < 0.01$
(ε^2)	11.5489	$p < 0.01$

Clearly then there are significant or highly significant differences between male and female language use on a number of variables. There is however, only one significant difference between mean *area* scores. This occurs in the figure for the variable (I) ($F = 6.1130$, $p < 0.01$). Scores for this variable are highest in the Hammer and lowest in the Clonard. (Area means: $B = 2.0104$; $C = 1.8333$; $H = 2.2000$). The same variable also shows a significant difference between means for the two *age* groups (40–55 years, 1.9083; 18–25 years 2.1208; $F = 6.1572$, $p < 0.05$). The younger age group therefore scores significantly higher than the older.

Since four of the five variables in Table 5.1 show a *highly significant* difference between the male and female groups, while ($\wedge^1$) shows a *significant* difference, we may conclude that all these phonological elements function as sex markers in the communities. We may also conclude for the moment (in this study at least, and using this method), that it is easier to demonstrate sex differences in language use, than age or area differences.

Unfortunately however, the manner in which speakers use language to express social values is not quite as simple as this analysis implies, nor can sociolinguistic variables be dismissed in this way as having unitary functions as sex or age or area markers. To demonstrate some of the complexities clearly, we look now at the scores for two of the variables already discussed, (a) and ($\wedge^2$), presented in graph form (Figures 5.4, 5.5).

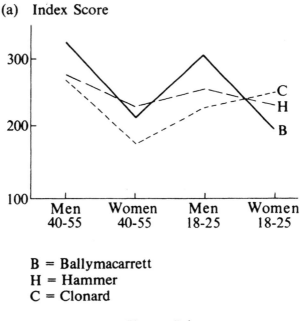

(a)   Index Score

B = Ballymacarrett
H = Hammer
C = Clonard

Figure 5.4

Clearly, Figure 5.4 confirms the results in Table 5.1 in that it shows a difference between male and female frequencies in the use of (a). Although the graph cannot really tell us whether this difference is significant, it does give us important information which is not apparent from any of the numerical scores so far considered. Particularly, the male/female difference in language use appears to be most regular in Ballymacarrett, almost non-existent in the Hammer, and actually to go in the *reverse* direction among the younger speakers in the Clonard.

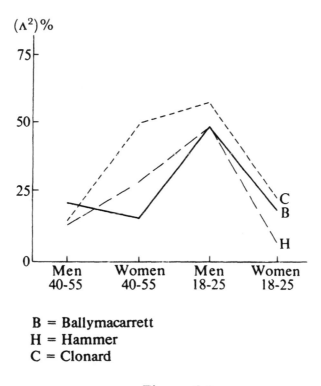

B = Ballymacarrett
H = Hammer
C = Clonard

Figure 5.5

Figures 5.4 and 5.5   *The distribution of two linguistic variables by age, sex and area in Belfast*

Since there are also *age* and *area* differences involved in the distribution of (a) through the community, further systematic analysis is needed. For although analysis of variance has so far not demonstrated a significant difference between age and area *means*, there certainly appears to be some difference in the way

(a) functions in the three areas, and in the Clonard a particularly complicated difference between the way in which the age groups and sexes use this variable.

If we now turn our attention to Figure 5.5, regularities which initial analysis has entirely failed to reveal are apparent: for the variable ($\wedge^2$) did not appear at all in the list of statistically significant differences between subgroups based on sex, age or area. Nevertheless, it is very clear from the graph that *young* speakers in all three areas show very regular patterns of variation according to whether they are male or female. With the *older* group the position is much less clear, except that in the Clonard the distinction between the sexes in the older age group goes in exactly the *reverse* direction, with the women using more of the vernacular variant than the men. What the graph cannot tell us, and what we seem to need at this point, is some kind of check on whether these complicated patterns of variation amongst sex, age and area *subgroups* in the community are significant. Analysis of variance can in fact give this information also. The F-ratio is able to indicate whether there is significant *interaction* of variables; that is whether variation (linguistic variation here) between subgroups in respect of one variable (sex, in Figure 5.5) is influenced significantly by variation between subgroups in respect of another (age, in this instance). It is best at this point to clarify what is meant by *interaction*, in its technical sense, by giving a simple non-linguistic example.

The following (constructed) set of data represents the mean number of cigarettes per day smoked by a sample of men and women in two age groups.

	Men	Women
40–55	20	10
18–25	10	20

If we simply compare the means for two age groups and both sexes separately (as was done for the linguistic variables), we would conclude that there is no difference in the smoking habits of the sexes, or of the two age groups, as the means are identical. Yet, such a conclusion misses the obvious point that young men smoke only half as much as older men, while young women smoke twice as much as older women. What has happened is that an *interaction effect* has levelled out differences between means when either age *or* sex are considered separately. It is an interaction effect of the same kind which masks patterns of variability in the distribution of both (a) and (Λ^2). In the case of (Λ^2) (Figure 5.5) it is the variables of age and sex which show an interaction effect, in the case of (a) (Figure 5.4) it is the variables of age, sex and area. For it is only the *young Clonard women* who reverse the expected pattern for the (a) variable. We have of course already seen patterns similar to those in Figures 5.4 and 5.5; Figure 5.4 is particularly reminiscent of the crossover pattern in the graph summarising the (r) data in New York City, and the (a) data in Norwich (Figures 5.1 and 5.2). Such a pattern is sometimes interpreted as typical of a linguistic change in progress (see p. 110 above).

However, before we can interpret the data of Figures 5.4 and 5.5 in *any* way, we really need to know whether the interactions are significant, or whether they are merely the result of chance variation—for we must remember that we are dealing with small subgroups (N = 4 for the young female group in the Clonard, for example). Since an analysis of variance technique takes account of the *size* of the subgroups being compared, we may conclude that there is indeed a real and reliable difference if a sufficiently high level of F to indicate a significant interaction is obtained. The procedure is that any given level of F indicates the *degree* of interaction; the t-test is then applied to check whether this degree of interaction is significant. An examination of the subgroup means can then indicate where the differences are located.

Before examining three variables whose distribution is in fact affected by significant interactions, it will be helpful to refer to a variable which does *not* show an interaction effect. Such a comparison demonstrates very clearly the extreme complexity of the (a) and (Λ^2) patterns.

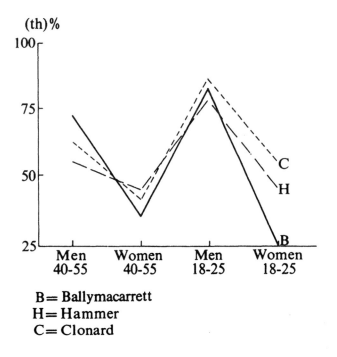

B = Ballymacarrett
H = Hammer
C = Clonard

Figure 5.6 *The distribution of (th) by age, sex and area in Belfast*

Figure 5.6 shows the distribution of (th) by age, sex and area in graph form. This is the pattern typical of the kind of variable Labov has aptly labelled 'a stable sociolinguistic marker', where no interaction effects are evident and which is not apparently participating actively in a linguistic change. Since the graph shows clearly that, in contrast with (a) and (Λ^2), there is little variation in age or area subgroups the results reported in Table 5.1 are an adequate account of the distribution of (th) through these communities.

INTERACTION EFFECTS IN THE DISTRIBUTION OF LINGUISTIC
VARIABLES

Table 5.2 *Linguistic variables showing significant interaction effects in their distribution*

Sociolinguistic variables	Interacting variables	F-ratio	Probability
(a)	area × sex	5.7593	$p < 0.01$
	sex × age	6.0003	$p < 0.05$
(Λ^2)	sex × age	16.8535	$p < 0.001$
(ε^1)	area × sex	3.6752	$p < 0.05$

We may infer generally from Table 5.2 that independent variables of age, sex and area can interact with each other in a complex way in controlling linguistic scores. The results for (a) and (Λ^2) largely confirm the impressions formed by Figures 5.4 and 5.5. The important point, however, is that we can be sure that the patterns revealed in the graphs are not simply the result of chance; the differences between the male and female (a) scores are not maintained in each area, and the frequencies in different areas are significantly different. The interaction effect of sex and area explains why this difference is not apparent if we compare area means (cf. the cigarette smoking example on p. 126 above). The significant interaction between sex and age is in fact largely due to the high scores of the young women in the Clonard. (We shall return to the distributional pattern for (a) when we consider network scores across the age, sex and area groups.) Similarly, if we look at the results for (Λ^2) we see a *very highly significant* interaction between sex and age. This reflects the fact that the two sexes behave in quite the reverse manner in different age groups in their use of (Λ^2), and that this difference cannot be attributed to chance variation in the sample. Although the graph suggests that the high female score in the older age group is particularly associated with the *Clonard*, the results of our analysis do not in this instance give grounds for thinking this link is more than accidental; for the F-ratio is not sufficiently high to indicate a significant *sex* by *area* or *age* by *area* interaction. All we are justified in concluding is that (contrary to what happens with younger speakers) in the older age group in general, the women use (Λ^2) at a higher level than the men. This is a particularly clear demonstration of the importance of submitting data to simple statistical checks: for it is hard to see otherwise how we could make a reliable statement about a complex distributional pattern like that of Figure 5.5.

Turning to (ε^1) (Table 5.2), we find once again that its function as a sex marker (see Table 5.1) is revealed by further analysis to be extremely complex. When we examine the means for the area and sex subgroups (see Table 5.3), we find that the area by sex interaction effect is produced by the differences between the sexes being much less in the Clonard and the Hammer, than in Ballymacarrett.

Table 5.3 *Mean scores for* (ε^1) *of both sexes in three areas*

	Men	Women
Ballymacarrett	100.0000	50.9421
Clonard	92.9763	78.8200
Hammer	93.5625	75.7138

This analysis reveals that the generalization formulated as a result of the overall scores reported in Table 5.1 requires some modification. Although (ε^1) functions as a sex marker in all three areas, with men always scoring higher, this function is very much clearer in Ballymacarrett where men *categorically* use the low vowel in words like *pet, neck, rent*. Ballymacarrett women on the other hand use a great deal less of it than women in the other two areas, where distribution is more nearly comparable. Note in passing that Ballymacarrett shows the sharpest patterns of sex differentiation in the distribution of (a) and (th) also; however, in the case of these two variables, the difference in distribution between areas is not sharp enough (cf. Table 5.3) to produce a significant sex by area interaction. We shall return shortly to the significance of these contrasting sociolinguistic patterns in the different communities.

What is clear so far from this analysis is that, even within a single social class group, different 'bits' of the language are associated with sex, area and age subgroups in an extremely complicated way, patterns of sex differentiation being particularly sharp. Yet, despite these linguistic differences which can be linked firmly to the variables of sex, age and area, there is a large residue of systematic variation between *individuals* which cannot be characterized in any clear way by dividing speakers into further subgroups. It is these individual differences in language use to which we now turn our attention.

SYSTEMATIC VARIATION BETWEEN INDIVIDUALS

For the very reason that so much variability is linked to factors such as age, sex and area, we need to know the general norms associated with these subgroups before we are in a position to assess the extent and significance of individual variation. For example, Table 5.4 lists the scores for eight variables of two middle-aged women from the Clonard. The consistency of the variation between them is all the more striking if we appreciate the extent to which variation on these same linguistic variables may be linked to categories of age, sex and area.

Table 5.4

Variables	1 (ai)	2 (a)	3 (ɪ).	4 (ʌ¹)	5 (th)	6 (ʌ²)	7 (ε¹)	8 (ε²)
Hannah McK	1.4	1.05	1.2	0	0	0	66.7	25.00
Paula C	2.4	2.63	2.5	9	58.34	70.48	100	47.83

Two speakers' scores for eight phonological variables. 1–3 are index scores; 4–8 represent percentages. A higher score indicates a relatively close approximation to vernacular norms.

The figures show that Paula quite consistently approximates closer to vernacular norms than Hannah. Yet, the objective social characteristics of the women are, by any commonly used standards, very similar. Both are married to unskilled workers, both are in unskilled jobs themselves, and both express satisfaction in the warmth and friendliness of life in the Clonard. Neither are educated beyond the minimum school-leaving age.

Any attempt to explain the consistency of the difference in linguistic scores in terms of some kind of social status index would, therefore, seem to be inappropriate. Yet, the differences *are* consistent enough to invite some kind of explanation, particularly since intragroup differences between individual speakers (see Appendix) are in very many cases consistent over a very large number of variables.

Before making any further attempt to account for patterns of variation like those in Table 5.4, it will be helpful to comment on previous work based on individual, rather than group, variation. The views of Le Page have already been discussed briefly earlier in this chapter.

Several linguists (for example, Gumperz, 1976b; Russell, 1982; Bickerton, 1975) have made very similar observations to those of Le Page (1968) when he remarks that 'the individual creates his system of verbal behaviour so as to resemble those common to the group or groups with which he wishes from time to time to be identified'. This hypothesis is strikingly similar to Giles' and Powesland's (1975) proposals for applying social psychology's accommodation theory to explain linguistic code-switching, and in fact, Le Page's interest in the function of language as a symbol of personal identity is shared by many social psychologists.

Labov (1966) notes considerable variation *within* social groups defined on the basis of age, class or sex, but argues convincingly that studies of the 'idiolect' are unlikely to reveal sociolinguistic structure as clearly as studies of the speech of whole social groups. The consistent patterns he himself uncovers are observable on this basis only; the size of Labov's sample in New York City, together with his method of aggregating data from all the individuals in the group, ensures that considerable variation between individual idiolects does not obscure more regular patterns of variation in the community as a whole. We should note here that Labov is not suggesting that individuals reveal only unstructured variations; he is showing specifically that the idiolect-based approach characteristic of earlier scholars (for example, Bloch, 1948; Hockett, 1958) is inadequate. Bloch and Hockett hoped that the idiolect would be revealed as a tightly structured self-consistent system, valid also for the wider community except perhaps for minor differences of detail. For many years now, sociolinguistics has shown that this deterministic approach is unprofitable, and we would not advocate it here. Nevertheless, as long as we do not expect to find in the language of the individual a perfect replica in miniature of his dialect grammar, there is no reason why a single speaker's output should be viewed as unstructured and unworthy of study. In fact, Bickerton, Le Page and Gumperz all take the individual as the basis of their descriptions of variation, principally because of the difficulty of defining corporate group boundaries. Le Page additionally is anxious to emphasize the individual's freedom of choice to use his language variably as a means of identifying with different groups at different times.

I do not suggest here that the practice of grouping informants to show patterns of linguistic variation is necessarily in any way an invalid procedure. On the contrary, clear patterns of variation have as we have seen often been revealed in this way. However, the fact remains that much systematic individual variation is still unaccounted for, and in undertaking a further level of analysis I would argue with Mitchell (1973) and Russell (1982), that the network of relationships within which an individual is embedded, and the corporate social groups to which he can be said to belong, are phenomena at different levels of abstraction.

It is now possible to relate views such as Le Page's in a systematic way to the kind of variability illustrated by Table 5.4. We should start by stating a clear hypothesis, which intuitively seems plausible, that closeness to vernacular speech norms correlates positively with the level of integration of the individual into local community networks. This hypothesis was formed originally as a result of observations of the everyday behaviour and the informal social ties of the residents of the three Belfast communities.

Paula and Hannah, for example, differ greatly in their level of integration into the local networks. Paula has a large family of her own, visits frequently with neighbours, and belongs to an informal bingo-playing group. Her neighbours are also her workmates. Hannah, on the other hand, has no children, or kin in the area (she is the child of a Protestant/Catholic mixed marriage). She belongs to no local informally constituted group of the kind we have described in Chapter 3 as a *high-density cluster*, and her workmates are not from the Clonard.

The idea that linguistic variability correlates with degree of integration into informally constituted groups is of course not a new one: we have already seen that Labov demonstrated this same pattern among adolescents in Harlem. However, the approach to be outlined here differs from Labov's in that it is not restricted to a study of adolescent peer groups. The method of analysis used to test the hypothesis differs from Labov's chiefly in two respects, both of which are linked to the different scope of the study. First, we can apply it to speakers (like Hannah) who are not members of a group or quasi-group with a clear core membership like the Jets, Cobras and T-Birds. Second, unlike Labov, we do not group speakers into core, secondary and peripheral members, but treat them individually. For this purpose, the concept of *social network* is used as an analytic tool.

APPLICATIONS OF SOCIAL NETWORK ANALYSIS

We begin by noting that, in principle, the content and structure of individual network ties can be both directly observed, and quantified; the formulae for computing *multiplexity* and *density* of individual personal networks were given in Chapter 3.

Further, the network concept was developed for the very purpose for which we require it now—to explain individual behaviour of various kinds which cannot be accounted for in terms of corporate group membership. Since scholars use the set of procedures generally labelled as network analysis to examine individual, mainly informal, relations between people, the method seems to be a promising approach to some kind of quantitative statement of what is meant by integration into the community. As we have seen, this is potentially an important independent variable.

To clarify what is meant by using the concept to *explain* behaviour, we look now in a little more detail at one of the classic network studies briefly discussed in Chapter 3.

Elizabeth Bott's report of an exploratory study of twenty London families, first published in 1957 but subjected to important revisions in 1971, is now a classic of the anthropological literature. Initially, the researchers set out to describe patterns of variation in the way husband and wife shared household tasks in terms of social class and neighbourhood (corporate group factors) but were forced to look for a more effective means of accounting for these patterns. Applying the concept of social network as developed by Barnes (1954), Bott found that clear separation of each spouse's area of responsibility and their degree of independence of each other, corresponded to the struture of their personal networks. Where the level of marital segregation was high and responsibility for tasks rigidly allocated (these conditions went together) each spouse tended to have contracted long-standing relationships with people who also knew each other. Where spouses were dependent on each other and did not allocate areas of responsibility as clearly, their personal networks were less 'dense'; their contacts did not normally know each other. Bott further commented that where the networks were dense, role relationships were usually multiplex; as we have seen, that meant that individuals interacted with each other in more than one capacity—a man's neighbour might also be his kinsman and his fellow employee.

At first sight it is difficult to see why there should be a link between marital segregation and network structure; but Bott argues convincingly that network structure is likely to be the causal factor, rather than vice versa. Dense, multiplex network ties have (she argues), been contracted prior to marriage, and such a network forms, in effect, a bounded group capable of imposing normative consensus on its members. Marriage partners are therefore kept relatively independent of each other, and more dependent on individuals in their own network. Absence of pressures applied by a dense, multiplex network results in greater interdependence between spouses and a sharing of tasks and responsibilities. Thus, level of marital segregation is explained in terms of the *capacity of a particular kind of network to act as a norm enforcement mechanism*; some kinds of personal network have a more powerful capacity to influence behaviour than others. Clearly then, a study such as Bott's does more than simply show a connection between a dependent and an independent variable. By looking at the characteristics of a particular network structure to influence behaviour, she is able to show in a concrete way that there are likely to be causal relationships between the two variables. We have already seen in Chapter 3 that a relatively dense multiplex network structure has the capacity to impose specifically *linguistic* norms upon its members.

Bott further pointed out the links between network structure and social class, which have already been discussed in some detail in this book.

Following up these observations, Frankenberg (1969) and Southall (1973) have used the concepts of network density and multiplexity to characterize a number of different types of community ranging from Irish and Welsh mountain settlements, through traditional working-class areas, to newly settled working- and middle-class suburban estates.

Although important modifications have been made to the original analysis, and both terminology and quantification procedures have been considerably refined, a number of Bott's observations have become accepted by scholars applying the network concept. It is now agreed that density and multiplexity usually go together, and that dense, multiplex networks act as norm enforcement mechanisms (Mayer, 1963; Kapferer, 1969; Boissevain, 1974; Cubitt, 1973); that a variable closely related to network density is geographical mobility (Turner, 1967). On the whole, networks in rural areas tend to density and multiplexity, and in urban areas to uniplexity and spareness. The exceptions to this generalization are of course the old established working-class areas such as those described by Young and Wilmott, Hannerz, Fried and Wiener. In these areas, often described as 'urban villages', personal networks tend to multiplexity and density.

Although he does not use the term explicitly, it seems to be this kind of network structure which Hymes has in mind in his definition of 'community' in terms of shared territory and primary interaction (see p. 15 above). A similar network structure probably also underlies Labov's notion of the importance of 'the category of local identity' in explaining linguistic variation in Martha's Vineyard.

One important modification to Bott's original view of network density as a norm enforcement mechanism is relevant to our own analytic procedures, and should be noted here. Cubitt's (1973) study of the networks of working- and middle-class Edinburgh families suggests that density in key *sectors* or *clusters* of the network—that is, compartments associated with specific fields of activity—is a more important means of compelling normative consensus than *overall* density. It is in practice extremely hard to measure overall density in a network of several hundred (or more) relationships, and where it is possible, Cubitt suggests that density is nearly always low. Specific clusters are isolated as being particularly important here, and varying significantly in density from one personal network to another, 'those of kinship, neighbourhood, work situation (both husband's and wife's) and voluntary association' (1973:81). In fact, the literature on traditional working-class communities, including the relevant parts of Bott's work, tends to support this view. In practice, most comment focuses on ties of kinship, neighbourhood, work and friendship.

Turning now to the use of this concept to account for variations in individual *linguistic* behaviour (as opposed to other kinds of social behaviour) it seems reasonable to adopt Boissevain's (1974) view that persons are capable of interacting meaningfully with each other, and that their behaviour does not entirely depend on their position in an abstraction we choose to call 'society'. The concept of network was developed in the first place because of this conviction that behaviour can often be accounted for by observation and analysis of individual interactions. Attempts to characterize it in terms of corporate group membership, culture and systems of values may sometimes be less satisfactory.

Boissevain's approach seems ideally adapted to the views of linguists such as Le Page who are anxious to stress the fluidity of individual behaviour and the range of choice open to people in their use of language as a means of symbolizing various identities. Of course, Le Page's comments refer mainly to a multilingual society; *mutatis mutandis* however, I see no reason why they should not be equally valid in an urban monolingual situation. People in cities of all kinds have vast resources of linguistic variability open to them which they may manipulate usually within the constraints permitted by a range of more general group norms such as those discussed at the beginning of this chapter.

It is of course clear that this dimension of variation—the manner in which people use the resources open to them—cannot be handled by the Labovian technique of aggregating scores. It is desirable that such a dimension should be studied systematically if at all possible, for it is a matter of commonsense observation that people do in fact use language (like dress, for example) to symbolize their adherence to informally constituted groups of many kinds. In the following chapter we examine quantitative techniques of correlating a speaker's language with the structure of his informal personal relationships—his social network.

6

The Language of the Individual Speaker: Patterns of Variation and Network Structure

The objective in this chapter will be to go some way towards accounting for patterns of variability at the level of the individual speaker by making further use of the concept of social network. Since a quantitative approach is required, in order to allow a direct comparison between the language of speaker A and of speaker B, we also need to find a means of *measuring* the network patterns of A and B so that we can examine possible links with linguistic patterns.

This in fact, as might be expected, is a complicated matter; but it is possible to construct a measure which we shall call a *network strength scale*. This measure consists of a six-point scale going from zero to five, and functions rather like a social class index (see Chapter 1) in that each individual is assigned a score at some point on the scale. The scale is constructed with reference to the key notions of relative *multiplexity* and *density* of personal networks, and makes use of several *indicators* of these two network attributes. It is best to consider, for a moment, the theoretical basis on which these indicators are selected.

The network studies discussed in previous chapters show clearly that density and multiplexity are excellent indicators of the pressures on a person to adopt the norms and values—including linguistic norms and values—of the 'local team'. Several other structural and content characteristics of a personal network may also be good indicators of the strength of pressures towards normative consensus. For example, degree of connection (number of contacts within a given time), centrality of position, intensity (affective value placed on relationships) are all apposite to any attempt to explain individual behaviour and are discussed by Mitchell (1969) and Boissevain (1974) in some detail.

However, most studies utilising the network concept have in practice found that *either* density of one or more of the clusters specified by Cubitt (whose work was discussed in Chapter 5) *or* relative multiplexity, offers powerful means of accounting for various behaviours. For example, problems as diverse as why individuals take one side in preference to another in a fight on the factory floor (Kapferer, 1969) and why patterns of gift exchange in an African community are variable (Trouwborst, 1973) are illuminated by analysis based on these two concepts. To some extent, multiplexity and density subsume other, less easily measurable variables. This can be demonstrated by referring to Elsie D, one of the older women in Ballymacarrett. Elsie D placed a low affective value on her relationships with her neighbours and appeared to reject 'local team' values. Devising a reliable measure for these attitudes would have been difficult and was in any event unnecessary, for the reason that the low level of multiplexity in her personal network ties formed what might be described as an 'objective correlative' to her subjective attitudes. She seemed to avoid multiplex ties with local people as far as possible, in that she did not interact with her neighbours on a friendly basis and avoided furthermore working with a cluster of neighbourhood women who were employed as domestics in a local school. Her kin ties in the area were not extensive. This pattern of social relationships seems to be very characteristic of people who reject 'local team' values, and it is worth noting in this context that *both* network patterns, *and* attitudinal factors suggest themselves as a basis for the measurement of degree of integration into the community. The network strength scale is in fact constructed on the basis of considerable accumulated evidence from several sources that multiplexity and density scores are important indicators of an individual's level of integration into the local community although, of course, it is not claimed that they are the *only* indicators. Two criteria were adopted in selecting the precise indicators to be used in constructing the scale.

1. They must reflect the conditions which have repeatedly been found important in a wide range of network studies, in predicting the extent to which normative pressures are applied by the local community (and of course accepted by the individual); it is specifically the capacity of some kinds of network to maintain consensus which may be significant here.

2. They must be recoverable from data collected in the field and easily verifiable. (For this second reason, affective measures are unlikely to be reliable.) A great deal of data on social relationships is, however, available; for all informants were extensively questioned about kin, place of work, corporate and informal group membership, and territorial loyalties. Each informant's behaviour was also closely observed over a period of about five weeks.

The implications of the second condition are important; for if we accept it, it follows that we cannot use multiplexity and density scores directly. As we have seen, both of these can be measured quantitatively. But the formulae require a quantitative statement of the size of a *total* personal network which very few researchers are in a position to provide. For the purposes of this study therefore, multiplexity and density are expressed indirectly only by indicators which are *readily verifiable from field data*, while at the same time reflecting a number of observations recurrent in a wide range of relevant network studies.

Bearing these problems in mind, we calculate an informant's network score by assigning him one point for each of the following conditions he fulfils:

1. Membership of a high-density, territorially based cluster.

2. Having substantial ties of kinship in the neighbour-

hood. (More than one household, in addition to his own nuclear family.)

3. Working at the same place as at least *two* others from the same area.

4. The same place of work as at least two others of the same sex from the area.

5. Voluntary association with workmates in leisure hours. This applies in practice only when conditions three and four are satisfied.

Condition one is designed as an indicator of density, and reflects Cubitt's insistence on the importance of taking account of the density of specific *clusters* in considering networks as norm enforcement mechanisms. (A cluster is defined as a portion of a personal network where relationships are denser internally than externally.) The Jets, Cobras and T-Birds described by Labov form clusters; many of the young men in the Belfast communities belong to similar clusters; some of the middle-aged women belong to clusters of six or seven individuals who meet frequently to drink tea, play cards and chat. Some individuals, on the other hand, avoid association with any group of this kind.

Conditions two, three, four and five are all indicators of multiplexity; if they are all satisfied, the proportion of the individual's interactions which are with members of the local community is inevitably very high. Three and four are intended to reflect the particular capacity of an area of homogeneous employment to encourage the development of dense, multiplex networks; four also reflects the fact that polarization of the sexes usually occurs when there is a large number of solidary relationships in a specific neighbourhood.

Readers may assume that multiplex ties of the kind reflected in conditions three, four and five are usually contracted by men, and that men would, therefore, automatically score higher on the network strength scale. In fact, since both the Hammer and the Clonard are areas of high *male* unemployment, individual women frequently score as high as, or higher than, men.

The scale is capable of differentiating individuals quite

sharply (see Appendix). Scores range from zero for someone who fulfils none of the conditions (although a zero score is rare), to five for several informants who fulfil them all. Such individuals must be considered extremely closely integrated into the community, in the sense that their kin, work and friendship ties are all contracted within it; additionally, they have formed particularly close ties with a corporate group (such as a football fans' club) or a less formal group based in the area. The defined territorial base associated with the kind of network structure which interests us is reflected in conditions one and two. This is very important, for as we saw in Chapter 4 of this book, geographical mobility has the capacity to destroy the structure of long-established networks.

Although choice of the precise indicators to be used in constructing the network strength scale has been governed by the two principles of verifiability and of building on the findings and implications of previous network studies, it is important to emphasize that an entirely different set of criteria for measuring network structure might, with equal validity, have been chosen. We shall see shortly that one study of a bilingual community (Gal, 1979), which correlates network type with language use, does in fact use an extremely simple measure of network type. Gal measures the 'peasantness' of a speaker's network by simply observing within a given period of time the proportion of his contacts who have peasant status. Although this approach is better adapted to a rural community of the kind which has relatively clear cultural categories of 'peasant' and 'non-peasant', Gal's work demonstrates that in Belfast a parallel approach might conceivably have been adopted which, for example, constructed a network measure based simply on the proportion of contacts within the community, or of a given status, over a limited period. However, as Gumperz has pointed out (1976b:14), personal network structure is influenced by a very large number of factors. It therefore follows that no investigation is likely to be able to identify and measure all of them, although it is important to be able to justify the approach which *has* been adopted. In the final chapter we will look a little more closely at this question in terms of theories of the social function of dense, multiplex, networks which underly the choice of indicators in this study. It is also possible, as we shall see, to assess the validity of the indicators in terms of the results of a statistical analysis.

THE DISTRIBUTION OF NETWORK SCORES BY AGE, SEX AND AREA

Since it is now possible to assign to each individual a numerical score (which, for the sake of brevity, will be referred to as his *network score*), we are in a position to examine systematically the effect of the variable of network structure on a speaker's language.

We have already considered the complex manner in which those other variables of sex, age and area interact with each other in influencing linguistic scores. We have also seen in Chapter 4, in a general way, that personal network structure as well as language structure is likely to be influenced by these same variables. For example, very dense, multiplex networks are associated particularly with men living in working-class communities of a traditional kind, with a locally-based homogeneous form of employment. More specifically, network structures in the three areas with which we are principally concerned seem likely to co-vary to some extent with factors like the stability of the area and availability of male employment locally. The men in Ballymacarrett lived in conditions particularly likely to favour the formation of dense, multiplex networks and polarization of the sexes. Conversely, the young women in the Clonard contrast with the men in being fully employed, and have developed solidary relationships of the kind usually associated with *men* of the same age.

Since it is likely then that network scores will vary in a complicated way across different area, age and sex subgroups, we must try to take account of this variability. For it would not be easy to interpret data showing a connection between language and personal network, without first having some idea of general network norms in the different subgroups.

Just as we explored the distribution of *linguistic* scores across

age, sex and area subgroups using an analysis of variance technique, we can in the same manner explore the distribution of
network scores. If this procedure seems complex, we should remind ourselves that it is no more than a reflection of the extreme
complexity of the manner in which speakers use language
variability for a range of social and individual purposes.

In applying an analysis of variance technique to look at the
links between network score on the one hand, and age, sex and
area on the other, we do not utilize the full range of the network
strength scale. For statistical reasons, only *high* and *low* network
scores are considered. High scores are those falling above the
median, low scores are those falling below (the median is considered to be 3.0 here) and median scores are omitted from this
part of the analysis.

The ratio statistic F indicates whether there is a significant
difference in network scores between sex, age and area groups,
and also whether there are significant interactions between any
of these independent variables (network is considered as the
dependent variable here). The results of this analysis are discussed briefly below. It will become clear shortly that this information is a necessary preliminary to a more direct investigation of the relationship between language and network.

Sex and Network: Interactions with Other Variables

As we might suspect, there is a significant difference between
male and female network scores (F = 9.964, p < 0.01). The
men score significantly higher than the women (means =
2.944 : 2.0278). The sex by age interaction is not significant:
that is, the sex difference in network scores is much the same for
both age groups. However, there is a significant *sex* by *area*
interaction (F = 8.025, p < 0.01). An examination of the male
and female means for the three areas tells us where this difference lies. There is in effect very *little* difference between male
and female means in two of the areas. In the Hammer, the men
score only slightly higher than the women (means = 2.125 :
1.875), while in the Clonard, the women actually score slightly

higher than the men (means = 2.75 : 2.875). However, these differences are very small in comparison with the very substantial differences between male and female scores in Ballymacarrett, where the men score very much higher than the women (means = 3.9583 : 1.3333). Only in Ballymacarrett, in fact, are network scores significantly different for men and women.

There is also a significant sex by age by area interaction (F = 6.154, p < 0.01), which can tell us more about the distribution of network scores across these various subgroups. If we are focusing mainly on the relationship between *sex* and network structure, as we are at the moment, this means that male and female network scores vary between different areas with each age group in an extremely complicated manner. Again, if we compare the various subgroup means, we can see where this difference lies. The young *Ballymacarrett* women have the *lowest* network scores of any subgroup (mean = 0.667) while the young *Clonard* women have the *highest* of any subgroup (mean = 4.75). Clearly, this is a very high score as the maximum is 5.0. The young Clonard women are in fact the only female group who have substantially higher scores than the men in the same age group. (The mean for the young Clonard men = 3.0.) Since the *older* Clonard age group shows the expected pattern with men scoring higher than women (means = 2.5 : 1.0), we can now see that the *overall* similarity between male and female scores in the Clonard is the result of the interaction effect of the variables of age and sex in this particular community.

It is already clear that these differences in the distribution of *network* scores co-vary, to some extent, with differences in the distribution of *linguistic* scores. Particularly, sharp and consistent sex differences in language score are associated with Ballymacarrett; the same area now emerges as showing sharp sex differences in *network* score. We shall consider the significance of these congruent distributions shortly.

Area and Network; Age and Network

Although many of the important points about the distribution of network scores across area and age subgroups have been dealt with in the previous section, a few further observations are relevant to our focal concern with the language/network relationship.

Although the differences between area means are not quite statistically significant (B = 2.6458: C = 2.8125: H = 2.0), it is worth noting the substantial difference between the score for the Hammer, and those for the other two areas, which are more nearly comparable. However, there is a significant interaction between *age* and *area* (F = 6.5592: p < 0.01) with the younger age groups scoring higher in Clonard and the Hammer, and the older age group scoring slightly higher in Ballymacarrett. The subgroup means are given in Table 6.1.

Table 6.1 *Mean network scores for two age groups in three areas*

Age	40–55	18–25
Ballymacarrett	2.8333	2.4583
Clonard	1.7500	3.8750
Hammer	1.1250	2.8750

Although *Ballymacarrett* shows very little difference between the network scores of the two age groups, the younger group considered overall (for all three areas together) scores significantly higher (means = 3.069 : 1.903). This difference is very substantial, and similar in size to the difference between the sexes.

It is possible to relate some of these sex, age and area differences in network scores to different social conditions in the three communities; for considered in the light of our discussion of the general social background in Chapter 4, some of these results are not unexpected. There is a good general account in Boissevain (1974) of the manner in which a very wide range of extrapersonal variables might influence the network structures of individuals.

Note first that only in Ballymacarrett are traditional *sex roles* retained in the form familiar from descriptions in the literature on working-class communities. The men are employed locally in a traditional and homogeneous form of employment (the shipyard) and contract solidary relationships associated with their work. The women are employed more diffusely, have fewer solidary relationships associated with work, but may contract multiplex relationships with kin and neighbours. The Clonard area, on the other hand, was experiencing severe male unemployment at the time of the interviews: both the Clonard and the Hammer had once been dependent on the now receding linen industry. Although unemployment was not quite as severe in the Hammer as in the Clonard, there was no local homogeneous form of employment.

These contrasting social conditions are reflected clearly in the big difference between male and female network scores in Ballymacarrett, a difference not found consistently in either of the other areas.

In the Clonard, the young women emerged as the only group who worked together and spent their leisure time together, contracting the kind of solidary relationships usually associated with working-class men. This socialization pattern is reflected clearly in the higher network scores of the young Clonard women—higher than those of the men—and it is also reflected in the complicated age by sex by area interaction effects, which level out the expected sex difference in network scores.

Although the Hammer area suffered similar but slightly less severe unemployment, no group emerged as having contracted particularly strong solidary relationships. The Hammer was notable principally for the geographical mobility of its residents: as a consequence of urban redevelopment, many had been allocated housing several miles from the Hammer. Although much social interaction was focused there in pubs, clubs, bingo sessions and corner-hanging groups, the residents had suffered a severe disruption of all the important sectors of their personal networks. This instability is reflected in generally low scores for the Hammer, and in very small differences between the sexes. For as we have seen, a clear pattern of men scoring high and women scoring low seems to be linked to a traditional working-class area with a homogeneous form of employment like Bally-macarrett, or like the mining community described by Dennis *et al.* (1957).

We may begin to suspect at this point that there is a fairly clear relationship between language scores and network scores: for the distributional patterns are remarkably similar in many important respects. First, we saw in Chapter 5 that the sharpest sex grading in language *also* was to be found in Ballymacarrett; this is true for several linguistic variables. Second, in respect of the variable (a), we find particularly striking parallels. The Hammer score shows very little difference between male and female scores—this can be seen clearly if we look at the presentation of the scores in graph form in Figure 5.4. Even more strikingly, the same interaction effect which influences the Clonard network scores (see p. 146 above) also influences the distribution of (a) scores in the younger Clonard age group. The young Clonard women emerge with unexpectedly high *linguistic* scores, in exactly the same way as they emerge with unexpectedly high *network* scores. We should note, however, that other linguistic variables do *not* necessarily reflect network structure in this way. For example (th) shows clear sex grading in much the same way for both age groups in all three areas. Nevertheless, we may suggest tentatively at this point that the distribution of the variable (a), at least, is more closely related to the network structure than to the sex of the speaker.

CORRELATIONS BETWEEN LANGUAGE SCORES AND NETWORK SCORES OF INDIVIDUAL SPEAKERS

Now that these general patterns of variability in network structure across the three communities have been established, the next step is to compare network scores directly with linguistic scores. The data described above, which were obtained from a comparison of group scores, already suggest that it will be possible to demonstrate a close connection between language use and personal network structure. To see just how close this connection is, we compare *individual* language and network scores, rather than group *means* in terms of a dichotomy between *high* and *low* network scores as we have done up to this point.

The basic hypothesis to be tested is that differences in network score are related to differences in linguistic score—specifically, that increasing linguistic variable scores are related to increasing network scores. The statistical test which measures, and gives a mathematical value to, relationships of this kind is known as *correlation*. The particular test used here is the *Spearman rank order correlation*. This test calculates how far the *rank order* of scores for each individual speaker on one factor (network) is similar to the rank order of scores on another (a linguistic variable). A statistic r is produced, which reflects how closely the rank orders of the two factors for all individual speakers match. The nearer r approaches to 1.0 (a one-to-one relationship between rankings), the closer the relationship between the two factors and the more likely that the statistic is not a result of chance variation in the sample.

It will be best at this point to demonstrate the principle of a correlation test based on rank ordering by using a simple set of (constructed) nonlinguistic data.

Let us suppose that a cigarette manufacturing firm marketed its product in seven different English cities and spent large amounts of revenue in promoting those sales. Each year, two sets of figures are returned by the marketing teams in each city: one set represents the number of cigarettes sold, the other the amount of money spent on advertising. Clearly, it would be of great interest for the firm to know how close a relationship existed between the amount of money spent on advertising, on the one hand, and the number of cigarettes sold, on the other. The two sets of figures (seven in each set) could be examined, and the rank order of each recorded. Assume that the Birmingham marketing team sold the most cigarettes, but spent the third highest amount of money on advertising; the other rank orders might be as follows:

	Advertising	Sales
Birmingham	3	1
Leicester	2	4
Newcastle	1	2
Nottingham	4	3
Manchester	6	5
Liverpool	5	7
Bradford	7	6

Clearly, there is not a perfect one-to-one correlation between rankings: but when the correlation test is applied (the formula is not given here) the result obtained is $r = 0.714$, which gives a measure of the relationship between advertising expenditure and sales. In just the same way, it is possible to list rank orders of network score and any given linguistic variable score, in order to test the closeness of the relationship between the two. Correlation is the appropriate technique wherever there are two sets of figures from a common source (an individual informant in our case), and the problem involved is to discover how closely the two sets are related. The tests carried out on the Belfast data use the figures given in the Appendix (pp. 204-5).

Although we know, in a general way, that the closer r comes to 1.0, the closer the relationship between the two sets of figures, we still need to know how to interpret r. The value of r is influenced by the number (N) of individuals in a sample tested, and it is important to know how much reliance can be placed on this value: that is, whether or not it can be said there is a relationship at a given level of r. To test the value—or significance—of r, the t-test is applied (in much the same way as it was applied in the analysis of variance to test the significance of the F-ratio there). The smaller the number of individuals in the sample, the more stringent the test of significance against chance. A significant result would mean that the probability of a given level of r occurring by chance was (as we have already

seen) less than one in twenty (p < 0.05). More highly significant results might also be obtained (p < 0.01; p < 0.001).
Thus, if a significant result is obtained we may conclude reliably
that language scores and network scores are related in a manner
which cannot be considered accidental. Note particularly that
this test does not involve averaging out scores or calculating
group scores for speakers: it deals always with *individual* scores.

CORRELATING NETWORK SCORES WITH LANGUAGE SCORES:
AN ILLUSTRATION

Clearly the analysis has already proceeded some way through a
very long process of linguistic and mathematical abstraction.
We have reached the point of being able to express *both* an
individual's language patterns, *and* his level of integration into
the community by sets of figures. Before proceeding to further
statistical analysis, it will be helpful to refer back to the two
women, Paula C and Hannah McK whose linguistic scores were
discussed in Chapter 5 (p. 131). We shall concentrate, for a
moment, on showing how network scores for these two women
were calculated and how closely they match variable linguistic
scores. A glance at Table 5.4 will remind the reader that although the social status of the two women was very similar
their patterns of language use were quite different. Measured
over eight different phonological variables, Paula's language
consistently approximated more closely than Hannah's to vernacular norms. It will also be recalled that Paula seemed to be
much more closely integrated than Hannah, in terms of kin,
work and friendship ties, into the local community (p. 134
above). In fact, Paula scores two and Hannah scores zero on
the network strength scale, reflecting this difference in the
character of their everyday social ties.

If each indicator is considered in turn (see p. 141 above), we
find that Paula fulfils conditions one and two; she is a member
of a local bingo-playing group and also has extensive kin ties in
the area. This produces her score of two. Hannah, however,

fulfils neither of these conditions. She has no kin in or near the Clonard, and has in fact lost touch with her family. She does not associate with any identifiable group in the area, tending to spend her evenings at home watching television. None of the conditions associated with work or workmates are fulfilled by either of the women. Both work some way outside the area isolated from other Clonard people. Paula looks after a crippled woman on the Protestant side of the sectarian divide, two miles from the Clonard. Hannah works in the canteen of the Royal Victoria Hospital, a specialist teaching hospital which employs domestic staff from various parts of West Belfast. Hannah does not meet in the canteen people she knows in any capacity except as workmates. Thus, although the network scores for both women are low, their rank ordering clearly reflects the rank ordering of linguistic scores. The younger Clonard women (already discussed in this chapter) contrast with both Paula and Hannah in scoring relatively high, because they fulfil the conditions associated with work. It may be helpful for the reader to look at all informants' scores as they are set out in the Appendix so that the general range of both linguistic scores and network scores may be appreciated. It is these network scores, calculated for each informant in turn in the same way as has been shown here, which are correlated with scores for each linguistic variable in turn. The results produced by these correlation tests will be the focus of discussion during the remainder of this chapter.

THE CORRELATION TESTS

A very large number of correlation tests were carried out. The tests revealed a positive and significant relationship between network scores and language scores on all the variables tested. However, three of the variables (ai), (ɪ) and (Λ^1) show this relationship only when the informants are divided into age and area subgroups, demonstrating once again the complexity of the manner in which speakers use language to convey social meanings. Table 6.2 below indicates correlations between language and network for those variables which show a significant correlation when all speakers are considered together—that is, when they are not subdivided according to age, sex or area.

Table 6.2 *Linguistic variables correlating with network scores for all subjects. N refers to the number of subjects tested for a given variable*

Variable	r	t	N	Level of significance
(a)	0.529	3.692	37	$0 < 0.01$
(th)	0.485	3.591	44	$0 < 0.01$
(Λ^2)	0.317	2.142	43	$p < 0.05$
(ε^1)	0.255	1.709	44	$p < 0.05$
(ε^2)	0.321	2.200	44	$p < 0.05$

These results show that there is in fact a real and reliable relationship between a speaker's language and the structure of his social network. As scores on the network scale increase, so do linguistic scores. Note that not all linguistic variables show an equally close relationship to network scores: the correlation is closest for (a) and (th).

We may suspect on the basis of previous analysis that not all speakers will relate these same linguistic variables to their personal network structure in the same way. It is likely that men and women, the young and the middle aged, and speakers from different areas will show different patterns in this respect. This seems inevitable when we remember that the network patterns of the sexes, age groups and areas are very different; however, complex interaction effects make any attempt to state these differences in a *general* way extremely difficult. In order to explore complexities of this kind, the subjects were divided into subgroups based on age, sex and area, and the relationships between linguistic scores and network scores re-tested. Tables 6.3 and 6.4 summarize the results of these tests. Each set of results is presented along with a brief comment on its interpretation. It is important to note that the test for significance against chance is very much more stringent where the N is small: that is, a higher level of r is required to demonstrate significance at all. Therefore, if a significant result is obtained when the N is very small—as when the subjects are divided into four subgroups according to age and sex—it can be said with confidence that the relationship between network and language is very strong indeed.

We begin by comparing the results of Table 6.2 with those reported in Table 6.3. Table 6.3 summarizes the results obtained when two correlation tests were carried out for each linguistic variable—one for male, and one for female subjects.

Table 6.3 *Correlations between network scores and language scores considered separately for male and female subjects*

Variable	Sex	r	t	N	Level of significance
(a)	M	0.485	2.287	19	$p < 0.05$
	F	0.683	3.741	18	$p < 0.01$
(th)	M	0.406	1.935	21	$p < 0.05$
	F	0.539	2.932	23	$p < 0.01$
(Λ^2)	M	0.411	1.966	23	$p < 0.05$
	F	0.171	0.777	22	$p > 0.05$
(ε^1)	M	0.292	1.368	22	$p > 0.05$
	F	0.085	0.381	22	$p > 0.05$
(ε^2)	M	0.276	1.283	22	$p > 0.05$
	F	0.210	0.963	22	$p > 0.05$

These results give much more information on the character of the language/network relationship. The variables (a) and (th) are shown to be sensitive to network structure for *both* sexes: however, the level of significance is greater for women than for men. In contrast, the results for (Λ^2) indicate a correlation only with *men's* network scores. We can now see that since the result for women does not reveal a significant correlation, the significant (Λ^2) result reported for *all subjects* in Table 6.2 depends on the larger N and conceals the fact that this variable functions as a network marker for men only. Since neither sex shows a significant r between either (ε^1) or (ε^2) and network scores, it is now clear that the significant overall result reported in Table 6.2 for these variables is attributable entirely to the higher N. However, note that higher rs for men on both variables indicates a *trend* towards a relationship with network. This trend is most clearly absent from women's (ε^1) scores. In other words, women show no tendency whatever to use (ε^1) (that is, high levels of the [æ] variant) as a symbol of community loyalty.

These results are particularly interesting if they are related to previous analysis which has examined separately distribution of *linguistic* scores and distribution of *network* scores throughout various subgroups in the community. Women in general had significantly *lower* network scores than men, and on a number of variables—we may refer particularly to (a) and (th) here— *lower* linguistic scores. These generally lower levels of use of the vernacular variants (a back variant of /a/ and the zero form of /ð/ in this case) do not however prevent *individual* women from using the (a) and (th) variables to symbolize their level of integration into the local community: the degree of 'fit' between network scores and language scores, for these variables, is greater for women than for men, despite the fact that high linguistic scores on the same variables are associated particularly with men. Thus, the degree of 'fit' between language and network may be seen as a completely different issue from that of the absolute level of *either* language scores *or* network scores. What seems to happen is that the variability found in women's speech is concentrated within relatively low levels of the vernacular variants, while still correlating closely with network structure. The position becomes even more complex when we turn our attention to the other variables. Recall that the (Λ^2) distribution was affected by a complex age and sex interaction, with younger men using the [ʌ] variant at a higher level than younger women; in the older age group exactly the reverse was true. The vernacular [æ] variant of both (ε^1) and (ε^2) on the other hand was used at a significantly higher level by men in *both* age groups. In this respect, these two variables function clearly as sex markers, like (a) and (th). Yet, unlike (a) and (th) but like (Λ^2), they seem to be used to symbolize level of integration into the community exclusively by *men*. While it appears then that 'bits' of the language can function simultaneously as sex markers and network markers, the two sexes may each select different variables to fulfil the latter function.

To summarize the facts, all five variables in Table 6.3 function as sex markers with men using higher levels of the vernacular variants than women, except for (Λ^2) where there is a sex by age interaction effect. Yet, the relationship between language and network is closer for women than for men when the variables (a) and (th) are tested, while for (Λ^2), (ε^1) and (ε^2) exactly the reverse is true. To some extent then, the social function of a linguistic variable as a network marker may be viewed as independent of its function as a sex marker.

When we move on to consider the effect that the *area* in which a speaker lives has on this relation between language and network structure, we find that it is considerable. Table 6.4 summarizes the relevant results. Note that two further linguistic variables (ɪ) and (ai) appear, showing significant correlations in one area only. Since we are not contrasting the scores for these variables with the *overall* scores reported in Table 6.2, only significant results for (ai) and (ɪ) are reported overleaf.

Some clear facts emerge from Table 6.4. First, one variable (ɪ), emerges as correlating with network in the Hammer. All other variables, including (ai) (neither (ɪ) nor (ai) have emerged as significant in any previous analysis), show a significant correlation *only* in Ballymacarrett. Thus, the overall correlations (Table 6.2) are seen to depend specifically on the high *r* in Ballymacarrett. The only variable which does *not* yield a significant result in Ballymacarrett is (Λ^2). However, the relatively high level of the Ballymacarrett *r* should be noted. It indicates a clear tendency for the level of use of the vernacular [Λ] variant to increase with network scores, but does not meet the 0.05 level of significance because of the relatively small N. We know that the small N is responsíble for this nonsignificant result, because the (Λ^2) r for Ballymacarrett is *greater* than the r for all subjects (Table 6.2): yet when all subjects were tested a significant result was obtained.

Table 6.4 *Correlations between network scores and linguistic variable scores calculated separately for three areas. B = Ballymacarrett, C = Clonard, H = Hammer*

Variable		r	t	N	Level of significance
(a)	B	0.930	8.360	13	$p < 0.01$
	C	0.345	2.287	15	$p > 0.05$
	H	−0.344	2.286	9	$p > 0.05$
(th)	B	0.816	4.679	13	$p < 0.01$
	C	0.011	0.039	15	$p > 0.05$
	H	0.346	1.379	16	$p > 0.05$
(Λ^2)	B	0.426	1.560	13	$p > 0.05$
	C	−0.042	0.151	15	$p > 0.05$
	H	0.247	0.920	15	$p > 0.05$
(ε^1)	B	0.771	4.016	13	$p < 0.01$
	C	−0.118	−0.429	15	$p > 0.05$
	H	0.053	−0.199	16	$p > 0.05$
(ε^2)	B	0.719	3.433	13	$p < 0.01$
	C	0.027	0.098	15	$p > 0.05$
	H	0.096	0.361	16	$p > 0.05$
(ai)	B	0.557	2.322	14	$p < 0.05$
(ɪ)	H	0.528	2.327	16	$p < 0.05$

Note particularly the very high r for (a). This is the closest correlation found in the entire investigation $(r = 0.93)$, representing an extremely close relationship between language and network scores. We have already seen (p. 149 above) that a tendency to use a great deal of the backed variants of /a/ corresponds even more closely with high network scores than, for example, high levels of the zero form of /ð/.

Again, these results are illuminated by reference to earlier analysis. In a previous section of this chapter, Ballymacarrett was shown to be the only area where there was a sharp contrast between male and female network scores, with the men scoring very much higher than the women. In the Hammer there was little difference between male and female scores while in the Clonard, complex sex and age interaction effects prevented any clear differentiation pattern as consistent as that found in Ballymacarrett.

In Ballymacarrett also, the sharpest and most consistent patterns of sex differentiation in *language* are often found (see Chapter 5, Figures 5.4; 5.5). It seems then, that where a community's social norms encourage the sexes to develop characteristically different *network* patterns, a clear correlation between network structure and language use is likely to be observable. Sex-based linguistic norms in Ballymacarrett appear to be more or less co-extensive with norms based on network: in other words, the same underlying sets of vernacular norms are likely to be most observable in the speech of men (because they use vernacular variants at a high level) and in the speech of those who are most firmly integrated into the community. In practice, those are usually men in Ballymacarrett, although women also use the vernacular at different levels depending on their network structure. However, *on average* they use the vernacular variably at a much lower level than men, although the 'fit' between network structure and language use for both sexes is very close.

If we turn our attention to the other two areas, we find that, despite the sharp contrast with Ballymacarrett (there is little significant correlation between language use and network structure), there are clear indications that patterns of language use depend *to some extent* on network structure. For example, only the Hammer shows a significant correlation between language scores on the variable (I) and personal network structure. In the Clonard there is, as we have seen earlier in this chapter, a clear similarity between the distribution of the variable (a) and the distribution of network scores. Although (a) also functions as a sex marker, the variable of personal network predicts the distribution of (a) scores more accurately than the sex of the speaker. However, while it must be acknowledged that these links between personal network structure and language certainly *exist* in the Hammer and the Clonard, the point is that they are less frequently than in Ballymacarrett consistent enough to emerge as significant when the relevant scores are subject to stringent correlation tests.

The contrast between the extreme regularity of the sex/network equivalence patterns in Ballymacarrett, and the absence of such regularities in the other two areas is shown particularly clearly in Figure 6.1. The diagram also shows the effect of these social patterns on language use by plotting the (th) scores for all speakers against their network scores. In Ballymacarrett, the men are all grouped near the top right-hand corner of the diagram, indicating both high network scores and a high level of use of the vernacular variant. The women are (with a single exception) grouped near the lower left-hand corner of the diagram, their low linguistic scores and low network scores being reflected by this arrangement. Although regression lines have not been marked on Figure 6.1, the tendency of the women to 'fit' their language use to their network structure more closely than the men is indicated by the position of those with the highest network scores further to the right of the diagram. The men show no clear tendency to group in this way.

One general conclusion which may be drawn with confidence from this complex, multidimensional analysis of language variability is that personal network structure is in these communities of very great importance in predicting language use: a dense, multiplex personal network structure predicts relative closeness to vernacular norms. However, the *constraints* on the capacity of network structure to influence language use are equally important, for the relationship between language and network is not absolute. It appears to exist in its most consistent form in the community where traditional sex/network equivalence patterns are preserved. Where these patterns are disturbed for any reason—such as geographical mobility or high

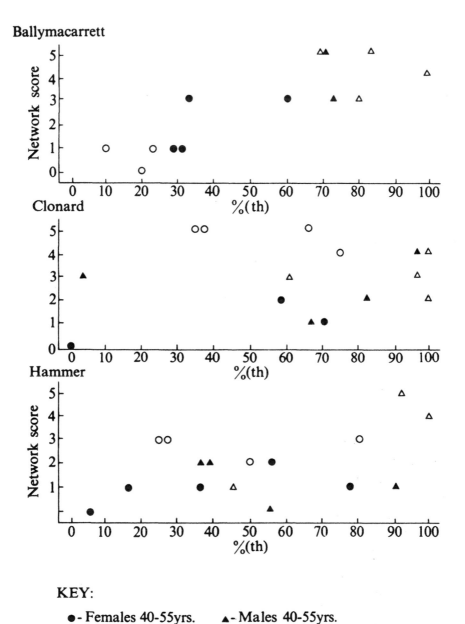

KEY:

● - Females 40-55yrs.   ▲ - Males 40-55yrs.

○ - Females 18-25yrs.   △ - Males 18-25yrs.

Figure 6.1 *Male and female scores for (th) against network scores*

levels of male unemployment—the relationship between language and network is less close. It is true that the variables of sex and network may have *different* effects on linguistic scores: sometimes a particular variable can be described meaningfully either as a sex marker or a network marker. But in considering the social mechanisms which impel some speakers to use very much higher levels of the vernacular than others, sex and network must be said to conspire with each other in a particularly intimate manner.

If we turn our attention to the question of how a language community maintains vernacular norms in the face of relentless pressure from the standard, the implications of the previous paragraph's argument are very far-reaching indeed. That vernacular norms *are* very persistently maintained in many communities everywhere is clear, and that nonstandard varieties and repertoires have important social functions is also clear. We saw in the early chapters of this book that Blom and Gumperz addressed themselves to the general exploration of the link between social values on the one hand, and language maintenance and shift on the other. Although they did not explore the direct social mechanisms which enabled speakers to maintain the language patterns congruent with their systems of social values, Blom and Gumperz did suggest a general link between high levels of dialect use and 'closed' network membership. One presumes from the description of the Hemnes community that such speakers would score high on a network strength scale such as one used in the Belfast study. The more detailed quantitative analysis of network structure carried out in Belfast reveals this language/network equivalence pattern to be most consistent in a traditional community with stable patterns of sex segregation which are themselves revealed both in network scores and language scores. It is clear from Blom and Gumperz's ethnographic descriptions that the Hemnes 'local team' members belonged to a community of this general type.

Since these studies seem to corroborate each other reasonably well, the way is now open to a consideration of the manner in which a break-up of these traditional sex-based network patterns might be an important social mechanism underlying linguistic change; conversely we may ask ourselves whether the same kind of network structure is the social mechanism whereby *vernacular* norms are maintained intact. This seems likely, as it is clear that the capacity of this network structure to maintain normative consensus is considerable. We shall return shortly to the connection between social network structure and patterns of linguistic maintenance and change.

LANGUAGE/NETWORK CORRELATIONS IN SUBGROUPS BASED ON AGE

So far it is clear that the correspondences between the social network structure of the individual, and the manner in which he uses the resources of variability open to him are best considered along with the variables of the speaker's sex, and the area in which he lives. As we have seen, this is partly because social conditions in different areas affect the network structures characteristic of the two sexes; particularly, the men in Ballymacarrett score very much higher than the women on the network strength scale, while this difference is not as clear or consistent in the other two areas, where traditional network patterns are disturbed. However, it is also possible to view the results of the analysis as indicating that particular 'bits' of the language are particularly significant—in terms of their social function—to different subgroups in the population. For example (1) carries a clear symbolic value in the Hammer, where a high level of use of vernacular variants correlates with high individual network scores. Since there is no evidence that this particular linguistic variable functions as a network marker elsewhere, we may link it firmly with the Hammer. This link is also suggested by the analysis of Chapter 5 which reveals a higher general level of use of vernacular variants of (1) in the Hammer than elsewhere (although it has been noted that there is no necessary connection between *absolute* level of language use and degree of 'fit' with network structure).

Similarly, we have seen that high scores on all variables are particularly associated with men; in view of previous work on male/female language differentiation in many different places this is not an unexpected finding. However, we have also seen that even though men use vernacular pronunciations more, women are capable of sometimes using variables particularly associated with men to symbolize their integration into local networks; the variables (a) and (th) correlate with female personal network structures more closely than they correlate with male network structures. The opposite is true for (Λ^2), (ε^1) and (ε^2). Therefore, we may quite meaningfully talk of some 'bits' of the language functioning as network markers for women, and others functioning as network markers for men, quite independently of any function these variables may have as sex markers. In the same way, it can be shown that further 'bits' of the language are linked in a complicated way with different *age* groups, at least in their function as network markers. This is done by further correlation tests which subdivide the population according to age. Since these results are not as consistently significant as those obtained when the population is divided into male and female groups only, or according to area only, it will be simplest to consider each linguistic variable in turn. Two tests were carried out for each variable: in the first the population was divided into two age groups; in the second into four groups, one male and one female subgroup for each age group. Only significant results are discussed below. Note that one further variable (Λ^1) emerges as being linked with the older age group only as a network marker. This variable has not appeared in any previous analysis of the language/network relationship, although the analysis in Chapter 5 revealed that it functioned as a *sex* marker for both age groups.

Variable

    (a)   1 *Highly significant* correlation with network in age group 40–55: ($r = 0.623$; $t = 3.188$; $N = 18$; $p < 0.01$).

                2 *Significant* correlation in age group 18–25: ($r = 0.475$; $t = 2.223$; $N = 19$; $p < 0.05$).

3 Further subdivision of subjects into male and female shows a correlation with network in the *older* female group only: ($r = 0.738$; $N = 9$; $p < 0.05$). Therefore, this variable as a network marker may be associated particularly with women, and particularly with the older age group.

(th)   1 *Significant* correlation with network in older age group only: ($r = 0.366$; $t = 1.758$; $N = 22$; $p < 0.05$).

2 Further subdivision of subjects into male and female shows a correlation with *female* networks in *both* age groups: (40–55: $r = 0.556$; $t = 2.114$; $N = 12$; $p < 0.05$; 18–25: $r = 0.631$; $t = 2.442$; $N = 11$; $p < 0.05$). This variable as a network marker may be associated particularly strongly with women, and more generally with the older age group.

(ε^1)   1 *Significant* correlation with network in age group 18–25 only: ($r = 0.413$; $t = 2.078$; $N = 23$; $p < 0.05$).

2 Further subdivision of subjects into male and female shows a correlation with *male* networks only in the age group 40–55. This variable can be associated generally both with the younger age group, and particularly with *men* in the older age group as a network marker.

(ε^2)   *High significant* correlation with male network structure in the age group 18–25 only: ($r = 0.658$; $t = 2.767$; $N = 12$; $p < 0.01$).

(Λ^1)   *Significant* correlation with network structure in *older* age group only: ($r = 0.474$; $t = 2.349$; $N = 21$; $p < 0.05$).

This final part of the analysis serves to demonstrate further the very great complexity of various sources of influence on a speaker's language. For example the variables (a) and (th) seem to carry multiple social values for everyone, to varying degrees: in their function as network markers, they are most salient in Ballymacarrett, for women, and for the older age group. The variables (ε^1) and (ε^2) on the other hand are linked particularly closely with *male* network structures, with the *young* male sub-group showing a strikingly close correlation between (ε^2) scores and network.

The social function of (Λ^1) is different, but equally complex: (Λ^1) scores correlate with network scores *only* for the older group, but, as we have seen (p. 103 above), this variable can be said to function also as a *sex marker* in a more general way. Thus, we appear to have a situation whereby the social function of a linguistic marker changes through time, as (Λ^1) does not appear to be used at all by the younger group as a symbol of community loyalty although its function as a sex marker in both age groups is quite clear. To express the facts in a more concrete way, we may say that a high level of (Λ^1)—that is, a relatively high frequency of the rounded variant [ɔ] of the vowel /ʌ/ (as in *cut*, | *bud*) at one time symbolized network loyalty, but has now come more specifically to symbolize masculinity. The (Λ^1) variable is particularly interesting in any discussion of linguistic change, as the rounded Belfast vernacular variant is also a well-known Hiberno–English *rural* stereotype: our analysis here is, therefore, capable of suggesting the manner in which the social meaning of specific 'bits' of the language may change, as populations migrate and social patterns change. This question will be discussed in a more general way in the concluding chapter.

VARYING APPROACHES TO THE LANGUAGE/NETWORK RELATIONSHIP

At this point, it is appropriate to consider the findings from the Belfast study in the context of other recent work which examines the relationship between a speaker's social network and his language use.

First, recall that Labov's study of adolescent peer group structure in Harlem (cf. p. 30 above) demonstrated a relationship parallel to the one we have shown here, between language use and closeness of integration into the vernacular culture. Although the conclusions from the Belfast and Harlem studies are broadly similar, Labov did not use the network concept explicitly, and his procedures differ in two important ways from those developed by the social anthropologists to whom the Belfast study is so heavily indebted. First, he examined relationships within a *bounded* group; the essence of the network approach is that it examines individual relationships without necessarily postulating group membership of any kind. Second, Labov's analytic method depends on a division of speakers into *groups* of core members, secondary members, peripheral members and lames. The position of these categories in the group structure is then correlated with *aggregated* linguistic scores. Again, the network concept offers a set of procedures essentially for the analysis of *individual* behaviour. However, despite these differences in approach, there are clearly many similarities between the Harlem peer group study and the Belfast study, both in the underlying hypothesis and in the general conclusions. In the concluding chapter of this book I return to compare Labov's and my own more general conclusions on the nature of the social mechanisms responsible for transmission and maintenance of the vernacular. It will be seen that the two sets of conclusions differ in certain respects.

Cheshire's (1982) Reading study of the relationship between language use and closeness to the vernacular culture is modelled on Labov's and arrives at similar conclusions. However, adolescent *girls* are included in the analysis and emerge as behaving differently from boys in that their degree of closeness to vernacular culture is a less accurate predictor of their language use. Interestingly (although Cheshire does not comment much on this finding) *one* of the two linguistic variables analysed correlates well with closeness to vernacular culture, while the other does not. This part of the study appears to corroborate an important conclusion which emerged from the correlation tests earlier in this chapter; although it was shown that in the Belfast communities *both* sexes use language as a symbol of loyalty to the local community, males and females may use *different* linguistic variables to express this function. Cheshire does not draw this conclusion specifically and, like Labov, examines group structure within a single cluster rather than a wider range of individual network ties; nevertheless, it seems likely that if the distribution of more than two linguistic variables were examined, *both* boys *and* girls might emerge as using language—but different 'bits' of language—as symbols of loyalty to the vernacular culture. For despite important differences in male and female adolescent peer group structure, it is clear that the Reading girls do use at least one linguistic variable in this way. We may conclude that any future study which examines the relation between vernacular loyalty and language use would benefit from consideration of a large number of linguistic variables.

One linguist who refers explicitly to the network concept a great deal in his work is John Gumperz. However, as in the Hemnes study, he does not use the concept quantitatively. A quantitative approach would involve, for example, specifying speaker A's network as being denser than speaker B's, and less dense than speaker C's. Rather, Gumperz makes a dichotomous distinction between 'open' and 'closed' network *types* (which he sees as characteristic of whole communities, or sections of communities) without necessary reference to the varying structure of *personal* networks. The closed type corresponds to the relatively dense, multiplex personal network structures with which we have been concerned in this book, while the open type is relatively spare and uniplex, and is characteristic of geographically and socially mobile individuals. Gumperz sees individuals who interact mostly within closed networks as sharing a number of 'communicative preferences'—as opposed to categorical rules —of a nonstandard kind. The network-specific communicative norms discussed in Chapter 4 would come under this heading. Gumperz himself pays particular attention to the social meanings speakers assign to network-specific code-switching patterns, prosodic contours and lexical choices: outsiders generally do not have access to these meanings (Gumperz, 1982). Typically, diglossic and bilingual communities are the focus of interest.

Gumperz's interest in the study of the particular communicative preferences characteristic of closed network groups leads to extremely detailed work on the manner in which misunderstanding of communicative intent between insiders and outsiders might arise (p. 172). The view that members of closed networks characteristically have access to nonstandard linguistc repertoires (in the sense that a nonlegitimized language, or a dialect, forms an important part of that repertoire) is of particular interest. Although Gumperz does not focus primarily on the social mechanisms of language maintenance, his view appears to be similar to the argument developed in this book that dense, close-knit network structures function as important mechanisms of *vernacular* maintenance, with a powerful capacity to resist the social pressures associated with the standard language.

Gumperz makes the important point that personal network structure is influenced by a very large number of factors, such as, for example, education, occupation, individual ambition or generation cohort (1982:71). For this reason, speakers of a very similar social background, even from the same family, may show very different patterns of language use. Therefore, *individual* patterns of variation in language use can often be accounted for better in terms of network membership than in terms of a speaker's rating on conventional social scales which measure his position hierarchically in relation to the rest of society (1982: 71). A similar point was made here in relation to the two women, Paula C and Hannah McK, whose language patterns and general social characteristics were outlined in Chapter 5 of this book, and discussed further in an earlier section of the present chapter.

Gumperz demonstrates the general link between a 'closed' network structure and preference for nonstandard patterns of language use particularly clearly in a community study of the Gail Valley area of Kärnten, Austria, a few miles from the Yugoslav and Austrian borders (p. 44). Slovenian and German have been in contact for many centuries in Kärnten, but for various social, political and economic reasons, Slovenian has generally given way to German in the area. However, in the Gail Valley, the situation has for some time been one of stable bilingualism, with Slovenian and German each representing different sets of social values. Gumperz explains this persistence of bilingualism in terms of the survival of 'the local system of overlapping kin, occupational, friendship and religious relationships' (p. 46). This is clearly the kind of network structure we have been concerned with in this book; and in the Gail Valley too it is associated with poverty. The land is poor and marginal, and the residents have not had access to social mobility for many generations. However, Gumperz's most recent data show the localized network structure changing as new economic opportunities arise for the Gail Valley residents. Many now travel outside the area to work, and outsiders in turn have moved in. The linguistic effect on the community is that the residents are rapidly becoming monoglot German speakers, with variation within German fulfilling the social functions once fulfilled by code-switching strategies. Thus, Gumperz sees changes in network structure as an important social mechanism of linguistic change.

Very similar conclusions emerge from Gal's (1979) study of the town of Oberwart, a German/Hungarian bilingual community near the Austrian border. Oberwart has been an agricultural community for centuries but, like the Gail Valley, has recently been subject to economic changes which give the residents opportunities to work in industries outside the area. An opposition of peasant/worker values is symbolized by the two languages, with Hungarian representing peasant values (*peasant* being an Oberwart cultural category) and German representing worker values. Most young Oberwarters wish to be considered as workers rather than peasants, and consequently prefer to think of themselves as monoglot German speakers, rather than as bilingual in both Hungarian and German.

However, everyone in the community is competent in both

languages, although the range of situations in which one, rather than the other (or a mixture of both), is used varies considerably. Gal measures the amount of language shift—that is, the extent of the preference for German over Hungarian—by looking at the preferences of thirty-two individual speakers in a range of social contexts. The most obvious factor which predicts language preference is age. Gal finds a 0.82 rank correlation between a speaker's age and his language choice, with the older speakers preferring Hungarian and the younger preferring German. Other factors are relevant to patterns of language choice, the most important being involvement in peasant life (given the social values assigned to the two languages). Gal measures this variable in two ways. First, the 'peasantness' of the individual's network is measured. This is done in a relatively simple way by specifying the percentage of his contacts within a given time (average seven days) who own animals. Speakers were ranked on this measure, and the correlation of this ranking with language choice was found to be 0.78. In addition, a much more complex index of each individual's *own* position on a peasant-to-worker continuum was constructed, using a large number of indicators to assign an index score to each speaker. The correlation between speaker-status and language choice was also reasonably good, but despite the complexity of the index, not as good as the correlation between the speaker's *social network*, measured on a very simple scale, and his language choice.

Several important points emerge from this study. First, the finding that a long-established network of the traditional type is associated with a nonstandard repertoire (monolingualism is the preferred norm in Austria) corroborates Gumperz's views. Second, the variable of network structure is a better predictor of patterns of variability at the *level of the individual speaker* than is the variable of the speaker's own social status. Third, the statistical technique of correlation is shown, as in Belfast, to be an excellent way of dealing with patterns of variation between individuals. Perhaps even more important, the Oberwart and Belfast studies together show that the network concept is capable of being applied in a sociolinguistic study of two quite different types of community. It is moreover clear, as we would expect, that the precise indicators of network type used in the correlation test may vary from one culture to another, and may be determined by careful observation. This is probably the only way in which the culturally relevant categories can be adequately defined (see further p. 173 below).

Gal gives some attention to the question of linguistic change, noting that the process of language shift (from Hungarian to German) is parallel to processes of phonological change (from phone A to phone B) in that the seeds of change are always to be found in synchronic variation in the speech community (1979:4). The comments in this chapter on the relationship between network structure and the maintenance of nonstandard patterns of use, whether in Belfast, the Gail Valley or Oberwart have in fact assumed this parallelism. The proposition that changes in network structure are important mechanisms of linguistic change will be considered in more detail in Chapter 7. Meantime, we conclude this section by looking at three more recent studies which, in different ways, have made use of the network concept.

It is clear from the discussion so far that although the network concept has certain limitations as a sociolinguistic research tool, principally as a basis for a *representative* account of patterns of language ability, it also has several rather obvious methodological advantages. These can be stated quite briefly. First, it provides a useful means of studying relatively small, self-contained groups in more detail than is possible within a large-scale survey framework. Second, it provides a means of approaching an analysis where the concept of *social class* is difficult to apply; this is a problem commonly encountered by researchers studying minority ethnic groups, migrants, rural populations or populations in non-industrialized societies (cf. Gal's Oberwart study, and see further Milroy, 1987; Horvath, 1985; Le Page and Tabouret-Keller, 1985). Finally, as we saw earlier in this chapter, network analysis offers a procedure for dealing with variation between speakers at the level of the individual rather than the group. These points are all relevant to the studies by Edwards (1986) of the language of British black adolescents; Bortoni-Ricardo (1985) of changes in the language of rural migrants to a Brazilian city; and Schmidt (1985) of the language of bilingual Australian Aboriginal adolescent groups.

One of the limitations on choice of method encountered by Edwards was that since there is no enumerated list of British black persons (even assuming that this is a well-defined category), a sample frame could not be constructed to allow speakers from the British black community to be systematically sampled from a range of social classes. Even if the use of social class as a speaker variable *were* feasible in this rather fundamental practical sense, it would in any case be unlikely to yield much insight into the interplay between social and linguistic differentiation. This is for the rather obvious reason that a social class index cannot distinguish in an illuminating way between members of a group who are mostly unemployed or concentrated in low status occupations. But since it seems to be possible to analyse the black community as a whole as consisting of overlapping sets of relatively close-knit groups, the network variable is rather more helpful in describing the relationship between linguistic variability and non-linguistic differences between speakers.

It was suggested earlier (p. 140) that the crucial variable (from a sociolinguist's point of view) underlying any measure of personal network structure is *degree of integration* into a close-knit group. It was also noted with reference to Gal's work (p. 171) that the same indicators were not necessarily relevant to different groups. Even if we confine our attention to Great Britain, membership of groups associated with religious institutions might well be irrelevant in a contemporary northern English coal-mining community, but highly relevant in a midlands black community, or a Welsh rural community (Thomas, 1986). In fact, the indicators used by Edwards were chosen for their capacity to distinguish between individuals who associated themselves to varying degrees with the norms and values of the black community; of particular importance is the distinction between black and non-black ethnicity. For this reason, Edwards's indicators were designed to measure in various ways the extent to which speakers had contact with black friends and neighbours and participated in black social activities. Whether or not the speakers were employed at all was also taken into account, since employment will almost always involve fairly extended interaction with non-black individuals. In fact, the index of integration into the black community which was constructed using these indicators correlated well with the extent to which the individual speakers used the *patois* characteristic of that community.

Bortoni-Ricardo's account of the sociolinguistic adjustment of rural migrants to Brazlandia, a satellite city of Brasilia, is a particularly interesting and innovative application of the network concept. A survey based on a stratificational analysis is not appropriate or feasible for a sociolinguistic study carried out in Brazil; the chief objections are that the notion of a continuum is neither congruent with the sharp distinction between rich and poor, nor does it adequately discriminate between the individuals studied, all of whom were relatively poor. Bortoni-Ricardo did not posit a linguistic movement by the migrants in the direction of an urban standardized norm of the kind familiar in studies using the social class variable (see further p. 175 below); taking the group's own linguistic norms as a starting point, she examined the extent to which speakers had moved away from their stigmatized Caipira dialect.

Bortoni-Ricardo's main hypothesis about change in *social structure* associated with the change from rural to urban life is that it involves a move from an *insulated* network consisting largely of kinsfolk and neighbours to an *integrated* urban network where the links will be less multiplex and associated with a wider range of social contexts. The linguistic counterpart of this process is analysed as one of *dialect diffuseness—* a movement away from the norms of the Caipira dialect. Two separate network indices are used to measure the changing patterns of the migrants' social relationships; the first is the *integration index* and the second the *urbanization index*. The integration index expresses numerically certain relevant characteristics of the three persons with whom each migrant most frequently interacts—for example whether or not they are kinsfolk, or whether the ties have been contracted in the pre-migration period. The score assigned to each migrant is intended to characterize progress in the transition from an insulated to an integrated type of network, and as such is a tool capable of investigating *loose-knit* types of personal network structure (see further p. 197 below). As Bortoni-Ricardo shows, integration scores are correlated with a *linguistic* movement away from the norms of the Caipira dialect.

The *urbanization index* is designed to supplement this structural measure, representing the extent to which the members of each migrant's personal network are integrated into urban life. A number of indicators are used to compute this index, two of which are educational level and occupational mobility; the indicators are selected for their capacity to measure the extent to which the persons with whom a migrant customarily interacts are integrated into (i.e. participate in) urban life. From both a methodological and a theoretical point of view, Bortoni-Ricardo's work is particularly interesting. In developing these two types of index it extends the application of the network variable beyond an analysis of small, close-knit groups of the kind with which we have been concerned in this book, to consider the extent to which individuals have detached themselves from such groups. The theoretical significance of this advance will be explored in Chapter 7.

Schmidt's study differs from both Edwards's and Bortoni-Ricardo's in that it does not quantify network structure at all, but uses the concept to account for differences between speakers which emerge from a quantitative analysis of *linguistic* data. The language of two small, close-knit groups of young Aboriginal women from a Queensland community (the Rock 'n Rollers and the Buckeroos) is studied against a background of societal bilingualism (Dyirbal and English) where Dyirbal is giving way, apparently fairly rapidly, to English. The young speakers mix the two languages in different ways and proportions and a number of creole-like characteristics are recorded, such as the Buckeroos' frequent use of *bin* as a past tense marker.

Schmidt's main interest is in a highly focused *peer group norm*, which is apparently a linguistically mixed code possessing characteristics both of Dyirbal and of English. This norm contrasts with that of the groups' careful speech which is very much closer to traditional Dyirbal (see Dixon, 1971 for a description). There is, for example, more evidence of intrusion from English in peer-group speech, and relatively low frequency of traditional Dyirbal morphological features, such as ergative inflexions. Thus, speakers who have productive control of Dyirbal morphology tend not to use it in peer-group situations. Schmidt reports two particularly interesting findings which emerge from a quantitative analysis of this mixed code peer-group norm. First, although there is considerable between-group variation, there is very little variation between the language of speakers *within* each group. Second, although the peer-group norm is characterized by speakers as Dyirbal rather than English, the extent of its Dyirbal admixture (sometimes only around 50 per cent) corresponds to the extent to which traditional Dyirbal features are controlled by the least fluent Dyirbal speaker in the group. Schmidt explains the group's ability to maintain this very homogeneous mixed code, the norms of which are apparently pragmatically determined, in terms of the capacity of close-knit networks to exert normative pressures upon individuals. This capacity has been seen rather generally by sociolinguists who have applied the network concept as forming the basis of an explanation of patterns of language maintenance. We shall look more closely in the concluding chapter at the theoretical implications of the link between a close-knit network structure and language maintenance and at its obvious corollary: that a loosening of close-knit ties is likely to be associated with linguistic change.

7

Conclusions and Theoretical Implications

A major premise of this book, elaborated in the early chapters, is that the study of the vernacular speech of the individual in its everyday social context is an important task for sociolinguistics. Since most current models of communicative competence and language structure rest on a rather narrow base derived from relatively formal styles or relatively educated varieties, it is particularly important to obtain more information about the facts of specifically *nonstandard* speech in a range of everyday contexts. *Not* to have such information is undesirable for practical as well as for theoretical reasons. For example, standardized language tests, which assess a very wide range of human traits, have frequently been criticized for their intrinsic bias against nonstandard speakers. Yet, in many regions of Britain nonstandard speakers comprise a majority of the population, and as Taylor has pointed out (1977), misassessment on this scale probably represents a considerable waste of human potential (see further Milroy and Milroy, 1985a).

Quite apart from the part played by the capacity of nonstandard speech to evoke unfavourable stereotyped reactions, a major reason for this imbalance in current linguistic knowledge is the operation of normal style-shifting mechanisms, which have the effect of making the vernacular speech of *any* individual extremely difficult to observe and record in its social context. The problem is compounded in the case of low-status nonstandard speakers who live in close-knit communities. Again as a result of the operation of normal sociostylistic mechanisms, such speakers will suppress all but their most careful linguistic styles unless special techniques of entering those communities and observing the everyday interaction of friends, kin and neighbours are designed.

In Belfast, a set of procedures based on the concept of the individual's social network was applied, in order to gain access to as wide a range as possible of everyday speech styles of nonstandard speakers. Note that the term *social network* refers quite simply to the informal social relationships contracted by an individual. Since all speakers everywhere contract informal social relationships, the network concept is in principle capable of universal application and so is less ethnocentric than, for example, notions of *class* or *caste*. Network studies have in fact been carried out by social anthropologists in societies of many kinds, ranging from middle- and working-class groups in Edinburgh, to shanty-town communities in Mexico City and rural or migrant communities in Africa. Since the network concept, unlike that of socio-economic class, is not limited by intercultural differences in economic or status systems, it is a valuable tool of *sociolinguistic* analysis also.

An individual's personal network may be analysed using the procedures described and exemplified by Boissevain (1974). It may be initially be characterized as relatively *dense* or *multiplex*, and individuals may be said to be linked to ego as *first* or *second order* contacts. As is to be expected from the findings of a number of anthropological studies, analysis based on these principles has proved to have important implications for fieldwork in working-class areas. This is because relatively dense, multiplex network ties contracted within a given territory are particularly associated with low-status groups, and give rise to a complicated nexus of rights and obligations which must be honoured by individual network members if they wish to preserve valued and useful relationships. To allow maximum involvement in this nexus, the fieldworker adopted a modified participant observation technique but defined her position as far as possible in relation to the network, rather than in relation to an outside research institution. A network-defined status as *friend of a friend* facilitated observation not only of a wide range of vernacular speech styles, but also of a number of more general communicative norms, both phatic and nonphatic.

Although the network concept may thus be seen to be of assistance in designing an explicitly principled fieldwork method for use outside an investigator's own community, its major contribution is to analysis of the manner in which individuals utilize the resources of linguistic variability available to them. The major hypothesis of the Belfast study was that even when variables of age, sex and social class are held constant, the closer an individual's network ties are with his local community, the closer his language approximates to localized vernacular norms.

This hypothesis was validated with the aid of statistical techniques, and Labov's similar conclusions from his Harlem study were extended in a number of ways. First, it is clear that the link between the closeness to vernacular culture and high frequency of key vernacular linguistic variables is general throughout the adult community; it is not merely adolescent groups who use language in this way. Second, the statistical technique of *correlation* allows us to demonstrate this link systematically by comparing the linguistic scores and network scores of individuals, thus avoiding a limitation of the investigation to the study of members of groups, or quasi-groups such as the Harlem street gangs. This is the main contribution of the statistical analysis; although the correlations tell us only that there is a relationship between language and network which is more than accidental, they do allow us to demonstrate that relationship in a highly systematic manner. If we wish to explain *why* that relationship exists, we must look elsewhere. The argument pursued in this book in answer to that important question depends fundamentally on the function of a close-knit network as a norm enforcement mechanism—a point originally argued in 1957 by Bott and now widely accepted by social anthropologists. Labov apparently takes the same view when he refers to the close supervision and control exercised by the peer group over its members; but he does not link this observation to its corollary—that the lames, who approximate *less* closely to the vernacular, are because of their peripheral position necessarily less subject to the supervision and control of the peer group. If we accept Labov's argument that the peer group acts as a norm enforcement mechanism and effectively *defines* the norms of Black English Vernacular (1972b: xiii), as I believe we must, the relatively low frequency of vernacular variants in the speech of the lames can be accounted for in at least two obvious ways.

First—and this is the view Labov appears to adopt, although he does not commit himself clearly on the issue—it may be argued that because of various factors such as parental persuasion, ill health, personal desires or institutional pressures, they have become involved in the upwardly mobile society on which the peer group members have turned their backs. This upward mobility is marked in their speech. Alternatively, their language may be viewed as not approximating particularly closely to the abstract norms of standard English—it is after all still extremely nonstandard. But because they are not constantly subject to the supervision and control of the peer group, they lack any social mechanism whereby a highly focused set of vernacular norms can be consistently maintained against the constant pressure of a competing set of institutionally legitimized norms, and so they drift away from that vernacular. In Le Page's terms, their language becomes more diffuse (Le Page, 1979). Now it may be objected that the second argument amounts to very much the same thing as the first. I shall try to show in this chapter that it does not, and that if we want to understand why people like the lames whose speech embodies *neither* abstract vernacular *nor* abstract standard norms in any highly focused form use language in the way they do, these important and probably universal underlying ideologies of status and solidarity must be considered in a more integrated way than has usually been the practice in sociolinguistic studies of urban speech. It has been amply demonstrated many times that both are clearly marked by patterns of language use: but except for a few studies of tiny parts of the sociolinguistic system such as the papers by Brown and Gilman (1960) and Brown and Levinson (1978) they are seldom conceived of as part of an *integrated* system of social values which can help to explain patterns of language use both at the level of the group and at the level of the individual in his relation to the group.

The implications of the Belfast findings (considered in conjunction with the converging findings of others) for these central problems of sociolinguistic theory are considerable. As I have indicated in several places we find related implications also for socially oriented theories of language maintenance and change, some of which are explored below.

CLOSE-KNIT NETWORKS AND LANGUAGE MAINTENANCE

A number of the studies discussed in this book have demonstrated an association between a close-knit, localized network structure and adherence to a vernacular or (more broadly) nonlegitimized norm. In Norway, such a network structure was linked with loyalty to a nonstandard dialect: in Oberwart and the Gail Valley with adherence to bilingualism. In both these latter communities bilingualism was a nonlegitimized norm of language use in a country where there was only one official language, and as such bilingualism may be seen in some respects as functionally equivalent to vernacular loyalty in a monolingual society, or to bidialectalism in a bidialectal community.

In Norway, as networks broke up some speakers (the students) showed signs of using the standard more extensively than 'local team' members; in Oberwart and the Gail Valley under parallel conditions speakers moved towards monolingual repertoires. Gumperz has made the point in many places that individuals whose networks are close-knit often share general 'communicative preferences' of a nonstandard kind, and is there referring apparently to phenomena such as those described in Chapter 4 of this book—patterns of phatic, proxemic and kinesic behaviour for example—as well as network-specific uses of code-switching strategies and prosodic patterns. Since these communicative patterns characteristically carry social meanings inaccessible to outsiders, to the extent that communicative intent may often be misunderstood, Gumperz attributes their persistence to a capacity to function as symbols of 'insider' status.

Thus a body of evidence emerges from several different kinds of society to suggest that a close-knit network structure is an important mechanism of *language maintenance*, in that speakers are able to form a cohesive group capable of resisting pressure, linguistic and social, from outside the group. If the individual's network structure becomes less close-knit, it follows that he will be robbed of an important mechanism of nonstandard norm maintenance; he will also be free of the constant supervision and control described by Labov.

The wider implications of these and related matters for sociolinguistic theory have been explored by Le Page in a number of papers (1975b; 1977; 1979). Le Page characteristically concentrates not on language variability, but on the concept of a linguistic norm, a phenomenon which he appears to view as a natural product of cultural *focusing*. He argues that a recognizably standard form of creole has developed for example in Belize, in a general situation of great cultural and linguistic *diffuseness*, 'because of the close daily interaction of its inhabitants in a confined space and under conditions of external threat which has made this act of identity on their part positive and necessary' (1979:176).

He further suggests that the emergence of standard languages (both at the present day and historically) is an aspect of cultural focusing which comes about under a number of conditions, 'partly through close daily interaction, partly by the need for solidarity under an external threat, partly through the models represented by powerful political or religious institutions'.

What makes Le Page's ideas particularly important is their generality, their avoidance of ethnocentric bias and their consequent applicability to linguistic groups of different statuses and cultures; he suggests for example that cultural focusing has taken place under much the same conditions as those described in Belize to produce the extremely consistent vernacular spoken by core members of the Harlem street gangs. Thus it appears likely that highly focused sets of linguistic norms may not only be maintained, but may also emerge in the first place, partly at least under the influence of the kind of group structure discussed in this book. We must look now at some of the implications of Le Page's contention that the same kinds of social processes operate on speakers from different cultures *and of different statuses* to produce a highly focused set of linguistic norms. Note particularly that Le Page lists the solidarity ethic, constant interaction and a confined territory as conditions favourig cultural focusing. All these conditions are commonly associated, as have seen, with a close-knit network structure.

FOCUSING AND DIFFUSENESS IN URBAN SPEECH

It is best to begin here by noting that Labov also recognizes the similarity of the social forces which produce two highly focused forms of English, each characteristic of groups greatly distant from each other both socially and geographically. Describing the close control exercised by the Harlem group members over the vernacular (1972b:257f), he compares it with the control exercised by public school networks in the use of RP amongst upper-class British speakers. I would add that structurally, upper-class networks resemble low-status close-knit networks in many ways. Upper-class Englishmen also generally lack social mobility (though for different reasons), occupy well-established territories, and are bound to each other by multiplex ties of kin, school, common financial interests and voluntary association. Élite equestrian sports may be viewed as the functional equivalent of working men's clubs; outsiders are commonly excluded from both. In a wide-ranging discussion of the function and structure of reciprocity networks, Lomnitz argues that they may form themselves *at any level of society where there is equality of wants*. The point is made vividly and clearly:

> One might think the rich would have no use for reciprocity networks when the advantages of the market economy are at their fingertips; such a view however does not take into account the real nature of reciprocity. The business of preservation of privilege at the top may be pursued with the same intensity and the same kind of urgency as the struggle for bare existence at the bottom. Goods and services that pass from hand to hand in a reciprocity network may range from a few beans to a hot tip on the stock exchange. The basic principle is the same. (1977:206)

In modern urban society, large socially and geographically mobile sections of the population will lack the conditions necessary for the formation and maintenance of reciprocity networks: as Lomnitz points out in the same analysis, individual mobility produces inequality of wants, as well as a collapse of well established territorial rights (p. 203).

Thus, pulling the strands of the argument together, it seems that cultural and linguistic focusing are associated with a close-knit network structure and can take place if the conditions are right at any stratum of society. In British (in which we must include Irish) society, social conditions have for some time encouraged the maintenance of highly focused language varieties at the highest and the lowest strata. An important difference between the two sets of norms is that the norms of RP are supralocal and are disseminated through institutional channels; differences within RP are structurally and phonetically minimal, and are not based on area. Belfast vernacular on the other hand, like Black English Vernacular, is an example of a highly focused variety at the lowest stratum, where many other localized and equally focused but linguistically divergent varieties are located. Both the low-status vernaculars and RP may be viewed as owing their relative stability to covert ideologies of solidarity and reciprocity; RP also draws its strength from *institutionally recognized* ideologies of status and upward mobility. It may further be argued that other sets of prestige norms, such as those described by Labov in the United States, have also emerged as the result of cultural focusing under much the same general conditions (given differences in social structure at the highest stratum) as a focused set of orthoepic norms first emerged from England. The social mechanisms of this focusing have yet to be explored, but a study of upper-class networks in American cities might well yield interesting information (see Kroch MS for a recent example of such a study).

As I have already suggested with reference to the linguistic patterns of Labov's lames (see p. 180 above), it is likely that the speech of the mobile section of an urban population can be characterized in terms of either or both of these abstract sets of norms (low-status as well as high-status); in Le Page's terms, the language patterns of the socially and geographically mobile are likely to be relatively *diffuse*. We will look now at the effect of these observations on our view of social-class variation in language by examining a small amount of data in a little detail.

In Belfast vernacular, the reflex of the /o/ vowel (*smoke*, *boat*, *home*) is a near-monophthongal, rounded, half-close, back vowel [o], varying in length from short to fully long, depending on phonetic environment. The RP reflex of the same vowel is clearly diphthongized [øʊ]. Some Belfast middle-class speakers use a diphthong with an unrounded first element which resembles the RP vowel fairly closely; others use a monophthong. It is difficult to understand why any native Belfast speaker should use a diphthong of this kind without referring to the ultimate influence of RP—the highly focused norm at the highest social stratum whose influence spreads by more or less conscious imitation. This is the kind of influence which Labov calls change from above (1972a:290).

We must contrast this with a kind of influence observable in pronunciations of a subclass of the /a/ vowel. For a word like *bag*, where /a/ is followed by a voiced velar, a very common 'corrected' Belfast pronunciation is [ba¹g]. This diphthong with its relatively low front vowel nucleus followed by a glide to a relatively high front position can be heard in the everyday speech of educated speakers, but also appears in the *careful* speech of vernacular speakers. On this occasion, we cannot account for the presence of a diphthong by referring to RP, where this item is pronounced with a more or less monophthongal front vowel [æ], any glide on the vowel is towards the centre. However, the stereotypical Belfast vernacular pronunciation has a *closing* diphthong; the nucleus of the vowel typically starts slightly higher than cardinal 3 and glides upwards [bɛ¹g]. If we appreciate that this pronunciation is stereotypical of a highly focused but heavily stigmatized local variety, we begin to understand why [ba¹g] appears in corrected speech, and not something closer to RP. What appears to be happening is that speakers are correcting *away from* the vernacular, a process accomplished by a strategy of lowering the nucleus of the diphthong while retaining the less auditorily salient closing glide. It is likely that RP pronunciation is blocked to these speakers because of its phonetic closeness to the stigmatized vernacular vowel; adopting the RP pronunciation would involve a complicated adjustment of the whole front vowel system by means of a chain shift mechanism if the RP vowel and the vernacular vowel were not to sound rather alike. Thus, one begins to see the complicated sociolinguistic and phonological constraints on the process of speech correction. Interestingly, the diphthongized reflex of /o/, which *does* show RP influence, does not collide in this way with any corresponding stereotypical vernacular vowel in the back series.

These examples demonstrate that the phonetic shape of the relatively diffuse speech characteristic of the more mobile section of the population can be most satisfactorily accounted for if *both* élite *and* vernacular norms are taken into consideration. The same principles apply, for example, to the 'intermediate' London and Norwich pronunciations of the word *home* cited by Trudgill (1983:42). The vernacular norms quoted for these two cities are [æʊm] and [ʊm] respectively. Two 'intermediate' forms are given for each city: [ʌʊm] and [hʌʊm] in London, and [hʊm] and [huːm] in Norwich. Although it is certainly possible to explain the presence of [h] in Norwich in terms of RP influence, the vowels are clearly derived from Norwich vernacular, the second variant probably representing an attempt to correct a stereotypical short vowel by resorting to a lengthening strategy in much the same way as the [baˡg] pronunciation in Belfast suggests correction of a stereotypical high vowel by means of a lowering strategy. In the London examples the low unrounded vowels show the clear influence of the vernacular; a strategy of backing the vernacular front nucleus appears to have been adopted here which still does not produce a vowel similar to the RP variant. The presence of [h] in [hʌʊm] can of course be attributed to more or less conscious imitation of RP.

It may be objected that Labov's concept of 'change from below' (1972b:290) adequately accounts for these relatively diffuse intermediate pronunciations; as Labov points out, historians of language such as H. C. Wyld have long been aware that lower-class forms often find their way into prestige varieties. However, Labov is quite clear in describing change from *below* as occurring below the level of consciousness, originating at any stratum of society (except presumably the highest), and as being most clearly observable in 'the unattended speech of daily life'. A good example of change from below in Labov's terms is (a) in Norwich (Figure 5.2), where the curvilinear pattern on the graph shows a lower-class form spreading into the *unmonitored* speech of the class above. This concept does not account for a pronunciation like [baˡg] which is observable in working-class speech as a *conscious correction*, and can be best explained at whatever stratum of society it occurs as a more or less conscious avoidance of a vernacular norm. It is not an imitation of a prestige norm on the one hand, nor an unconscious adoption of a nonprestige norm on the other. It may well be that some of the intermediate forms cited by Trudgill are best accounted for in the same terms.

It does not of course follow that clear sets of norms are to be found only at the highest and lowest strata although in this section we have considered only RP on the one hand and low-status vernacular norms on the other. However, Le Page's principle that cultural and linguistic focusing can take place at any stratum of society where social conditions are favourable implies that other sets of local norms may sometimes emerge and influence the phonetic shape of 'intermediate' forms. This kind of focusing is particularly clear in the case of Scottish English, where educated norms quite unlike those of RP are actually embodied in elocution handbooks (MacAllister, 1963). There is some indication that Patterson's linguistic prescriptions designed for Belfast speakers a century ago are influenced by similar Scottish norms, as well as by RP. Nor can we discount the possibility that the rapid social change of the last twenty years in Northern Ireland, involving as it has the displacement of the traditional RP speaking landowning political élite, may result in a cultural focusing which can in turn produce a recognizable set of specifically *local* prestige norms.

Our major concern here, however, is not with the emergence of 'intermediate' norms, but with the influence of the vernacular on the speech of higher status groups. It appears that this influence may take two distinctly different forms. First, there is the kind of influence Labov calls change from below, and second the negative influence described here, a more or less conscious *avoidance of stigma*. It cannot be assumed that consciously corrected forms are always explicable in terms of the influence of a prestige norm only. Although in some cases, such as in accounting for the copula deletion patterns in the speech of the Harlem lames, avoidance of stigma and adoption of prestige norms may come to much the same thing, it is sometimes important to make the distinction and acknowledge explicitly the strong *negative* influence of the vernacular on the speech of the upwardly mobile. Such a theoretical framework might have helped Macaulay, for example, in a practical way in his investigation of Glasgow speech. Acknowledging both the irrelevance of the RP norm for many speakers and the fact that some corrections such as [hom] for [hem] (*home*) seem to be the result of conscious suppression of the Scots vowel, he nevertheless follows the early Labovian model of describing variability in terms of a highly focused supra-local set of prestige norms (1977:28). This leads to some near absurdities, such as the exclusion from the (a) variable of items which belong to the /u/ class in RP despite the fact that many Scottish speakers have a single /a/ vowel. Macaulay freely acknowledges these problems; but their solution probably lies primarily in describing variability in terms of the vernacular (also taking into account MacAllister's norms of correctness) rather than in terms of a set of prestige norms with obviously English associations whose influence may be difficult to predict.

In general Labov's 1966 model appears to require some modification if used to deal with northern varieties of British English. This is probably partly because of their long history of separateness from RP, and partly because of the existence of a highly focused set of specifically Scottish prestige norms (whose sphere of influence stretched into northern England) embodied in the conventional spelling system used in Scottish literature of the Middle Ages and after. One consequence of this sociolinguistic history is a sharp disjunction between prestige and vernacular varieties; Johnston (1983) has described communities with this kind of sociolinguistic structure as 'divergent dialect' communities, and argued that quantitative methods cannot be used there successfully without radical adaptation of Labov's standard paradigm.

NETWORK STRUCTURE AND LINGUISTIC CHANGE

The main orientation of this book has been towards questions not of linguistic change, but of linguistic stability. In this chapter so far attention has been given to the association between a close-knit network structure and two related linguistic phenomena: the maintenance of consistent nonstandard linguistic norms, and the emergence in principle at any level of society of a highly focused set of norms. It has furthermore been argued that the influence of a focused set of norms, at whatever stratum of society they appear, should be taken into account in describing the relatively diffuse language patterns characteristic of large numbers of socially and geographically mobile speakers.

One important corollary to the link between language maintenance and a close-knit territorially-based network structure is that linguistic change will be associated with a break-up of such a structure. It is likely that two effects of the processes of urbanization and industrialization will be to disperse traditional close-knit networks, and to accelerate linguistic standardization.

In a wide-ranging discussion of processes and problems of standardization, Haugen hints at one obvious linguistic consequence of these changes in network structure, noting that 'the modern nation state . . . extends some of the loyalties of the family and the neighbourhood or the clan to the whole state. Language and nation have become inextricably intertwined' (1966:103). If, as Haugen implies, these categories of identity cease to be as important as they are in, for example, Hemnes or Ballymacarrett, we may expect some of the social values associated with localized vernaculars, and which play an important part in maintaining them, to be transferred to a less localized linguistic code. Thus, complex attitudinal factors, in addition to more obvious ones such as upward mobility, are probably involved in the association between a loosened network structure and a movement towards a more standardized norm. As we shall see shortly, change in network structure alone does not appear to be a sufficient condition for change *towards* a *standard*, although it does appear to trigger off some kind of change in the vernacular. In Oberwart and the Gail Valley, however, changes in work location and consequently network structure, appear to be important factors in the movement towards the legitimized monolingual norm of the nation-state. In Oberwart, as Gal points out, this change provides the impetus for change within German; monolingual speakers gradually adapt their linguistic repertoires in such a way that varieties of German are able to take the place of Hungarian in fulfilling a range of social functions.

Although there are clearly large-scale links of this kind between language change and network structure, it is possible to infer from the Belfast data some rather more subtle influences. The interpretation of the linguistic facts proposed in this section depends crucially on the significant correlations between language structure and network structure described in Chapter 6, and to a lesser extent on the acceptance of these statistical facts as a reflection of the capacity of a close-knit network to impose linguistic norms upon its members in much the manner described in Labov's account of peer group behaviour. It is of course possible to interpret the correlations in other ways also.

First, by referring to the distributional patterns of the variable (Λ^1) one may see how changes in the *social value* ascribed to this phonological element are associated with changes in network structure. Standing apart from the Belfast data for a moment, we may note that the vernacular rounded variant [ɔ] of the /ʌ/ vowel in *hut, cup, bud,* is also a well-known *rural* stereotype, beloved of exponents of stage Irish and tellers of Irish jokes. The statistical evidence in Chapter 5 indicates that this variable functions generally as a sex marker with the men predictably using the vernacular variant significantly more than the women. There are no significant distributional differences according to either age or area.

However, the correlation tests of Chapter 6, which measure

fit between language use and network structure rather than absolute *levels* of language use, indicate that there is a significant relationship between high network scores and high levels of use of the vernacular variant *in the older age group only*. Pulling these various strands of information together, I would suggest, slightly speculatively, that the original migrants to Belfast (in some cases the parents of middle-aged informants) brought the stereotypical /ɔ/ pronunciation with them from the countryside, *possibly in its function as a marker of network loyalty*. As these migrant networks broke up and new urban networks reformed, the [ɔ] variant apparently lost this function: for there is no tendency for /ɔ/ scores to correlate with network scores in the younger age groups. However, the same phonological element now functions quite clearly as a *sex* marker, while others, such as (a) and (th) now fulfil its former function. Trudgill (1985:118) discusses a similar 'social redistribution' of variants, which in Norwich as in Belfast is associated with the emergence of an urban dialect.

Second, the process Le Page describes as focusing—the formation of a recognizable set of linguistic norms—is in itself an aspect of linguistic change. The Belfast material provides some interesting evidence of the linguistic reflexes of focusing. Since Belfast is a relatively young city, some of the Clonard informants having migrated there as children, we would expect a characteristic Belfast vernacular to have emerged in its most focused form in Ballymacarrett, the oldest and most stable of the three communities studied. In fact, in Ballymacarrett the sex differentiation pattern is characteristically parallel for both age groups over a range of important phonological elements (see Chapter 5), suggesting that the language patterns of two generations are governed by a single agreed set of norms. Clonard speakers of different generations, on the other hand, do not always evaluate vernacular phonological elements in the same way. It is these local differences in the social value ascribed to the (Λ^2) and (a) variables which produce the age by sex and age by sex by area interactions shown in graph form in Figures 5.3 and

5.4. Moreover, residual *rural* linguistic features (also evaluated as rural by the younger speakers) such as [*t*]: (*butter, train, petrol*) and [kj]: (*cat, cap, car*) are quite prominent in the speech of men over the age of about forty in the Clonard, but have almost vanished from the vernacular of their wives and sons (Milroy and Milroy, 1978:36). Thus, the degree of linguistic focusing we find in Ballymacarrett does not yet appear to have taken place in the Clonard.

The Ballymacarrett pattern further suggests that sharp sex differentiation in language may be part and parcel of a highly focused vernacular structure; we have seen that it is also linked with stable network patterns. Interestingly, in the Hammer, where *network* scores are generally low, with little difference between male and female scores, consistent differentiation in language use according to sex is very much less sharp than in Ballymacarrett. Bearing in mind Frankenberg's remark (p. 253) that in general sex roles become more blurred as networks become loose-knit, I would suggest that one linguistic effect of the break-up of close-knit networks may be the blurring of sex differentiation in language. It is not at all clear what changes in individual patterns of language use are involved here, and it seems unlikely that sex differentiation in language will fail to reappear in some form even where networks are loose-knit. The important point is that the Hammer and Ballymacarrett patterns are different in a consistent enough way to suggest that the blurring of sex differentiation patterns is another kind of linguistic change which may be linked with network structure.

Finally, perhaps the most interesting link of this kind emerging from the Belfast data is a rather negative one. There is clear evidence, even from this one-class study, that a number of word classes are undergoing systematic linguistic change. Those taking place in the small /ʌ/ ~ /ʉ/ word class (*pull, took, foot*, among others) and the much larger /ɛ/ word class (*bed, leather, rent*) are particularly interesting. We shall look at the smaller word class first.

It has been shown elsewhere (Milroy and Milroy, 1978)

that the lexical set involved in this alternation has diminished in size since the mid nineteenth century, cetain words having stabilized in the /ʉ/ class. We now no longer find *wool, hood* and *wood* alternating in Belfast, although they still do so in the rural hinterland. Thus, the process of linguistic change in this case is one of lexical transfer, whereby items which alternate between two lexical classes gradually stabilize, a few at a time, in the /ʉ/ class.

Now, only eighteen items were recorded in 1975 as alternating in this way in Belfast; but what is particularly interesting is the powerful capacity of the [ʌ] variant of this small number of very common words to carry social values associated with the vernacular culture. The [ʌ] variant is very much more likely to be used by men than women—particularly in the younger age groups—and is frequently cited by informants as a stereotypical Belfast pronunciation. It also functions as a network marker specifically for men; unlike the patterns for some other variables, there is no correlation between *women's* network scores and level of use of [ʌ].

It therefore appears probable that a strong tendency to linguistic change is inhibited—that is, a small number of residual items are prevented from stabilizing in the (ʉ) class—by the powerful capacity of the two variants to express contrasting social values, particularly to indicate loyalty to the local community as opposed to the 'official culture'.

The manner in which the variables of sex and network may interact in either inhibiting or enabling linguistic change can be demonstrated by further analysis of the social distribution of the variants of the Belfast variables (a), (ε^1) and (ε^2) (see p. 130). For the purpose of this discussion, (ε^1) and (ε^2) are treated as a single variable, (ε), variants of which appear in both monosyllabic and polysyllabic tokens of /ɛ/ (as for example in *red* and *ready*; cf. p. 120 above). We also need to take into account data which have not so far been presented in this book, from community studies carried out in 1980 of Andersonstown (West Belfast) and Braniel (East

Belfast). These studies employed methods similar to those described in Chapter 3 and the communities are best seen as somewhat higher status counterparts of Clonard and Ballymacarrett respectively. Also relevant to the argument here are rural dialect and real time data which in earlier chapters have been referred to only very generally. Further details of this material and of the later community studies may be found in Harris (1985), Milroy and Milroy (1985b) and Milroy (1987).

We saw in Chapters 5 and 6 that both (a) and (ε) were strongly affected by the speaker variable of *sex*. Raised, lengthened variants of (ε) were associated principally with women, and backed variants of (a) with men. It is clear from the historical and dialectological data presented by Patterson (1860), Staples (1898), Williams (1903) and Gregg (1972) that /a/ raising and /ε/ backing are both relatively recent phenomena in Belfast, but are characteristic of modern Scots and originate in the Ulster–Scots speaking dialect area of Down and Antrim (as distinct from the Mid- and West-Ulster non-Scots hinterland). East Belfast adjoins the Ulster-Scots region of North Down, whereas West Belfast points south-west down the Lagan Valley, the speech of which is Mid-Ulster, with less Scots influence. Furthermore, immigration to West Belfast is recent, largely from a Mid- and West-Ulster hinterland (cf. p. 78 above). Present day sociolinguistic evidence suggests that the incoming variants of (ε) and (a) are diffusing from East to West of the city; remember that scores for /a/ backing are higher for Ballymacarrett men than for any other group studied, while Ballymacarrett women used the low, conservative variants of (ε) less than any other group (p. 130). As might be predicted from this pattern of sex differentiation in the inner city, the higher status Andersonstown and Braniel speakers exhibit a similar pattern of sex differentiation but use the incoming variants of (ε) more frequently, and the incoming variants of (a) less frequently than Ballymacarrett and Clonard speakers.

In summary, raised variants of (ε) are in the inner city

associated particularly with women (and, we might add, with careful speech styles). They are also associated generally with slightly more prestigious outer city speech; data collected by survey methods from a large and more heterogeneous samples of the Belfast population confirms that the higher the status of the speaker the more likely he or she is to use raised variants (Milroy *et al*, 1983). Incoming variants of (a) show an almost perfectly converse pattern of social distribution, being associated with male, vernacular inner city speech. Taking this evidence together with the historical and geographical data outlined above, we may conclude that although incoming variants of both vowels appear to have originated in the same hinterland Scots dialect, each has assumed a diametrically opposed *social* value in its new urban setting.

The relationship between speaker choice of variant and individual network structure adds a further complexity to this pattern. As we saw in Chapter 6, choice of variant correlates with network structure amongst some inner city subgroups, but the social patterns are quite different for each vowel. Although (a) is generally sensitive to network structure, choice of variant is more closely correlated with network structure for women than for men, despite the fact that on average they use incoming backed variants much less frequently than men. The converse is true of (ε); while men use incoming raised variants much less on average than women, the correlation between choice of variant and network structure is higher for men (cf. p. 156). We can thus argue that (ε) functions particularly clearly for men and (a) for women as a network marker, and note that in each case *it is the group for whom the vowel has less significance as a network marker which seems to be leading the linguistic change.* This complex relationship between sex of speaker, network structure and language use is summarized below (see Table 7.1).

It has been argued throughout this book that a close-knit network functions as a conservative force, resisting pressures for change originating from outside the network; those whose ties are weakest approximate least closely to vernacular

Table 7.1 *Contrasting patterns of distribution of two vowels involved in change, according to sex of speaker, relative frequency of innovatory variants and level of correlation with network strength.*

	Change led by	High correlation with network strength
(a)	men	women
(ε)	women	men

norms, and are most exposed to external pressures for change. We have also seen that the innovatory variants of (a) and (ε) have a common dialectal point of origin, but have taken on very different *social* values in their new urban setting. The analysis presented in this section and in Chapter 6 suggests that the vernacular speakers associated most strongly with the innovation are in each case those for whom the vowel functions least prominently as a network marker. It is as if a strong relationship between the network structure of a given group and choice of phonetic realization of a particular vowel disqualifies that group from fulfilling the role of innovators with respect to that vowel. Conversely, the dissolution of the language/network relationship with respect to a group of speakers may be a necessary precondition of that group fulfilling the role of linguistic innovators.

These observations suggest that since network structure seems to be implicated in a rather negative way in linguistic change, a closer examination of *weak* network ties would be profitable. We proceed in the following section to explore the sociolinguistic significance of loose-knit networks.

LOOSE-KNIT NETWORKS AND LINGUISTIC CHANGE

A general methodological problem associated with the use of the network variable is that although it can be readily operationalized to study speakers whose networks are of a relatively close-knit type, it cannot easily handle socially and geographically mobile speakers whose personal network ties are not predominantly dense or multiplex; yet, such persons make up a substantial proportion of the population in a post-industrial society. Loose-knit networks are hard to deal with chiefly because a multi-valued speaker variable like social network involves comparing speakers who differ from each other in certain respects—let us say in respect of the multiplexity of the ties which they have contracted at the workplace (cf. p. 143 above)—but are still similar enough to each other in other related respects to make such a comparison meaningful. For example, it is evident that relative to someone who has changed jobs and houses several times, the networks of the Belfast inner-city speakers which were compared in Chapter 6 are *all* close-knit. While we might make this general point and follow through its implications when we want to compare, for example, the Braniel group with the Ballymacarrett group, it is much less easy to see how the relatively loose-knit network structures of *individual* Braniel residents might meaningfully be compared with each other.

Many of the Braniel people who participated in the community study owned cars and telephones, which they used as a means of maintaining important personal ties over long distances; the capacity of these ties to influence their behaviour (linguistic or otherwise) is not clear. Other speakers seemed to be relatively exposed to standardizing mainstream influences, in that they had contracted few personal ties which were likely to exert normative pressure on their behaviour; but in any case the geographical spread of the ties contracted by most Braniel speakers made them difficult to investigate. While we might readily hypothesize that these individuals were generally less likely than Ballymacarrett people to be subject to the pressures of their personal networks and more likely to be subject to a less localized outside influence, it is hard to suggest dimensions on which a number of loose-knit networks, which differed greatly from each other, might be systematically compared.

Although loose-knit networks are difficult to handle at the operational level (but see the discussion on p. 174 above of Bortoni-Ricardo's study of rural immigrants to a Brazilian city) it was argued at the end of Chapter 6 that at the level of theory they are likely to be important. As is the case so often in this area, we find that anthropological and sociological studies of small scale communities illuminate the issue. On the basis of evidence from a number of such studies, Mewett (1982) has argued that class differences begin to emerge as the proportion of multiplex relationships declines, multiplexity being an important characteristic of a close-knit type of network structure (cf. p. 51 above). This observation suggests a framework for linking network studies with larger scale class-based studies in formulating a more coherent multi-level sociolinguistic theory than we have at present. Furthermore, Granovetter (1973) has argued in a stimulating and suggestive paper (upon which the argument in this section is heavily dependent) that 'weak' and uniplex interpersonal ties are important channels through which innovation and influence flow from one close-knit group to another, linking such groups to the wider society. This rather larger-scale aspect of the social function of weak ties has important implications for a socially accountable theory of linguistic change and diffusion.

Granovetter's working definition of 'weak' and 'strong' ties is as follows:

> the strength of a tie is a (probably linear) combination of the amount of time, the emotional intensity, the intimacy (mutual confiding) and the reciprocal services which characterise a tie. (p. 1361)

Although rather vague, this characterization is probably sufficient to satisfy most people's intuitive sense of what might be meant by a 'weak' or 'strong' interpersonal tie, corresponding approximately to an everyday distinction between an acquaintance and a friend. It is certainly satisfactory for our purposes here, and corresponds fairly well to the measures of network strength used in the Belfast inner city communities (pp. 141–2 above). Although *strength of tie* is a continuous variable, for the purpose of exposition Granovetter treats it as if it were discrete. His basic point is that weak ties *between* groups regularly provide bridges through which information and influence are diffused, and are more likely than strong ties, which tend to be concentrated *within* groups, to fulfil this function. Thus, while strong ties give rise to a *local* cohesion of the kind which has been explored in this book, they lead paradoxically to overall fragmentation.

Granovetter argues in some detail that there is a structural reason why weak rather than strong ties form bridges between cohesive groups, deriving from the positive relationship between the strength of a tie binding two arbitrarily selected individuals, A and B, and the degree of overlap in their personal networks. As a consequence of this relationship, the ties between *non-overlapping* groups through which information and influence flow are likely to be weak. Emphasizing the significance of the relationship between strength of tie and network overlap, Granovetter suggests that *no strong tie can be a bridge*. A bridge is defined as the sole link between two close-knit groups, and since in practice there will probably be many such links, the notion is best treated as a theoretical construct.

The important point (from the perspective of this book) which follows from Granovetter's argument is that weak intergroup ties are likely to be critical in transmitting innovations from one group to another, despite the common-sense assumption that *strong* ties fulfil this role. For example, Downes (1984:155) suggests that the network concept is important in developing a theory of linguistic diffusion, but assumes that it is strong ties which will be critical. This assumption seems to be shared by linguists who have considered the matter at all; indeed, in his recent work on linguistic change and diffusion Labov (1980:261) presents a model very different from the one proposed here, of the innovator as an individual with strong ties both inside *and* outside a local group.

Although at first sight Granovetter's principle might seem counter-intuitive and paradoxical, a little thought suggests that it works out well empirically. First of all, it is likely (in the networks of mobile individuals at least) that weak ties are more numerous than strong ties. Second, many more individuals can be reached through weak ties than through strong ties; consider for example the bridges set up by participants at academic conferences, which link cohesive groups associated with each institution and through which new ideas and information pass. Conversely, information relayed through strong ties tends not be innovatory, since those linked by strong ties tend to share contacts (i.e. to belong to overlapping networks).

This general principle entails that mobile individuals who have contracted many weak ties, but as a consequence of their mobility occupy a position marginal to any given cohesive group, are in a particularly strong position to diffuse innovation. Interestingly, this contention is in line with the traditional assumption of historians of language that the emergent, mobile merchant class were largely responsible for the appearance of Northern (and other) dialectal innovations in Early Modern (Standard) English; see, for example, Strang (1970:214f), Ekwall (1956); Baugh and Cable (1978:194).

It might appear that Granovetter's relatively clear hypothesis could easily be supported or refuted empirically; but unfortunately network or sociometric studies cannot readily be used as a source of corroboratory or disconfirmatory evidence, simply because their design usually entails relative neglect of weak ties. Thus, for example, when persons are asked to name others from whom they have received information (or friendship, as in Labov 1972b) the number of permitted choices is usually restricted so that the naming of weak ties is effectively inhibited. Even if the research design permits identification of persons with weak ties to specified others (as does the Belfast inner city study) it is extremely hard to study those ties simply because they are weak and perceived as unimportant (see p. 198 above for an outline of other methodological difficulties). Where evidence *can* be extracted from network studies it tends to be complex and indirect, such as the distributional patterns of the innovatory variants of (a) and (ε) described in the previous section.

Empirical evidence to support the general idea that innovations first reach groups via weak ties may however be extracted from a large body of research on the diffusion of innovations, collected by Rogers and Shoemaker (1971). An important distinction which emerges from Rogers's and Shoemaker's discussion is between the *innovators* and the *early adopters* of an innovation. Innovators generally seem to be marginal to the innovation-adopting group, often being perceived as under-conforming to the point of deviance. Early adopters on the other hand are central members of the group within which they have contracted strong ties, and conform closely to group norms. They frequently provide a model for other non-innovative members of the group. After its adoption by these central figures from more marginal persons, an innovation is typically disseminated from the inside outwards with increasing speed, showing an S-curve of adopter distribution through time. While it is clear that linguistic innovations differ in a number of respects from, say, technical innovations, they do not appear to be *diffused* by mechanisms markedly different from those which control the diffusion of innovations generally. For linguistic innovations also have frequently been observed to show this characteristic S-curve of distribution through time (Chambers and Trudgill, 1980:176–81; Bailey, 1973).

In view of the norm-enforcing capacities of groups built up mainly of strong ties, it is easy to see why innovators are likely to be persons weakly linked to the group. Susceptibility to outside influence is likely to increase in inverse proportion to strength of tie with the group (measured in the Belfast communities by a network strength scale). Where groups are loose-knit—that is, linked mainly by weak ties—they are likely to be generally more susceptible to innovation. This is consistent with Labov's principle that innovating groups are located centrally in the social hierarchy, characterized by him as upper-working or lower-middle class (Labov, 1980:254; Kroch, 1978). For it is likely that in British (and probably also American) society close-knit networks are located primarily at the highest and lowest strata, with a majority of socially and geographically mobile speakers falling between these two points (cf. p. 181).

One apparent difficulty with a theory which argues that innovators are only marginally linked to the group is in explaining how they can successfully diffuse innovations to central members of the group; two related points are relevant here. First, we may surmise with Granovetter that since resistance to innovation is likely to be strong in a norm-conforming group, a large number of persons will have to be exposed to it and adopt it in the early stages for it to spread succesfully. Now in a mobile society like ours, weak ties are likely to be very much more numerous than strong ties, and some of them are likely to function as bridges through which innovations flow. Thus, an innovation like the Cockney merger between /v/ and /ð/ and /f/:/θ/ reported in Norwich teenage speech (Trudgill, 1986:54ff) is likely to be transmitted through a great many weak links between Londoners and Norwich speakers; Trudgill suggests tourists and football supporters as individuals who might contract such links. Quite simply, before it stands any chance of acceptance by central members of a group, the links through which it is originally transmitted *need* to be numerous (cf. Granovetter, 1973:1367; also Granovetter, 1982).

The second point we need to make in explaining the success of marginal members of a group in innovating is that persons central to a close-knit, norm-enforcing group are likely to find innovation a risky business; but adopting an innovation which is already widespread on the fringes of the group is very much less risky. Thus, instead of asking how central members of a group are induced to accept an innovation from marginal members, we can view this as a sensible strategy on their part. For it is likely that a necessary (but not sufficient) condition for the ultimate adoption of a candidate innovation is that it is positively evaluated, either overtly or covertly. Thus, Norwich speakers, whether they are central or marginal to their local groups, in some sense view vernacular London speech as desirable—more desirable than the speech of other cities. Central members of a group diminish the risk of potentially deviant activity by adopting an innovation from persons who are already linked to the group, rather than by direct importation.

The details and implications of this 'weak tie' model of linguistic change are discussed in detail by Milroy and Milroy (1985b) and Milroy (forthcoming). The model is shown to be capable of accounting for some puzzling patterns of variation and change (in Belfast and elsewhere) which are difficult to explain in terms of the usual unqualified assumption that linguistic change is encouraged by frequency of contact and relatively open channels of communication, and discouraged by boundaries of one sort or another, or weaknesses in lines of communication.

THE TRANSMISSION OF VERNACULAR NORMS

The capacity of a close-knit network structure to inhibit some kinds of linguistic change, and to maintain vernacular norms in a highly focused form, is relevant to a theoretical issue raised by Labov concerning the transmission of a low-status vernacular. The question is, how does Black English Vernacular (and also, it could be added, other vernaculars) maintain itself in such a strikingly consistent form across time and space when its heaviest users are adolescent peer group members whose speech patterns often become more diffuse as they grow older?

It is likely that everywhere adolescents are heavy users of nonstandard vernaculars. Observations in Belfast corroborate others made in many places in suggesting that they are more consistent vernacular speakers than the adults with whom

we have been mainly concerned in this book. The language/
network hypothesis would in fact predict something of this
sort since peer group networks seem to be the most close-
knit around the age of sixteen; subsequently pressures of
work, independence and mobility (both geographical and
social) inevitably lead to greater variability in personal
network structure. It is the fact of relatively few adults
retaining the strong orientation to vernacular culture found
in the peer groups, and of this changed orientation being
marked in their speech, which leads Labov to wonder how
vernacular norms can be maintained intact when they seem
to be transmitted through successive peer groups and to be
relatively diffuse in the adult population. What prevents
Black English Vernacular from splitting in many different
directions?

I would begin by suggesting that Labov oversimplifies
the character of the contrast between the strongly focused
vernacular of the peer groups and the more diffuse speech of
the adult population. If he had carried out a detailed small-
scale study (as opposed to a survey) of the adult population
of Harlem, parallel to the famous study of the adolescent
peer groups, this might well have become apparent. In fact
the Belfast study, focusing as it does on the adult population,
suggests a partial if somewhat complicated answer to Labov's
question.

The series of statistical analyses reported in Chapters 5
and 6 of this book reveal the distribution of vernacular
phonological elements through the adult population to be
extremely complex, particularly in relation to the independent
variables of sex and network structure. Using the concept of
statistical significance, it is possible as we have seen to
designate some linguistic elements as *sex* markers, in the sense
that men and women use them at significantly different levels.
Others appear to function as *network* markers in the sense
that they correlate significantly with the network patterns of
the individual. Sometimes a linguistic element may be
associated with both variables, sometimes only with one of

them, and sometimes it is linked significantly to these variables in only one age group.

Even more subtly—and I believe this is the key to a solution of Labov's problem—it is possible for a group of speakers to use a particular vernacular variant at a *relatively low level*, and still to show a significant correlation (a good fit) between network scores and linguistic scores. This is what happens with the vernacular zero variant of (th), for example. Figure 6.1 shows clearly that women use zero very much less than men, but do in fact relate their level of use *within the female norms* more closely than men to their network structure. Thus a low level of use of particular vernacular variant, calculated in terms of the average score of a social group, does not necessarily imply that the vernacular variant has no clear social function for the speakers in that group (cf. also p.196 above).

It is worth noting also that several of the men whose scores are plotted on Figure 6.1 use the zero form well over 90 per cent of the time. Therefore, although the generally low female scores probably mean that *on average* adolescents use this important vernacular variant more than adults, we should not lose sight of the fact that some adult speakers appear to be extremely heavy users of the vernacular.

In making a contrast between the linguistic patterns of adults and adolescents Labov, whose quantitative methods generally involve grouping and averaging linguistic scores, is probably referring simply to *average* differences in *group* scores. However, the significant distributions revealed in the Belfast data (by the use of slightly more elaborate quantitative methods) suggest that simple comparisons of average group scores do not adequately characterize the extremely subtle manner in which the resources of the vernacular are used by the adult population. Although in this group the base of the vernacular is certainly narrow in terms of the number of speakers using it at a high level, the fact is that some individuals do use it functionally at extremely high levels to express various meanings of loyalty and identity. The social messages encoded by these speakers can be interpreted only in relation to the messages encoded by those who use the vernacular at a low level, and vice versa. This becomes clear if analytic methods are used which reveal the important distinction between, on the one hand absolute levels of use of the vernacular, and on the other closeness of fit between language use and loyalty to the vernacular culture. It is inevitable that many adult speakers will use the vernacular at a low level if it is to function effectively for those who use it at a high level as a symbol of solidarity or masculinity, as well as no doubt a number of other aspects of identity. The point is, that although the average level of use of the vernacular may as Labov perceives be low outside the adolescent peer group culture, an extremely complex distribution of vernacular phonological elements closely reflects the greater heterogeneity of values and of informal social relationships in the adult population. The association of the vernacular with important values of local loyalty and solidarity which are often explicitly perceived as opposed to institutionalized provincial or national values should, as Blom and Gumperz have shown in Hemnes, ensure its survival and transmission in a highly focused form.

STATUS AND SOLIDARITY

It is clear that the general conclusions emerging from the Belfast study in no way contradict others from the sociolinguistic work of the past two decades. On the contrary, a small-scale network-based analysis of language variability seems likely to yield some insight into the nature of the social mechanisms which give rise to stratification of language by age, sex and social class. As we saw earlier, Mewett (1982) has proposed that the disappearance of multiplex ties in small communities is associated with the emergence of a clear social class system, and Granovetter suggests that loose ties fulfil an important function in linking small, cohesive groups to a wider stratified society. Dense, multiplex network ties do, however, seem to be associated particularly with low status groups, men and adolescents, and a large number of studies where informants are sampled from a range of social classes have repeatedly shown that these speakers approximate on average more closely to urban vernaculars than higher-status groups, women and middle-aged speakers. Thus, although there is still a good deal worth exploring on the nature of the relationship between network structure and class structure, the findings of network studies are entirely consistent with those of sociolinguistic surveys.

One important reason for the language/network link has been pointed out by linguists and psychologists many times (for example, Trudgill, 1972; Ryan, 1979): that is a highly focused set of vernacular norms is able to symbolize solidarity and loyalty to a set of values of a non-institutional kind. Another reason is the capacity of a close-knit network, noted by Labov in his Harlem study, to exercise control over its members so as to ensure that they maintain this set of norms in a highly focused form. The independent work of a number of social anthropologists would also lead us to expect a close-knit network to have this effect on individual behaviour.

An awareness that what might be called *the solidarity factor* has an important influence on patterns of language use should not lead us to play down the importance of the more obvious influence of the status factor. Although this orientation is not always made fully explicit, a status-based model assuming the influence of upward mobility on language use generally underlies large-scale surveys such as those of Labov (1966) or Trudgill (1974). Although the same scholars have indicated elsewhere that they are keenly conscious of the existence of *competing* sets of vernacular norms, no unitary model has yet emerged which attempts to account for these two opposing ideologies of status and solidarity in an integrated way. Typically, work focusing on the linguistic effects of the status factor is carried out by means of a large-scale survey method, while work on the solidarity factor (such as Labov's Martha's

Vineyard and Harlem peer groups studies) involves detailed analyses of the speech of groups of individuals within a given territory or a single social group. Yet, as I have tried to show in a previous section of this chapter, competing sets of linguistic norms which reflect the influence of both factors need to be taken into account if the relatively diffuse language patterns of the mobile section of an urban population are to be adequately described.

I would not claim here to offer anything approaching a fully integrated model of the kind which seems to be required. But it is possible to contribute towards the formulation of a model of sociolinguistic structure which takes into account the influence of these competing ideologies by suggesting how they may interact with each other in controlling individual language behaviour. First, it is worth making explicit a further corollary to the main argument of this book: if a speaker's personal network is relatively loose-knit it will not constitute a bounded group capable of enforcing a focused set of linguistic norms. His speech may then be more liable to influence from a publicly legitimized norm disseminated through institutional channels. It is a matter of common observation that speakers of nonstandard vernaculars frequently change their speech in this way when they move away from the areas where well-established close-knit networks are located; such a movement is often associated with upward social mobility. Even though speakers may status-code their language when upward mobility is associated with a change in network structure, it is important to note in passing that change in network structure alone does not appear to be a sufficient condition to predict a movement towards any clearly defined legitimized norm. This becomes clear if we consider evidence from the Hammer area of Belfast. Although networks in this area have become relatively loose-knit due to enforced relocation, it is not possible to argue in any meaningful way that Hammer speakers are more standardized than Ballymacarrett or Clonard speakers. The main effect of the change in network structure on patterns of language use seems to have been the blurring of sex differentiation, but any linguistic 'drift' which has taken place does not seem to have been in the direction of a prestige norm. The correct generalization therefore appears to be that speakers with loose-knit networks are relatively more *exposed* to the influence of a prestige norm: a change in network structure in itself does not predict this influence.

We touch here on controversial matters; it has in fact been noted already in Chapter 4 (pp. 82f) that social theorists do not agree on the nature of the relationship between the collapse of reciprocity networks and individual social mobility. Arguments have been advanced on the one hand that reciprocity networks are dysfunctional for individuals who attain social mobility, and on the other that individuals whose network resources are destroyed compensate for their loss by seeking status and rewards of a more public kind. Clearly it is important at least to consider questions such as these if we want to move towards an understanding of the manner in which status and solidarity factors interact with each other in influencing the speech patterns of individuals. Some of Labov's remarks on peer group members, as well as my own observations in Belfast do, in a limited way, illuminate this issue.

Frequently, a clear tension between status-based and solidarity-based influences on the social behaviour of individuals is evident. Labov notes, for example, that highly intelligent peer group members often deliberately turn their backs on the upwardly mobile society outside their own close-knit community: for them the solidarity factor wins out and they remain close to the vernacular culture, solidarity-coding this orientation in their speech. A number of adolescents in the Hammer rejected upward mobility in a parallel manner. For example, three children from one large family had refused grammar school scholarships, preferring to attend the local low-status secondary school in order to maintain ties with kin and friends. Their elder cousin had recently left the sixth form of a high-prestige grammar school and at the time of the fieldwork was unemployed. He had rejected the attempts of the school careers master to place him in white-collar employment, preferring to wait for a low-grade clerical job to turn up in the local textile engineering firm where many of the Hammer youngsters hoped eventually to find work. Despite his grammar school education, a preference for solidarity over status was clearly marked in his speech.

Many counter examples of individuals who actively seek upward mobility can of course be quoted. Some of the Belfast informants deliberately avoided close ties with the local community because they saw them as detrimental to their own or their children's opportunities for social advancement. For example, several people from the older of the age groups studied carefully directed their sons away from local peer groups; these adults, whose own involvement in local networks was usually also minimal, tended as we have seen to mark this orientation towards the status factor in their speech. At a relatively abstract level of social structure there appears to be an association between the collapse of close-knit networks and the emergence of a class structure; however, at the level of the individual any attempt to generalize on the links between a loose-knit network structure and upward mobility is difficult, since upward mobility is not the only factor giving rise to a loose-knit network structure. Forced relocation, lack of kin and absence of local employment opportunities may all contribute. Labov similarly noted that working-class adolescents could become lames and involved in a status-orientated values system for many reasons, ranging from school and parental pressures to personal weakness or ill health or simply personal preferences.

It seems then impossible at present to characterize the relationship between network structure and social mobility in any clear way. What is clear from these examples is that individuals may find themselves on the periphery of localized networks for many reasons, some of which may be quite outside their control. *Whatever* the reasons however, a low level of integration into the network is likely to be marked linguistically by relative distance from the vernacular. Although it is not at present possible to formulate a coherent theory of the manner in which status and solidarity factors interact in influencing a speaker's language, we must recognize that for all speakers (with the exception of those in the highest-status groups) these two ideologies are likely to be symbolized by divergent sets of linguistic norms. Each individual is able, to some extent, to show by his choice of language how he has reconciled the two.

THE CONCEPT OF NETWORK AND THEORIES OF VARIABILITY

If hypotheses concerning the relationship between patterns of language use and the structure of informal social ties are to be tested (as I hope they will) in different kinds of community, it is important to find adequate ways of characterizing and measuring network structure. One way of approaching the question of how to apply the network concept in different locations is to look as specifically as possible at the implications of selecting indicators of network structure such as those used in the Belfast study rather than, for example, the single indicator used by Gal in Oberwart.

First we should note that since personal network structure is influenced universally by a great many factors including, for example, territorial stability, location of work and kin, age, sex and personal affinity, one cannot hope to identify and measure all relevant factors. The range of choice actually available to an investigator depends on the local cultural categories which reflect more abstract properties of network structure such as multiplexity and density; but we also need to acknowledge that indicators are likely to be selected in accordance with theoretical orientation and analytic purpose. This becomes clear if the methods of the Belfast and Oberwart studies are compared.

One operational objective in the Belfast study was to find a means of measuring indirectly the relative density and multiplexity of personal networks, and the indicators selected ensured that the highest scores could be achieved only if a high proportion of an individual's interactions in the important sectors of kin, neighbourhood work and friendship were with a limited number of people in a limited territory. This approach reflects an acceptance of the conclusions of such social anthropologists as Bott and Cubitt who insist on the social function universality of a close-knit territorially-based network as a norm maintenance mechanism. In turn, these conclusions have been seen as particularly relevant to sociolinguistic enquiry because they reflect the common-sense observation that individuals have a variable capacity to influence each others' behaviour, including some aspects of linguistic behaviour.

Throughout this book the question of how (rather than why) highly focused sets of vernacular norms are maintained has been considered. It has been argued that speakers are able to retain this orientation, despite counter-pressures from the standard, partly at least because the kind of close-knit network with which many vernacular speakers are associated has the capacity (as Labov has noted of specifically adolescent peer groups) to exercise close supervision and control over its members. In the previous section the ultimate question of *why* some speakers were more closely integrated into local networks than others was raised, but as we might expect, not satisfactorily answered. Our inability to provide a firm answer is useful however in suggesting some limitations on how the significant correlations between language use and network structure should be interpreted. The use of the concept in the first place, quite apart from the results of the analysis, raises a number of pertinent questions. Are we subscribing to an implicit linguistic determinism by adding yet another constraint on variability to the better known ones such as ethnic group, social class, age and sex? Does a person *choose* to be more or less closely integrated into his community and to signal his choice when he speaks? If this does happen should a personal network score be interpreted as reflecting a psychological fact, or simply as characterizing in a neutral way the structure of a speaker's informal social relationships?

It is clear from the network patterns of some of the individuals discussed in the previous section that it is not possible to give firm ‚and categorical answers to these questions. Some individuals appear to extricate themselves deliberately from close ties with the local network; others seem to be separated from it by the force of circumstances. Sometimes on the other hand individuals deliberately retain close-knit ties, turning their backs on upward mobility, while others seem to retain these ties out of necessity rather than choice. So although an individual's network score may certainly reflect closely his personal affinities and attitudes to the vernacular culture, it cannot be said to do so in any consistent or reliable way. Therefore, although this conclusion does not deny the capacity of the individual to choose his orientation to a close-knit group and to signal that orientation linguistically by manipulating the resources of phonological variability available to him, it is important to interpret the network measure used in this book as one of social structure. It cannot claim, unfortunately, to reflect consistently an individual's attitude to status or solidarity ideologies although many would consider that characterizing the relationship between these attitudes and language use was a task of fundamental importance. Although it may be possible in practice to interpret some speakers' network scores in this way, a much more reliable conclusion to draw from the Belfast analysis is that whatever the social or psychological factors may be which influence an individual's network structure, that structure is likely to be reflected in patterns of language use.

In contrast to the Belfast study, Gal's choice of network measure is less explicitly influenced by theories of the social function of close-knit networks. Nor is her analytic purpose to examine in detail the influence of personal network structure on patterns of language use. Rather, it is to evaluate the relative effect of a number of speaker variables (network, age, status) on patterns of language choice. For this purpose, a comparatively simple measure of the content of a person's network—its relative 'peasantness'—was used.

The norm-enforcing capacities of the Oberwart peasant networks are clear from Gal's acount of the constraints on language choice experienced by young peasant wives (1979:144). However, her use of the network concept is in general less influenced than mine by theories of social function. Certainly, her underlying view of the relationship between the variables of network and status seems to be different. While Gal appears to view these as alternative modes of analysis which might be compared and evaluated, I have adopted the view (taken also by Russell (1982)) that the informal relationships in which a person is enmeshed and the status group to which he or she may be said to belong are phenomena at different levels of abstraction.

Although then it is clear that individual theoretical orientation and analytical purpose may lead investigators to make use of the network concept in different ways, both the Belfast and the Oberwart studies used statistical correlations to compare the language patterns of individuals. Although different indicators were used in each of these studies, it is important to note that the statistically significant correlations are themselves evidence of the validity of the indicators of network structure used in the quantitative measures. This is not to deny that other equally valid indicators could be found or that all five indicators used in the Belfast study are of equal validity; but what can be said with assurance is that a wholly irrelevant measure of network structure (such as one based on an individual's height or weight) would not produce significant or highly significant results *when rigorous statistical procedures were applied.* Thus, one important advantage of using a correlation technique is that the investigator can be confident, if the relationship between language and network variables emerges as significant and so unlikely to have occurred by chance, that he has not selected his network indicators entirely wrongly and arbitrarily. This point is methodologically important since it is likely that a convincing case could be made, not capable of resolution by means of argument and counter-argument, for using several different kinds of indicator.[1] If we take into account other network studies in different types of community such as those of Bortoni-Ricardo, Edwards, Thomas and Schmidt, the network concept may be claimed to have a very general and possibly universal applicability. However, the indicators which may be said to reflect the underlying structure of personal relationships will vary in accordance with the investigator's perception of the most relevant and easily measurable cultural categories. Looking some distance into the future it could be argued that widely applicable concepts of this kind are precisely what are needed if we are to succeed in integrating the findings of scholars with common interests but working in different traditions—such as creolists, linguistic anthropologists and urban dialectologists. Following a similar line of reasoning, Le Page has criticized the ethnocentric and doctrinaire approach of much linguistic and sociolinguistic theory, seeing the most important task of scholars as being to formulate what he describes as *laws*: 'statements of the necessary inherent relationships between individual behaviour, the rules of social behaviour and individual and social identity' (1977:173). The purpose of this book has been to contribute to our ability to make statements of this kind.

[1] Gal does in fact apply statistical tests to determine whether personal network structure or personal status correlates better with language choice; she finds that network gives a better correlation. There is no reason why this procedure should not be adopted to determine which *indicators* of, for example, network or social class correlate best with linguistic patterns.

Appendix

Linguistic variable scores for forty-six speakers

Women: 1. Ballymacarrett   2. Clonard   3. Hammer

	NSS	(ai)	(Λ^1)	(th)	(Λ^2)	(a)	(ϵ^1)	(ϵ^2)	(o)	(ɪ)
					Linguistic Variables					
1. *40–55*										
M B	3	2.3	47.0	60.26	30.80	2.33	75.00	63.64	86.3	2.1
M T	1	2.4	52.4	28.57	0.00	1.73	63.64	50.98	72.2	1.6
B M	3	2.3	33.3	33.33	30.71	2.48	46.67	38.89	90.9	1.8
E D	1	2.0	—	29.17	5.50	2.13	0.00	5.50	90.0	1.9
18–25										
L S	1	2.3	26.7	10.00	39.77	2.16	50.00	62.50	95.4	2.4
A W	1	1.9	10.5	23.61	11.61	2.38	66.67	54.55	100	1.8
R L	0	1.5	46.7	20.00	15.56	1.45	50.00	30.33	100	1.8
2. *40–55*										
P C	2	2.4	9.0	58.34	70.48	2.63	100	47.83	50.0	2.5
L C	1	2.4	52.9	70.46	83.34	1.75	100	92.86	90.9	1.8
H McK	0	1.4	0.0	0.00	0.00	1.05	66.67	25.00	20.0	1.2
18–25										
N McK	5	2.2	46.7	66.67	36.00	2.75	100	100	100	2.1
M McK	5	2.0	18.7	37.92	21.77	2.70	83.33	63.64	100	2.1
B C	4	1.9	33.3	75.00	19.38	2.35	66.67	69.57	90.8	1.8
M C	5	2.2	36.4	35.00	19.04	2.33	25.00	26.92	66.6	1.6
3. *40–55*										
M H	1	2.4	28.6	16.67	24.25	—	71.43	63.16	100	2.2
M M	2	2.9	59.0	56.64	27.87	2.25	78.57	52.94	100	2.2
L M	1	2.2	50.0	77.50	61.88	2.42	100	76.19	100	2.2
J D	1	2.4	—	36.77	0.00	—	78.57	52.94	100	—
A H	0	2.4	23.0	5.00	—	—	—	—	—	2.1

(Appendix cont'd.)

	NSS	(ai)	(Λ^1)	(th)	(Λ^2)	(a)	(ϵ^1)	(ϵ^2)	(o)	(ı)
				Linguistic Variables						
18–25										
L X	3	2.8	50.0	80.00	10.00	2.50	100	58.33	100	2.6
C M	3	2.3	33.3	25.00	0.00	—	57.14	36.84	100	2.4
S M	2	2.3	47.0	50.00	5.21	2.78	80.00	80.00	100	1.9
C McC	3	3.0	25.0	26.70	12.50	—	40.00	29.41	100	1.9

Men: 1. Ballymacarrett   2. Clonard   3. Hammer

	NSS	(ai)	(Λ^1)	(th)	(Λ^2)	(a)	(ϵ^1)	(ϵ^2)	(o)	(ı)
1. 40–55										
D B	3	1.9	53.0	73.13	32.50	2.83	100	77.50	73.2	1.9
G K	5	2.2	66.7	72.23	10.85	3.78	100	61.70	64.3	2.1
S S	3	2.1	40.0	—	—	—	—	—	85.8	2.1
18–25										
T D	3	2.4	88.9	81.99	33.30	3.13	100	79.31	100	2.5
S M	5	2.4	36.4	70.84	30.80	3.43	100	83.33	100	1.8
B B	5	2.5	54.6	84.38	42.70	3.15	100	89.29	100	2.1
J H	4	2.7	45.8	100	83.69	3.03	100	64.00	95.0	2.3
2. 40–55										
M C	3	2.3	71.4	3.13	19.88	2.75	100	94.44	88.7	1.3
E C	4	2.2	68.2	96.43	23.22	3.03	100	75.76	87.5	1.8
J McK	1	2.0	66.7	67.71	21.43	2.65	100	77.27	66.7	1.6
T M	2	2.6	22.7	82.11	2.09	2.73	86.67	76.47	80.0	1.1
18–25										
E C	4	2.4	26.7	100	83.04	2.30	100	91.30	100	2.2
M C	2	1.9	6.70	100	60.15	2.45	71.43	79.92	100	2.3
G McD	3	2.2	62.5	60.72	52.16	2.55	85.71	72.41	100	1.9
G M	3	3.0	78.9	96.43	44.87	2.12	100	57.14	100	2.2
3. 40–55										
A H	1	2.2	30.8	90.39	1.93	2.85	100	88.24	100	2.1
H M	2	2.1	57.9	36.58	34.11	3.05	91.67	85.00	100	2.2
M H	0	1.6	36.8	55.56	3.85	—	100	53.85	—	2.1
J X	2	2.5	80.0	38.10	9.53	2.73	92.86	75.00	96.4	2.1
18–25										
E D	5	1.9	66.7	92.86	50.35	2.78	100	90.48	100	2.4
T C	4	2.8	30.8	100	58.34	2.18	95.00	75.00	100	2.5
J C	2	2.3	20.0	—	—	—	100	71.43	100	2.4
S McC	1	2.6	37.5	45.64	36.19	—	68.97	36.19	81.9	1.9

References

Bailey, C. J. (1973) *Variation and Linguistic Theory*. Washington DC: Center for Applied Linguistics.

Barnes, J. A. (1954) Class and committees in a Norwegian island parish. *Human Relations 7* (1).

Basso, K. H. (1970) 'To give up on words': silence in Western Apache culture. In Giglioli (ed.), 67–85.

Baugh, A. C. and Cable, T. (1978) *History of the English Language*. (3rd edn) London: Routledge and Kegan Paul.

Bauman, R. and Sherzer, J. (1974) *Explorations in the Ethnography of Speaking*. Cambridge: Cambridge University Press.

Bell, C. and Newby, H. (1974) *Readings in Sociology of Community*. London: Cassell.

Bickerton, D. (1975) *Dynamics of a Creole System*. Cambridge: Cambridge University Press.

Bloch, B. (1948) A set of postulates for phonemic analysis. *Language 24*, 3–46.

Blom, J. P. and Gumperz, J. (1972) Social meaning in linguistic structures: code switching in Norway. In Gumperz and Hymes (eds), 407–34.

Boal, F. W. (1978) Territoriality on the Shankhill–Falls divide, Belfast: the perspective from 1976. In Lanegran and Palm (eds), 58–77.

Boal, F. W. and Poole, M. A. (1972) Religious residential segregation in Belfast in mid-1969: a multi-level analysis. In Clark and Gleave (eds), 1–40.

Boal, F. W., Doherty, P. and Pringle, D. G. (1974) The spatial distribution of some social problems in the Belfast urban area. Belfast: Northern Ireland Community Relations Commission.

Boal, F. W., Doherty, P. and Pringle, D. G. (1978) *Social Problems in the Belfast Urban Area*. Occasional Paper 12, Dept. of Geography, Queen Mary College, London.

Boissevain, J. (1974) *Friends of Friends: Networks, Manipulators and Coalitions*. Oxford, Blackwell.

Boissevain, J. and Mitchell J. C. (eds) (1973) *Network Analysis: Studies in Human Interaction.* The Hague: Mouton.

Bortoni-Ricardo, S. M. (1985) *The urbanisation of rural dialect speakers: a sociolinguistic study in Brazil.* Cambridge: Cambridge University Press.

Bott, E. (1971) *Family and Social Network* (rev. ed.). London: Tavistock.

Bouvier, J.-C. and Martel, C. (1973) Les effets de la palatalisation de K-, G— + A sur le système consonantique des parlers Nord-provençaux. In Straka (ed.), 211–31.

Brown, P. and Levinson, S. C. (1978) Universals in language usage: politeness phenomena. In Goody (ed.), 56–289.

Brown, R. and Gilman, A. (1960) Pronouns of power and solidarity. In Sebeok (ed.), 253–75.

Burroughs, G. E. R. (1971) *Design and Analysis in Educational Research.* Oxford: Alden and Mowbray.

Cazden, C. B., John, V. P. and Hymes, D. (1972) *Functions of Language in the Classroom.* University of Columbia: Teachers' College Press.

Chambers, J. K. and Trudgill, P. (1980) *Dialectology.* Cambridge: Cambridge University Press.

Cheshire, J. (1982) *Variation in an English Dialect: a Sociolinguistic Study.* Cambridge: Cambridge University Press.

Clark, B. D. and Gleave, M. B. (eds) (1972) *Social Patterns in Cities.* London: Inst. of British Geographers.

Cohen, A. (ed.) (1982) *Belonging.* Manchester: Manchester University Press.

Coulthard, M. (1977) *An Introduction to Discourse Analysis.* London: Longmans.

Cubitt, T. (1973) Network density among urban families. In Boissevain and Mitchell (eds), 67–82.

Dennis, N., Henriques, F. M. and Slaughter, C. (1957) *Coal Is Our Life.* London: Eyre and Spottiswoode.

Dittmar, N. (1976) *Sociolinguistics.* London: Arnold.

Dixon, R. M. W. (1971) *The Dyirbal Language of North Queensland.* Cambridge: Cambridge University Press.

Douglas-Cowie, E. (1978) Linguistic codeswitching in a Northern Irish village: social interaction and social ambition. In Trudgill (ed.), 37–51.

Downes, W. (1984) *Language and Society.* London: Fontana.

Edwards, V. (1986) *Language in a Black Community*. Clevedon, Avon: Multilingual Matters.

Ekwall, E. (1956) *Studies on the Population of Mediaeval London*. Lund: Lund Studies in English.

Ervin-Tripp, S. (1972) On sociolingustic rules: alternation and co-occurrence. In Gumperz and Hymes (eds), 213–50.

Evans, E. E. (1944) Belfast: the site and the city. *Ulster Journal of Archaeology*, 7.

Fasold, R. W. (1978) Language variation and linguistic competence. In Sankoff (ed.), 85–96.

Ferguson, C. A. (1977) Linguistics as anthropology. In Saville-Troike (ed.), 1–12.

Finnegan, R. (1970) *Oral Literature in Africa*. Oxford: Clarendon.

Frankenberg, R. (1969) *Communities in Britain*. Harmondsworth: Penguin.

Fried, M. (1973) *The World of the Urban Working Class*. Cambridge, Mass.: Harvard University Press.

Gal, S. (1978) Variation and change in patterns of speaking: language shift in Austria. In Sankoff (ed.), 227–38.

Gal, S. (1979) *Language Shift: Social Determinants of Linguistic Change in Bilingual Austria*. New York: Academic Press.

Gauchat, L. (1905) L'unité phonétique dans le patois d'une commune. Halle: Max Niemeyer.

Giglioli, P. P. (ed.) (1972) *Language and Social Context*. Harmondsworth: Penguin.

Giles, H. and Powesland, P. F. (1975) *Speech Style and Social Evaluation*. New York and London: Academic Press.

Giles, H. and St Clair, R. (eds) (1979) *Language and Social Psychology*. Oxford: Blackwell.

Giles, H. and Smith, P. M. (1979) Accommodation theory: optimal levels of convergence. In Giles and St Clair (eds), 45–65.

Goffman, E. (1976) Replies and responses. *Language in Society*, 5, 257–313.

Goody, E. N. (ed.) (1978) *Questions and Politeness*. Cambridge: Cambridge University Press.

Goody, J. and Watt, I. (1963) The consequences of literacy. In Giglioli (ed.), 311–57.

Granovetter, M. (1973) The strength of weak ties. *American Journal of Sociology*, 78, 1360–80.

Granovetter, M. (1982) The strength of weak ties: a network theory revisited. In P. V. Marsden and N. Lin (eds), *Social structure and network analysis*. London: Sage.

Gregg, R. J. (1972) The Scotch–Irish dialect boundaries of Ulster. In Wakelin (ed.), 109–39.

Gumperz, J. and Hymes, D. (1972) *Directions in Sociolinguistics*. New York: Holt Rinehart & Winston.

Gumperz, J. J. (1970) Sociolinguistics and communication in small groups. In Pride and Holmes (eds), 203–23.

Gumperz, J. J. and Hernandez, E. (1969) Cognitive aspects of bilingual communication. *Working Paper 28*, Language Behaviour Research Laboratory, Berkeley.

Gumperz, J. J. (1968) The speech community. In Pride and Holmes (eds), 219–30.

Gumperz, J. J. (1972) Introduction to Gumperz and Hymes (eds), 219–30.

Gumperz, J. J. (1976a) Social network and language shift. *Working Paper 46*, Language Behaviour Research Laboratory, Berkeley.

Gumperz, J. J. (1976b) The sociolinguistic significance of conversational codeswitching. *Working Paper 46*, Language Behaviour Research Laboratory, Berkeley.

Gumperz, J. J. (1977a) The conversational analysis of interethnic communication. Mimeo: University of Berkeley.

Gumperz, J. J. (1977b) Sociocultural knowledge in conversational inference. In Saville-Troike (ed.), 191–211.

Gumperz, J. J. (1982) *Discourse strategies*. Cambridge: Cambridge University Press.

Hall, E. T. (1963) A system for the notation of proxemic behaviour. *American Anthropologist, 65*, 1003–26.

Hannerz, U. (1974) Black ghetto culture and community. In Bell and Newby (eds), 149–74.

Harris, J. (1985) *Phonological variation and change*. Cambridge: Cambridge University Press.

Harris, R. (1972) *Prejudice and Tolerance in Ulster*. Manchester: Manchester University Press.

Haugen, E. (1966) Dialect, language, nation. In Pride and Holmes (eds), 97–111.

Hockett, C. F. (1958) *A Course in Modern Linguistics*. New York: Macmillan.

Homans, George (1958) Social behaviour as exchange. *American Journal of Sociology, 62*, 597–606.

Hudson, R. A. (1980) *Sociolinguistics*. Cambridge: Cambridge University Press.

Hymes, D. (1967) Models of the interaction of language and social setting. *Journal of Social Issues, 23* (2), 8–28.

Hymes, D. (1972) Models of the interaction of language and social life. In Gumperz and Hymes (eds), 35–71.

Hymes, D. (1974) *Foundations in Sociolinguistics: An Ethnographic Approach*. Philadelphia: University of Pennsylvania Press.

Johnston, P. (1983) Irregular style variation patterns in Edinburgh speech. *Scottish Language, 2,* 1–19.

Kapferer, B. (1969) Norms and the manipulation of relationships in a work context. In Mitchell (ed.), 181–244.

Kendon, A., Harris, R. M. and Key, M. R (eds), (1975) *The Organisation of Behaviour in Face to Face Interaction*. Mouton: The Hague.

Knowles, G. O. (1978) The nature of phonological variables in Scouse. In Trudgill (ed.), 80–90.

Kroch, A. S. (1978) Towards a theory of social dialect variation. *Language in Society, 7,* 17–36.

Kroch, A. S. (1979) Dialect and style in the speech of upper class Philadelphia. Mimeo: University of Pennsylvania.

Kurath, Hans, Bloch, Bernard and others (1939–43) *Linguistic Atlas of New England* (3 vols). Providence: Brown University Press.

Labov, W. (1966) *The Social Stratification of English in New York City*. Washington, D.C.: Center for Applied Linguistics.

Labov, W. (1971) Variation in language. In Reed (ed.), 187–221.

Labov, W. (1972a) *Sociolinguistic Patterns*. Philadelphia: Pennsylvania University Press; Oxford: Blackwell.

Labov, W. (1972b) *Language in the Inner City*. Philadelphia: Pennsylvania University Press: Oxford: Blackwell.

Labov, W. (1972c) The design of a sociolinguistic research project (mimeo).

Labov, W. (1978) (Draft). Field methods used by the research project on linguistic change and variation. Mimeo: University of Pennsylvania.

Labov, W. (ed.) (1980) *Locating Language in Time and Space*. New York: Academic Press.

Labov, W. (1981) Field methods used by the project on linguistic change and variation. *Sociolinguistic Working Paper, 81,* Austin, Texas: South Western Educational Development Laboratory.

Labov, W., Cohen, P., Robins, C. and Lewis, J. (1968) *A Study of the Nonstandard English Negro and Puerto-Rican Speakers in New York City*. Report on Co-operative Research Project 3288. New York: Columbia University.

Labov, W., Yaeger, M. and Steiner, R. (1972) *A Quantitative Study of Sound Change in Progress*. Report on NSF Project no. GS-3287.

Lambert, W. E. (1979) Language as a factor in inter-group relations. In Giles and St Clair (eds), 186–92.

Lanegran, D. A. and Palm, R. (eds) (1978) *An Invitation to Geography* (second edition). New York: McGraw-Hill.

Laver, J. (1975) Communicative functions of phatic communion. In Kendon *et al.* (eds), 215–38.

Laver, J. and Hutcheson, S. (eds) (1972) *Communication in Face to Face Interaction*. Harmondsworth: Penguin.

Le Page, R. B. (1968) Problems of description in multilingual communities. *Transactions of the Philological Society*, 189–212.

Le Page, R. B. (1975a) 'Projection, focussing, diffusion', or, steps towards a sociolinguistic theory of language. Mimeo: University of York.

Le Page, R. B. (1975b) Polarizing factors—political cultural economic—operating on the individual's choice of identity through language use in British Honduras. In Savard, J.-G. and Vigneault, R. (eds), *Les états multilingues*, 537–52. Quebec: Laval University Press.

Le Page, R. B. (1976) The multi-dimensional nature of sociolinguistic space. Mimeo: University of York.

Le Page, R. B. (1977) Processes of pidginization and creolization. In Valdeman, A. (ed.), *Pidgin and Creole Linguistics*. Urbana: University of Illinois Press.

Le Page, R. B. (1979) Review of Dell Hymes—*Foundations in Sociolinguistics* and Norbert Dittmar—*Sociolinguistics, Journal of Linguistics*, *15*, 168–79.

Le Page, R. B. and Tabouret-Keller, A. (1985) *Acts of Identity*. Cambridge: Cambridge University Press.

Levinson, S. C. (1978) Sociolinguistic universals. Mimeo.

Lloyd, P. (1979) *Slums of Hope?* Harmondsworth: Penguin.

Lomnitz, L. A. (1977) *Networks and Marginality*. New York: Academic Press.

MacAllister, A. H. (1963) *A Year's Course in Speech Training* (9th ed.). London: University of London Press.

Macaulay, R. K. S. (1977) *Language, Social Class and Education.* Edinburgh: Edinburgh University Press.

Maclaren, R. (1976) The variable (ʌ): a relic form with social correlates. *Belfast Working Papers, 1,* 45–68.

Mather, J. Y. (1972) Linguistic geography and the traditional drift net fishery of the Scottish east coast. In Wakelin (ed.), 7–31.

Mayer, P. (1963) *Townsmen or Tribesmen: Conservatism and the Process of Urbanisation in a South African City.* Cape Town: Oxford University Press.

Mewett, P. (1982) Associational categories and the social location of relationships in a Lewis crofting community. In Cohen (ed.), 101–30.

Milroy, J. (1976) Length and height variations in the vowels of Belfast vernacular. *Belfast Working Papers in Language and Linguistics, 1, 3.*

Milroy, J. (1980) Lexical alternation and the history of English. In Traugott (ed.), 355–62.

Milroy, J. (1981) *Regional Accents of English.* Belfast: Blackstaff.

Milroy, J. (forthcoming) *Society and Language Change.* Oxford: Blackwell.

Milroy, J. and Milroy, L. (1978) Belfast: Change and variation in an urban vernacular. In Trudgill (ed.), 19–36.

Milroy, J. and Milroy, L. (1985a) *Authority in Language.* London: Routledge and Kegan Paul.

Milroy, J. and Milroy, L. (1985b) Linguistic change, social network and speaker innovation. *Journal of Linguistics, 21,* 339–84.

Milroy, J., Milroy, L., Gunn, B., Pitts, A. and Policansky, L. (1983) Sociolinguistic variation and linguistic change in Belfast. Report to the Social Science Research Council (Grant no. HR5777).

Milroy, L. (1976) Investigating linguistic variation in three Belfast working-class communities. *In Proceedings of the Third Annual Conference.* Belfast: Sociological Association of Ireland.

Milroy, L. (1978) Network ties on an upper-middle-class housing estate. MS.

Milroy, L. (1987) *Observing and Analysing Natural Language.* Oxford: Blackwell.

Milroy, L. and Milroy, J. (1977a) Speech and context in an urban setting. *Belfast Working Papers in Language and Linguistics, 2, 1.*

Milroy, J. and Milroy, L. (1977b) Speech community and language variety in Belfast. Report to the SSRC.

Mitchell, J. Clyde (ed.). (1969) *Social Networks in Urban Situations*. Manchester: Manchester University Press.

Mitchell, J. C. (1973) Networks, norms and institutions. In Boissevain and Mitchell (eds), 15–36.

Northern Ireland General Register Office (1971) *Census of Population*. Belfast: HMSO.

Opie, I. and Opie, P. (1959) *The Lore and Language of School Children*. Oxford: Oxford University Press.

Orton, H. (1962) *Survey of English Dialects: Introduction*. Leeds: E. J. Arnold & Son.

Orton, H., Sanderson, S. and Widdowson, J. (1978) *Linguistic Atlas of England*. London: Croom Helm.

Pahl, R. E. (1975) *Whose City?* Harmondsworth: Penguin.

Patterson, D. (1860) *Provincialisms of Belfast*. Belfast.

Petyt, M. (1978) Secondary contractions in West Yorkshire negatives. In Trudgill (ed.), 91–100.

Philips, S. (1972) Participant structures and communicative competence: Warm Springs children in community and classroom. In Cazden, John and Hymes (eds), 370–94.

Philips, S. (1976) Some sources of cultural viability in the regulation of talk. *Language in Society*, 5, 81–95.

Pride, J. B. and Holmes, S. (eds) (1972) *Sociolinguistics*. Harmondsworth: Penguin.

Reed, C. E. (ed.) (1971) *The Learning of Language*. New York: NCTE.

Reid, E. (1978) Social and stylistic variation in the speech of children: some evidence from Edinburgh. In Trudgill (ed.), 158–71.

Rogers, E. M. and Shoemaker, F. F. (1971) *Communication of Innovations* (2nd ed.). New York: Academic Press.

Romaine, S. (1978a) Post vocalic /r/ in Scottish English: sound change in progress? In Trudgill (ed.), 144–57.

Romaine, S. (1978b) Problems in the investigation of linguistic attitudes in Scotland. *Work in Progress, 11–29*. Dept of Linguistics, University of Edinburgh.

Romaine, S. (ed.) (1982) *Sociolinguistic Variation in Speech Communities*. London: Arnold.

Russell, J. (1982) Networks and sociolinguistic variation in an African urban setting. In Romaine (ed.), 125–40.

Ryan, E. B. (1979) Why do low-prestige language varieties persist? In Giles and St Clair (eds), 145–57.

Sacks, H. Aspects of the sequential organisation of conversation. (MS).

Salisbury, R. F. (1962) Notes on bilingualism and linguistic change in New Guinea. In Pride and Holmes (eds), 52–64.

Sankoff, D. (ed.) (1978) *Linguistic Variation: Models and Methods*. New York: Academic Press.

Sankoff, G. (1971) Language use in multilingual societies. In Pride and Holmes (eds), 33–51.

Sankoff, G. (1974) A quantitative paradigm for the study of communicative competence. In Bauman and Sherzer (eds), 18–49.

Saville-Troike, M. (ed.) (1977) *Linguistics and Anthropology*. Washington D.C.: Georgetown University Press.

Scheflen, A. E. (1964) The significance of posture in communication systems. In Laver and Hutcheson (eds), 225–46.

Scheflen, A. E. and Ashcraft, N. (1976) *Human Territories: How We Behave in Space–Time*. Englewood Cliffs: Prentice Hall.

Schegloff, E. A. (1972) Notes on a conversational practice: formulating place. In D. Sudnow (ed.) *Studies in Social Interaction*. New York: Free Press.

Schmidt, A. (1985) *Young People's Dyirbal*. Cambridge: Cambridge University Press.

Sebeok, T. A. (ed.) (1960) *Style in Language*. Boston: MIT Press.

Sherzer, J. (1977) The ethnography of speaking: a critical appraisal. In Saville-Troike (ed.), 43–57.

Shuy, R. W., Wolfram, W. A. and Riley, W. K. (1968) *Field Techniques in an Urban Language Study*. Arlington: CAL.

Sinclair, J. M. and Coulthard, M. (1975) *Towards an Analysis of Discourse*. London: Oxford University Press.

Southall, A. (ed.) (1973) *Urban Anthropology*. London: Oxford University Press.

Southall, A. (1973) The density of role relationships as a universal index of urbanisation. In Southall (ed.), 71–106.

Staples, J. H. (1898) Notes on Ulster English dialect. *Transactions of the Philological Society*, 357–87.

Straka, G. (ed.) (1973) *Les Dialects Romans de France*. Paris: CNRS.

Strang, B. M. H. (1970) *A history of English*. London: Methuen.

Taylor, O. (1977) The sociolinguistic dimension in standardized testing. In Saville-Troike (ed.), 257–66.

Thomas, B. (1986) Differences of sex and sects: linguistic variation and social networks in a Welsh mining village. Paper presented at the Sixth Sociolinguistics Symposium, University of Newcastle upon Tyne.

Traugott, E. *et al.* (eds). (1980) *Papers from the Fourth International Congress in Historical Linguistics*. Amsterdam: Benjamins.

Trouwborst, A. (1973) Two types of partial network in Burundi. In Boissevain and Mitchell (eds), 111–25.

Trudgill, P. (1972) Sex, covert prestige and linguistic change in the urban British English of Norwich. *Language in Society, 1,* 179–95.

Trudgill, P. (1974) *The Social Differentiation of English in Norwich*. Cambridge: Cambridge University Press.

Trudgill, P. (1983) *Sociolinguistics* (2nd ed.) Harmondsworth: Penguin.

Trudgill, P. (ed.) (1978) *Sociolinguistic Patterns in British English*. London: Arnold.

Trudgill, P. (1986) *Dialects in Contact*. Oxford: Blackwell.

Turner, C. (1967) Conjugal roles and social networks. *Human Relations, 20,* 121–30.

Wakelin, M. (ed.) (1972) *Patterns in the Folk Speech of the British Isles*. London: Athlone.

Watson, O. M. and Graves, T. D. (1966) Quantitative research in proxemic behaviour. *American Anthropologist, 68,* 971–85.

Whyte, W. F. (1955) *Street Corner Society: the Social Structure of an Italian Slum*. Chicago: University of Chicago Press.

Widdowson, John, D. (1972) Proverbs and sayings from Filey. In Wakelin (ed.), 50–72.

Wiener, R. (1976) *The Rape and Plunder of the Shankill*. Belfast: Notaems.

Williams, R. A. (1903) Remarks on Northern Irish pronunciation of English. *Modern Language Quarterly, 6,* 129–35.

Wolfson, N. (1976) Speech events and natural speech: some implications for sociolinguistic methodology. *Language in Society, 5,* 189–209.

Wright, P. (1972) Coal-mining language: a recent investigation. In Wakelin (ed.), 32–49.

Wyld, H. C. (1936) *A History of Modern Colloquial English*. Oxford: Blackwell.

Young, M. and Wilmott, P. (1962) *Family and Kinship in East London*. Harmondsworth: Penguin.

Index

134, 138; and theories of variability, 212–16; as a norm enforcement mechanism, 52, 86, 108, 136–7, 179, 213

Sociolinguistic methods, 2, 6

Sociolinguistic variable, 10; as marker of social identity, 157, 164, 166; in Belfast, 101–4, 116–20, 123–30, 154–66, 205–6; in New York City, 10–11; problems with the concept of, 11; with lexically limited distribution, 24, 118

Solidarity, as an independent variable, 83–4; amongst men, 80, 144; amongst women, 144; and cultural focusing, 183; and network structure, 82–3; and status ideologies, 84, 180, 184, 186–7; ethic of in low status communities, 73–4, 211

Speech community, 40; as defined by Gumperz, 85, 94, 107; as defined by Labov, 13; problems in concept of, 75–6, 105

Speech events, 2, 67–9 *passim*; examples of, 86–7

Speech style, as independent variable, 10, 11, 111; analysed multi-dimensionally, 17, 58–9, 63–4, 66–9; analysed on linear continuum, 101–2; isolation of, during interview, 9, 25–6; *see also* Spontaneous styles; Stylistic analysis

Spelling pronunciation, 104

Spontaneous styles, 5, 8–9, 63–4, 67–8; contrasted with interview style, 66, 101–6

Standardized codes, 17, 182, 190–1; *see also* Prestige linguistic norms

Statistical analysis, 102–3, 120–31; methodological importance of, 215–16

Statistical significance, 103; importance of checking, 121; method of establishing, 122–3

Status, and solidarity as competing ideologies, 207–10; aspects of which influence behaviour, 83; models of sociolinguistic description based on, 208–9

Stereotypes, 118, 192

Stylistic analysis, of conversation, 62–8; *see also* Discourse structure

Territoriality, 16; and network structure, 54, 86; and ethnic segregation, 72, 76, 77; in Belfast, 79, 84; reflected in network strength scale, 142–3

Traditional dialectology, 2–6 *passim*; and formal speech styles, 26

Transactions, 47–8

Urbanization index, 175

Vernacular, and young speakers, 114; as data base for sociolinguistic analysis, 23–4, 75, 114; loyalty to, 19, 167–8; low status of, 18–19; of a city, 24; of individuals, 12, 177; phonological structure of, in Belfast, 116–19; recorded in Belfast, 58–60, 69; recorded by means of group sessions, 26–31; symbolizing group identity, 18, 206–7

Vernacular norms, 184, 186–8; and network structure, 160, 162, 163; as symbols of solidarity, 184, 186–8, 207, 208; transmission of, 204–7; *see also* Linguistic norms; Prestige linguistic norms

Working class, 72–3, 75; network structure in, 137

LIBRARY, UNIVERSITY OF CHESTER